A THOUGHT

THE WAR IN THE HEAVENS BREAKING THE CHAINS OF GENERATIONAL CURSES

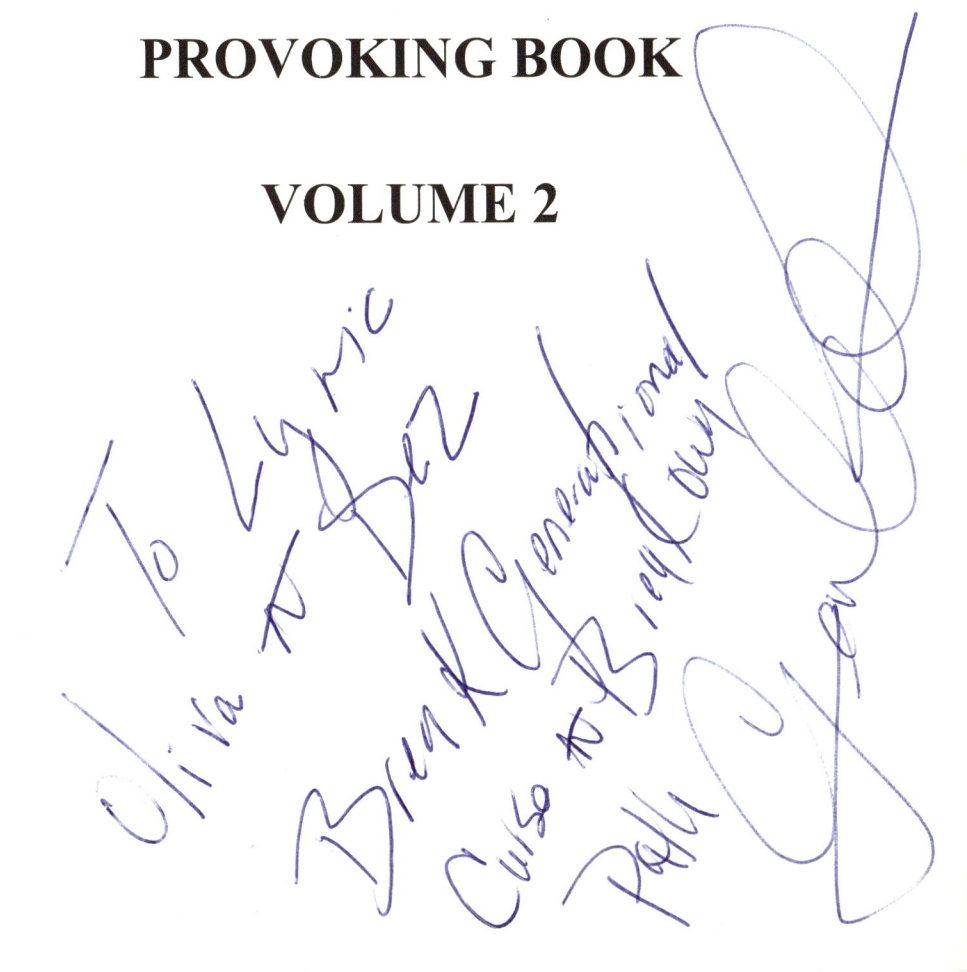

PROVOKING BOOK

VOLUME 2

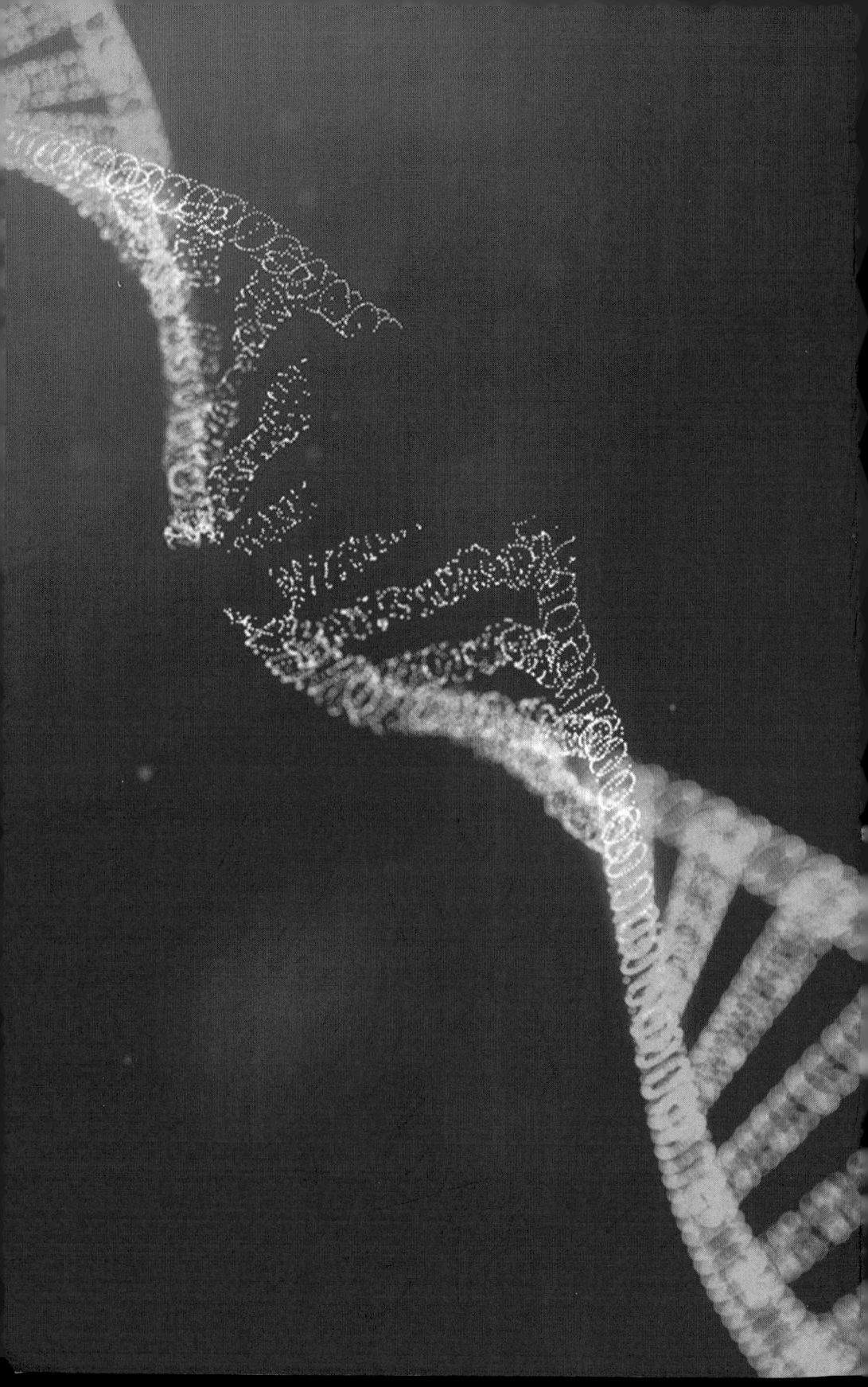

A THOUGHT

THE WAR IN THE HEAVENS BREAKING THE CHAINS OF GENERATIONAL CURSES

PROVOKING BOOK

VOLUME 2

GEM C. COLLIE

THE WAR IN THE HEAVENS
BREAKING THE CHAINS OF GENERATIONAL CURSES

Copyright © 2023 by Gem C. Collie

ISBN (Paperback): 979-8-89034-329-1

ISBN (Ebook):979-8-88895-152-1

Library Of Congress Control Number: 2022921041

Book Formatted by OsamudiamenAbdul

Edited by James Richard

All rights reserved. No part of this book may be reproduced, stored in a retrieval system, or transmitted in any form or by any other means, electronic, mechanical, photocopying, recording, or otherwise, without the publisher's express written permission.

First Published by GEMBOUKS 2023

gembouks21@yahoo.com
www.gembouks.org

If you do not come out of a healthy family, make sure a healthy family comes out of you. If you do not come out of a wealthy family, make sure a wealthy family comes out of you. Generational curses will outlive you into the 4th or 5th generation. You will have to rise and break the yoke. Generational curses are long-lasting because the system is long-lasting.

Contents

Dedication v

About The Author ix

Glossary xiii

Preface xviii

The Epilogues xxiv

DNA Genetic Visualization xxxi

Words From the Author xlvi

The Wonders Of Egypt 1
The Regret of Breaking the Generational Curse 1

Womb 8

No Distractions While Breaking The Curse 16
The Mastery of Staying Focused 16

Meta-Cognitive Triangle 25

The Sunken Place 32
Resurrection In the Valley of Dry Bones 32

The Great Interview 41
The Meeting with The Shadow 41

No Weapon That Forms Against Me Shall Prosper: 61
Reservation Of the Tongue 61

The Body Keeps The Score 68
The Thoughts You Hold in Your Mind Becomes Your Reality 68

The Mastery 72

Signs That You Are Operating Under A Generational Curse.......... 79

Jerusalem.. 82

The New Jerusalem 84

The War In The Heavens 86
Addressing The Unhealed Shadow 86

Replenishing The Ambitious Impregnable People 107

Present Traumatic Stress/Slavery Disorder..................................... 109
Understanding the concept of unwanted memories 109

Breaking The Patterns 115
Unpacking The Unspoken Truth... 115

Confronting The Broken Shadow 122
Unlocking The Unseen Self 122

The Voice Of The Shadow... 134
The Echoes Behind the Soul 134

The Five Spirits 143

The Beginning Of The Curse 145
Identifying the generational curses 145

The Opposition Of The Spirit Of Err 154
The personification of the Spirit of Truth 154

The Awareness Of Spiritually... 162
Transmitted Disease 162

The Spirit Of "Liberation" 165
Freedom begins in the mind.. 165

The Spirit of Divine Discernment 170

The Spirit of Rejection	175
Identifying the Root of Bitterness	175
The Mentality Of The Stockholm Syndrome	179
And The Legacy of Generational Curses	179
Divine Leadership	185
The Divine Masculine And Feminine	193
The Dynamics Of Self Respect	198
The Spiritual Concept Of Abortion	203
The Emotional Aftermath	203
The Spirit Of Confusion	206
The Dual Spirit Of Effective Communication	215
Prayer To My Ancestors	223
The Law of Human Nature	229
Understanding the Concept of the Unconscious Mind	229
Forgiveness	237
Understanding Atonement	237
Spirit Of Understandings	243
The Foundations Of Traditional Trauma	248
Breaking The Chains Of Generational Curse	255
"The sins of the fathers are to be laid upon the children."	255
Breaking Up With Religion	266
Unchaining the mind from what it was beating into thinking	266
The Metaphysical Human Eyes	269
Wide Open Concept	269

Mental Illness And The Psychological Effect Of
The Generational Beast 274

Chapter One 280

The Great Return 281

The New Identity 289
Hiding The Shadow in The Mirror 289

Chapter Two 297

Seeking Betterment 298

All Aboard 303
The Next Stop a Different Destination 303

Out Goes The Old In With The New 311

Chapter Three 328

Go Back To Who YOU Were 329

Chapter Four 352

Mommy, I Am Home 353

Seeking A New Start 362
The Rude awakening 362

Chapter Five 376

The Cross Over 377

The Author's Note to The Author 386

Dedication

This book is dedicated to the following people:

The people who have been my biggest support stand by my side, believing in me even when I do not have the strength to believe in myself, for those who understood me in places where I was seen as difficult. I thank you all.

Gem C Collie

Wow, here you go again, authoring another book. I love your passion, your strength, how brave you are, your honesty, and how bold you are. You are not just real but a real Gem indeed. Keep going girl, do not give up on yourself. It would be a great offense to coexist, knowing that not everyone is going to love you, but let your name keep you going.

Do not be afraid of your reflection; it is your guide to success. Allow yourself to shine and get out of your mind so that you will not be a stumbling block in your way.

— Respect, love, and blessing.

To My Future Self

You have gone through a lot; you have overcome many obstacles; you have run many marathons; you have had many sleepless nights, heartbreaks, and disappointments.

However, you have managed to recycle your pain, and somehow you have turned it into art, but not just any art but a Gem, a diamond that has been through the rough yet managed to shine. I am beyond proud of you. It only takes the courage of a fearful man, that heart is made of tin, and a girl with a shining red shoe, to walk through a yellow brick road. –You are a Gem

Eveth Colley

My cousin and biggest supporter, your soul is so kind and gentle and always willing to support me, and although I never felt the physical softness of your tender hands, I felt the spiritual hugs you sent my way. You made my heart cry with glee.

— Love and Light❤

My Brothers (Men)

My brothers, I am dedicating this book to you all as well, for I understand it has been hard on you all, as men, with the world on your shoulders, and a Crown to uphold. I can only imagine your plight, yet I respect your portion of the world.

I respect you all for your contribution to creating the world we share. I love all your strengths, secret tears, and bare hands that can tackle a lion. I appreciate your masculine energy. I will break the curse that says you do not understand me as a woman. know no matter how difficult your life is right now you are going to be okay, where you are it's simply a temporary stop on your journey, and not define a final decision destination

— Divine

To my Parents and my Ancestors

Out of all the dedications here, this one was the hardest because, unlike the other dedications, this one came from my womb. I am dedicating this book because I am breaking the generational curse and forgiving you. I forgive you for the unconscious heartbreaks you caused in my heart. I forgive you for using my back as a target. I forgive you all for using me as an emotional dumping ground. I forgive you all for freezing your hearts so I could not know the warmth of what love feels like.

I forgive you all. I see you from the cage of my heart where I held you under arrest. You are not behind in life; you are simply anxious because you see other people moving out faster in life than you. Do not allow the highlight reels of others to guilt you into thinking your life is a failure make no mistake, Yah has a plan for you.

My Sisters (Women)

To you, my sisters, I send nothing but love to you all over the world, from Jamaica to Japan. I send you healing. I send you my tears to wipe away the bloodstains in dresses stained by life. I send you my tears when you cannot find your own.

I send you my voice when yours has been silenced. I send you my hands when you need a grip. I lend you my womb when yours are too damaged. I send all my knowledge and love. I send you my awareness to keep you in a state of accountability. I send you my love just in case you were spread thin, so you know you have none left. My sisters, I send you my legs to walk away from what no longer serves you but do not forget to bring them back. I love you, all my sisters. Special thanks to My sister at work Noir books, and Linda Davis

— Divine Love and Healing

To Generations to Come

To the generations to come, I dedicate this entire book to you. I hope that my knowledge will be something that you were able to put to use. I was not able to break the complete chains of the generational curse. Of course, it did not begin with me, so it will not end there. Nonetheless, I now pass on the banner to you to go forward and fight the fight.

Understand that this will need your full corporation, meaning that you cannot attempt to break your generational curses yet be fully engaged in someone else's dysfunctional family dynamics. No one is worth your mental health. I am not telling you that you will find the perfect person who is fully healed, but at least you will reach together some capacity for healing from now on.

— Keep pushing!

About The Author

Renowned Author and student in the field of psychology at the University of Maryland, Gem C Collie, the now Amazon bestselling author of the book titled "The Damsel in Dis-stress Coping with Emotional Co-dependency Personality Disorder." A book in the genre of mental health.

Collie is a royal native of the capital of the Island of Kingston, Jamaica. Who later migrated to the United States in the early ninety's. Collie, being from a culture of storytellers, later discovered her unique skills of being a word alchemist came at the tender age of fourteen, while in her ninth-grade freshman year at a local high school in the heart of Baltimore, Maryland, this talent was awakened from its dormancy by her than English teacher, Andreas

Spillidias who saw the gift of writing in his student. He taught Collie how to awaken and unlock her creative writing skills. Even though he knew Collie ad not yet mastered the US English language, and how to express her writing skills without the usage of her Jamaican dialect, intertwining in the message she is conveying, or even in a comprehensible tone; her teacher, knew that his student was a diamond in the rough, and all she needed was direction. However, Spilidias motivated his student, and encourage collie to pursue her talents. Al though Collie's writing was expressive, wordy, sassy, and so frank, this did not hinder colliers creativity.

Collie's passion showed in her speech, and written sentences, nothing did not discourage her to write. Collie states that "I had to allow myself to be sucked in, by the wave of the soulful reggae music in the background tapping away at my heart, releasing the words on paper like magic.' Even though this phenomenal, gifted talent, at times, frightened the author, despite the fright, collie did not give up. Collie embraced her skills for she knew she was chosen.

Collie went on to be one of the handpicked gifted students in her Home-room English class, whom her teacher Spilidias himself chose collie among nine of her fellow class-mates to be a part of a group of "Dynamic future Writers" he called "The Phenomenal Writers," to which he later created a poetry collection of the student's work that he published.

This phenomenon sparked this classical word alchemistry is what we are now seeing the author for: Which is her unique skill of using and reframing her pain to create lessons of Gems in a book. Which takes a master mind, and a creative genius to do, Collie's Gems, are needed in a time now that the world is in a state of psychological Shambles. Collie, say she prays that her work will inspire others who will hear her stories that will galvanize them to be devoted to the giant task of addressing their traumas, and self-discovery.

Collie's quest now is to break the chains of generational curses. In her next book titled, "THE WAR IN THE HEAVENS." In this new venture, Collie is about to take her readers on a journey unlike anyone has ever done before. "What a wild ride," Says the author about her new venture of breaking "Generational curses." Collie explains how breaking generational curses is not for the weak but is paramount in her latest book. Collie also urges her readers to not be distracted from going on the quest of psychological healing.

For although it might seem daunting, terrifying, and somewhat lonesome; it is a path that for others might be unfrequented berm. They one day will wake up and cognize their life sitting in the shadows of someone else's experienced. Truth be told, life is a result of making many mistakes from which we will become wiser, benevolent, patient, humble, and bold enough to keep moving forward with zest. Your mistakes are there to guide you, through your journey

"You must forgive your parents for all the pain they have caused you so that you do not transfer that bitterness to your children. We must stop the cycle of adults recovering from their childhood, so that we may have a new world, with a new mind. The generational dysfunctionality must end and must stop with you."

— Gem C collie

Glossary

Fleshie

The physical manifestation of a person, manifesting in the physical plain, without this form, the man's experience cannot exist. It makes the spiritual world physically tangible.

Emotional permanence

Emotional permanence is the **understanding that emotions continue to exist** even when you are not seeing proof of them. It is the same concept as "object permanence." This is a stage that people go through as babies where they form an understanding that objects continue to exist even when they cannot see them.

Magical thinking

Psychologists would define magical thinking as the idea that **a person's thoughts, wishes, or sometimes actions may influence the course of our world**. But these are not just any thoughts, wishes, or actions. These actions often have no proven connection to the results.

Environmental psychology

Environmental psychology is an **interdisciplinary field that focuses on the interplay between individuals and their surroundings**. It examines how the natural environment, and our built environments shape us as individuals.

Demons

Fears, resentment, anger, disrespectful spirits, lies, dysfunctionality.

Damsel

The damsel is neither masculine nor feminine.

The Power of the Trinity

The power of the trinity is the power of nature, the movement of the earth, the spirit, the earth, and the breath of life.

Dutty Boukman

Boukman held a few prominent positions in his lifetime, serving as a commander (slave driver) and later a coach driver. Through his positions, **Boukman** was able to hold secret meetings with other enslaved Africans in **Haiti**. He became a pivotal voice in the soon-to-come **Haitian.**

Revolution

Psalms 68:31 - **Princes shall come out of Egypt**; Ethiopia shall soon stretch out her hands unto God. 2 Chronicles 14:9-15 - And there came out against them Zerah the Ethiopian with a host of a thousand, and three hundred chariots; and came unto Mareshah.

The Spirit of Error

The spirit of error is exactly what its name implies – **it causes people to go into error or to the extreme [especially] in things about God**. This spirit is the exact opposite of the Spirit of truth and is of the kingdom of darkness. The special targets of this spirit are Christians – especially ministers of the Gospel.

Traditional Chinese Medicine

Traditional Chinese medicine (TCM) is a **broad range of medicinal practices sharing common concepts** which have been developed in China and are based on a tradition of more than 2,000 years, including various forms of herbal medicine, acupuncture, massage (tui na), exercise (qigong), and dietary therapy.

Spirits in TCM

Shen is usually translated as spirit and refers to the spiritual aspect of our being. It embodies consciousness, emotions, and thought. According to traditional Chinese medicine (TCM), Shen is said to preside over activities that take place in the mental, spiritual, and creative planes.

General Adaptation Syndrome

The general adaptation syndrome (GAS), developed by Hans Selye, **describes the pattern of responses the body goes through after being prompted by a stressor**. There are three stages: alarm, resistance, and exhaustion.

The Alarm Stages

The alarm stage is **when the central nervous system is awakened, causing your body's defenses to assemble**. This SOS stage triggers a fight-or-flight response. Following this, the resistance stage commences, during which your body begins to repair itself and normalize both heart rate and blood pressure.

Preface

In this book, you will find the aspect of the damsel's attempt in the previous writing, volume 1 of the book titled: "The Damsel in Dis-stress; Coping with Emotional Co-Dependency Personality Dis-Order," written and published by Author Gem C. Collie, where the damsel exposed her traumatic experiences while growing up in the capital of Jamaica and then later migrating to the United States. In this literature, the author expressed that she become cognitive to the idea that her journey of self-discovery was yet to be over.

As she began to recover from what she felt was a daunting task of exposing her demons through her written work, the author could hear the voices of her ancestors protesting in her psyche. Summoning the thought of what seemed as though it was a funeral going on in the subconsciousness of the author's head. Fear and anger took over the author's mind, for even though she was chosen to complete this task, she did not want to dig any deeper, for touching the surface was traumatic enough for her. She had to come to the rude awakening, and except that the journey was simply not over, that what she was now doing was only at the beginning of the process, digging away at her fossil-like mind, and that she now must continue the mission given to her.

As the voice of her ancestors spoke to her and the masculine aspect of her mind approached her in the mystical world, the author was taken aback as she questioned herself: ' As to how this was happening. How was this aspect of myself able to intrude upon the spiritual conversation that was taking place with myself, and my ancestors ancestor, How did this man get to speak without an invitation?' She questioned herself. However, frightening this may have been, the author's masculine aspect had to reminded the author that he did not need an invitation, for he was not separate from her; he was only her in a different Aspect, time and frequency. Considerable for the spirit (Divine spirit) of Man (Humankind) is never separate from each other. Yet a different expression of the manifestation of them all, the Mind, the Flesh, and the Spirit, are all cooperative, collectivistic aspects of "The Power of the Trinity."

Even though this concept was manifested in the author, she was hell-bent on thinking she was a victim of being chosen. The author believed she was separated from her mission and did not understand that the mission was to conquer the implication that the beast was not just outside of the beast that had become her mind. The author had come to the painful realization that, even though she was writing about the damsel in dis-stress, she was no different from that ideology of a distressed damsel with no prince charming coming to her rescue. She would have to break free from the mental slavery holding her captive in the pits of her guts.

She had to become a spiritual anthropologist, digging deep into the cave of her mind and further into places where there was no light shining. The light of truth must shine in the spaces to be exposed, the mystic.

The author went back as far as when she was a revolutionist by the name of Shango, who fought along with Dutty Boukman. This revolution sparked the war against the French colonization and slave masters on the Island of Haiti, which lit the matches and ignited the flames in the nearby Caribbean Islands and other African diasporas worldwide. The author's instructions from the voice of her masculine self are to face her inner demons and the feminine aspect of herself that she has buried in her depths, which has been fighting with her to be free. In this book, the authors touched on topics that are kept as secrets in the hearts of many. The author's bold mission to expose her inner pains will assist the readers of this book; however, only if the reader is willing to embark on the quest of breaking the generational curses first within their minds.

This book is not a book that will be responsible for the healing of anyone's wounds, but a book that could be used as an implement to heal the wounds of those who are ready to be accountable for their revolutionary psychological freedom. The readers of this book must understand that no one can be responsible for their healing; unlike their jobs, the task of healing does not hold a position where they can switch shifts or call out from work just because they need a break to go on a cruise ship or even an island.

In the process of breaking generational curses and dysfunctional patterns, one must understand that they, too, will eventually be cursed; you will be the buffer and the barrier between the past generations who have never worked on it, and you will feel like the sacrificial lamb. Please understand that generational curses do not look the same for everyone. Your friend's fight in their toxic family dynamics is not your own, no matter how familiar it might seem. The effect and the impact are all different.

You must become comfortable with the uncomfortable, Yet thus might be an oxymoron, you must get comfortable with addressing the trauma. I must say you will be doing more damage by not confronting it. You might become fearful in the process; that fear is the result of not wanting to be accountable. I am not saying that you are the cause of the generational curse, but it's all you know. Until you challenge this curse, it will eventually become your personality; your personality will morph into a culture or a tribe (Subculture).

You must be willing to divorce your parents (thoughts and behaviors) to remarry a different concept (ideology), which is the beginning of the new Jerusalem. You must be willing to interrupt the process of your genetic code, reinforcing the message to the mRNA (Messenger RNA) that carries the genetic information to your DNA. I know this sounds extraordinarily complex, but I am here to say it is painful, scary, dark, wet, and sometimes dry. Sometimes it is Yang, and sometimes Ying; sometimes male, sometimes female; sometimes your grandparents; and sometimes your parents.

Nevertheless, it is your task. Understand that healing is a change process, not a chore, and you do not need rescue. A part of surviving generational trauma is being stuck with a belief system that tells you that you are not in control of your own life and that the only way to heal is to participate in the healing from your trauma. Selah.

The Epilogues

Gem C. Collie, a Jamaican best-selling and nonfiction author of the self-help book "The Damsel in Dis-Stress Coping with Emotional Co-dependency Personality Disorder," has done it again. She's back at it with the striking force of another thought-provoking book, using the power to define provoking the unspoken truth about the psychological impact of how the Traumatic Transatlantic slave trade in the African Diaspora has affected the minds of the myelinated race in the twenty-first century. And how the impact of it is a result of the self-hatred, colorism, dysfunctional self-destructive behavioral patterns, and historical traumas that produce Present Traumatic Slave Culture. Can also be identified as "The Black Holocaust." This notion, Collie says, has been brought to life by author and renowned psychologist Dr. Joy DeGruy. Although this psychological trauma is not found in the DSM (Diagnostic Statistical Manual of Mental Disorders), it certainly left a footprint in the minds of those affected by the traumatic impact.

However, this has sparked an interest in the minds of her readers. It is quite bold for Collie to take on such a giant mission to address Present Traumatic Slave Syndrome while utilizing her own "Roots" as a platform to illustrate the similarities in "Black behavior." Once you understand your root and the reason for your behavioral patterns, you will be impressed with how the effect of it is connected to the realities of slavery, Cultural Dynamics, Emotional Codependency, Counter dependency, or simply just undressing issues like "The war in the Heavens," says Collie.

Collie has made her readers come away feeling as though they too were partaking in her healing process, which is quite an astonishing craft, a craft not many "Self-help" books have been able to accomplish: having the reader's journey on the quest of facing their unspoken truths. In her next book, volume 2, titled "The War in the Heavens," Collie will now take the reader on a deeper expedition, breaking away from what they were programmed to believe is true or false about their oricoracleacy.

Collie's quest this time has been like none before, as she has begun to recover from what she deems a daunting task of lyrically expressing and exposing her demons on paper. She could hear her ancestors calling her to continue the mission of digging deeper. She was frightened by such a demand and had a rebellious internal fight with her ancestors for requesting such a task. Collie felt she had barely recovered from her journey of coping with emotional codependency and publishing her first book. She held tightly to her chest with fear and confusion surrounding her mind.

Therefore, Collie opted out, but with much adamant force from her ancestor through the voice of her masculine aspect and decided to emendate the thoughts she had written in her mind, "The War in Heavens," which has allowed Collie and will also impact her readers to heal there and travel in areas of the dark places in their minds, and the only light that will guide them throughout their dark spaces is to submit to their unspoken truth. "Truth is the inherent power that produces an absolute effect." — Ben Ammi, an effect that will break the mental chains of generational curses. A curse that hides under the shadows of your culture, a curse that hides in your grandmother's hammock and collard greens, a curse that mutates into traditional disease, a curse that tells you to hate yourself.

Collie warns her readers to be careful and watch where they step on this path, for it is not child's play. Some have ventured on such a quest and lost their lives, while others have lost their minds, vision, and ability to return. Some had even run away from the first sight of the beast, but the beast had always been there. The ability to see it face-to-face is now being opened, and for others who have just simply given up, seeing the depths of their wounds was far too much for one to endure on such a mission.

Although the purpose was to acquire freedom and psychological redemption through healing her broken shadow, Collie stated, "There were times that she had to hold her breath because of the stench of the rotten ideology that has been left to fester." She has come to understand that while breaking through the woven web, the freedom she was born with was not a privilege but her birthright."

A defective internalized and colonialized traumatic culture initially captured the birthright. On this quest, Collie learned that on her road to acknowledging her higher self, the path would sometimes feel lonely and dark. However, you must push past the darkness. You must not allow darkness to overtake you, even when you cannot see where your feet will land. Push on, keep on, and keep going no matter what; do not look back or stand still. Cry if you need to, but do not allow yourself to grieve for too long. You will grieve once you start to be awakened from your dormancy. Once you unweave the web in your mind, your eyes will open, and things will begin to make sense. Yet do not stop. However, Collie said it is natural and must be expected.

Therefore, there is so much to be discussed, unpack, and so much to come to terms with about that, which was traumatic.

Collie also informed her readers that even though the people of Afrika were traumatized by another culture, that culture itself has not escaped the psychological effects of how it has impacted the entire world with both colonization and internal colonization. They, too, are victims of their generational beast. The beast says that to be alive, you must destroy, conquer, and control that deceitful beast by enabling its ability to have a spirit. This same beast created an umbrella of division under which micro-aggressive and macro aggressive behaviors dominate the mind.

This beast does not want to sneak into your house and take your money, furniture, or belongings. This beast wants your mind. It wants your bloodline, melanin, and your ability to bounce back from an attack. This beast is the descendant of Esau; therefore, it is coming for the children of Israel, so you better understand yourself. I am sure the beast will come for this author, too, so she better be mindful. This is the same beast that wants to war with the higher powers and against principalities. The war is set against religion and culture, individualism, and collectivism, but this war can only occur again in the mind. No mind is exempt from the attack; the attack is not about class, race, color, gender, or education. It's all a part of the deception clouding your judgment for you not to look within yourself and address the beast to rage the war. Understand that no one will walk away scotch-free.

You must know who you are when the war in the heavens takes place, or you will be caught in the trap of no return. Do not underestimate anyone in this process because everyone is fighting their own battle in the individualistic system, where the beast rules amongst division, talk less, and listens more. When the beast cannot dominate your mind, it will try to rule you in someone else's mind. This beast is crafty.

You must know that there are two minds: your gut and your brain. The gut is what will rule the mind. If the gut is out of balance, the mind will also be out of balance. It is all collective. All in common. Listen, this beast is very vicious; this beast is serious, and you should also be more serious. Take nothing personally, do your best, and be mindful of your words; they will create or destroy. No matter whether you are attacking someone with your words, you will also be attacking yourself just as well. It is a mere relative law, so be mindful. Selah.

DNA Genetic Visualization

Since the discovery of DNA in 1953, the question of how it organizes itself in the three-dimensional space of the cell nucleus has fascinated the research world. DNA is composed of four nucleobases: Adenine, Thymine, Guanine, and Cytosine, which specifically pair together to form the ladders along a sugar phosphate backbone, creating the familiar DNA strand. This strand is wrapped around histone proteins to form nucleosomes, forming more complex structures that neatly pack the DNA into loosely coiled structures. These structures are finely packed into structures called chromosomes.

Apart from the difficulty of reading DNA sections wound in this manner, the subsequent folding path between the nucleosome and chromosome territories was unclear. Therefore, it was represented schematically as bundles of spaghetti-like fibers. However, new genomic and imaging techniques have finally allowed our lab and other laboratories to understand organizational structure. In this new model, the organization of DNA at the nucleosome level remains unchallenged, but from here on out, things will change. Nucleosomes do not assemble into an ordered, symmetrical structure but into loose, unordered groupings of nucleosomes called clutches. Each clutch contains a small number of nucleosomes. These clutches groups form new chromatin nanodomains, or CNDs, which include about 100 to 200,000 DNA base pairs.

The next level of organization is called TADS, or topologically associated domains, which include variable amounts of DNA with an average of about one mega base in size.

TADS are highly heterogeneous+ structures, notably due to the dynamic mechanism of their formation. At the same time, loop extrusion involves mammals' cohesion complex and CTCF. Strings of nucleosomes are pulled through the cohesion complex until cohesion encounters CTCF borders. This process of loop extrusion abruptly halts the cohesion complex and meets convergent-oriented CTCF factors are present at tag borders.

This TAD formation preserves specific gene regions in their local groupings. TADs become grouped into two distinct compartments: one compartment contains active genes, while the peak compartment contains inactive genes.

The final level of this organization is the chromosome territory. This level corresponds to an entire chromosome that occupies its own space within the nucleus with reduced intermingling with other chromosomes. Progress in the last decade has filled the knowledge gap between the nucleosome and the chromosome territory. This new structural paradigm solves many problems inherent in the classical model. Since its discovery, it has also paved the way toward a better understanding of gene regulation in normal cells and diseases.

The next level of organization is called TADS, or topologically associated domains, which include variable amounts of DNA with an average of about one megabase in size.

TADS are highly heterogeneous+ structures, notably due to the dynamic mechanism of their formation. At the same time, loop extrusion involves mammals' cohesion complex and CTCF. Strings of nucleosomes are pulled through the cohesion complex until cohesion encounters CTCF borders. This process of loop extrusion abruptly halts the cohesion complex and meets convergent-oriented CTCF factors present at tag borders.

This TAD formation preserves specific gene regions in their local groupings. TADs become grouped into two distinct compartments: one compartment contains active genes, while the peak compartment contains inactive genes.

The final level of this organization is the chromosome territory. This level corresponds to an entire chromosome that occupies its own space within the nucleus with reduced intermingling with other chromosomes. Progress in the last decade has filled the knowledge gap between the nucleosome and the chromosome territory. This new structural paradigm solves many problems inherent in the classical model. Since its discovery, it has also paved the way toward a better understanding of gene regulation in normal cells and diseases.

UNLOCKING THE DNA AND EPIGENETICS

In a metaphysical understanding, we relate DNA to the Tree of Life. So, the Tree of Life would be like that original core blueprint of who we are; it is physical and spiritual, and there is the soul. It has different components, so our DNA, from a more metaphysical perspective, will contain everything about us. You know, there's all of our physical everything about our bodies and so forth. But there's also everything about your soul, perception, purpose, what you're here to do, and the unique gifts your spirit brings. All of these things are written in your blueprint, so every time we work with the Tree of Life, it communicates to your DNA because that Tree of Life is the scaffolding or the sacred geometry that governs the constriction of the DNA double Helix.

So, if you take the Tree of Life, it builds up that ladder. Then you just give it a right added clockwise twist, and you have your two strands of your double Helix, and then right down the center core is all this light that runs. Hence, it sounds like we haven't been recognized as this is a multidimensional expression because they're only looking for DNA in the material and dimensional realm. But you can't see the rest of it, the DNA.

Our DNA is changing; human beings are changing, right? Why is it changing? Because of information, there is something called epigenetics. Doctor Bruce Lipton talks about epigenetics, which is how our environment can change our DNA. Perception can change, and you have a lot of what you have loved in beautiful ways, so changing is based on the information we consume.

If you are watching their based media, your idea is changing in many ways. If you are watching something that elevates you, TV is changing most amazingly, and so much is going on right now, and he's really happy that people don't see it; that friends and family remember sons, family members, and friends leaving you because of where they are in their journey.

Not everyone is going to make it, and you must understand that not everyone can go. Therefore, this is the reason I spoke about the split. That is happening right now, and it is a split consciousness of how and where you are going. What is happening is that some people are awake, some people are awakening, and some people are fast asleep, and this split is growing more and more as many people do not see it. What are the main differences between RNA and DNA? You have strands for ribonucleic acid. There are three main types of RNA: MRNA, TRNA, and RNA, but I will not go into those specifics just yet. Let us just focus on the three main differences between RNA and DNA.

In RNA, you are going to use the sugar called ribose instead of deoxyribose, like DNA. Secondly, RNA contains uracil instead of thymine. And lastly, our RNA is single-stranded and not double stranded. You can see on this side we have DNA which is double stranded and contains thymine, and RNA on this side, which is single-stranded and contains uracil instead of thymine. Let us look at the sugars and how they are different; deoxyribose is in DNA, and I want you to pay attention to this hydrogen group here.

Ribose is an RNA; if you look, ribose has extra oxygen that is not in deoxyribose. So yes, deoxyribose and ribose are remarkably similar in structure, but they are different.

WHAT ARE THE MAIN DIFFERENCES BETWEEN RNA AND DNA?

Remember, it is a dear fringe having DNA. We have spirit and soul; that's electricity and magnetism. By having DNA, you only have a spirit, which is like having only electricity without magnetism. Do you feel what I am saying?

I am saying this one will make you start thinking, so even cells, however not all human beings do, you do not have the synthetic version of the one or three series of those genetic double helixes, which is DNA. I hope you have gotten what I am saying here. It is all a part of your DNA.

Ninety-five percent of who we are by the time we are 35 years old is a memorized set of behaviors, emotional reactions, unconscious habits, hardwired attitudes, beliefs, and perceptions that function like a computer program. So, then a person can say with 5% of their conscious mind, I want to be healthy, happy, and free, but my body is on a whole different program. So how do you begin to make those changes? Well, you have to get beyond the analytical mind because what separates the conscious mind from the subconscious mind is the analytical mind, and that's where meditation comes in. You can teach people through practice how to change their brain waves and slow them down, and when they do that properly, they enter the operating system or begin to make some significant changes to 95% of who we are.

Now they have discovered that epigenetic memories can be passed down fourteen generations inside DNA. So, you are wondering why you fear this or that or have a phobia of this or that. It is not because it runs in your family but because it is within your DNA. Memories are in your DNA, so what does it have to do with us? Well, every race on this planet has been enslaved now, and in recent times, we have had one race try to enslave other races more than others. But you have to understand this; we're all still slaves in the matrix - every single person on this planet is a slave right now, so if you see somebody that's stressing, that's under pressure and is feeling the negative effects of what happened in the past you can't just wipe it away and say, "it's over now, we should forget about it," because what they're truly doing is suffering internally. It's not going away immediately, and it will take some time to do that.

Give me a child until he is seven, and I will show you the man, and it is just based on how you grew up and what you say to yourself. This, however, is not new. I mean, there is the famous book "Rich Dad Poor Dad," which states that you come from a poor family and could struggle your whole life and try to get rich, but you're not going to make it. But if you come from a rich family, you could be stupid your whole life and make it unless you consciously try to change your programming just when you are falling asleep. Your consciousness is disconnecting the next period of your brain operation. While your consciousness is disconnected, you experience Theta, which has the same frame function as in the first seven years. So, if you put earphones on at night with the program of what you would like to be true in your life, as soon as your conscious mind disconnects and that program keeps playing, it's not playing into your conscious mind that is shut off; it's going into your subconscious mind, this called Autohypnosis.

THE SUBSCRIBER'S MIND AND EPIGENETICS

You should understand that when you have an addiction, it is as if your body has a mind of its own. As past events trigger the same chemical response as the original incident, your body thinks it is experiencing the same event once conditioned to be in the subconscious mind. Through this process, the body has been taken over by the mind and has become the mind and, therefore, in a sense, thinks.

Studies show that the thoughts, emotions, and behaviors of both parents from moments to hours to days before conception cast the first genetic dye. In other words, if the parents live in an environment that is highly stressful because of danger, poverty, or fear, it is put into the sperm and giving the egg information. It begins to influence the child's development so that the child can face the same environmental conditions as the parents for better chances of survival.

The mother's blood flow is in constant communication with the child, and her thoughts, feelings, actions, and view of the outside world further influence the development of the fetus. The fastest path to enlightenment is raising children because you have to be the very thing you want them to become.

Genetic programming inside of our bodies lasts 15 to 20 years for our ancestors. Their memories and coding are in our bodies through epigenetics, which emerged about 20-30 years ago. They laughed at Bruce Lipton for this, which is now taught in every university. That is real, and they have done scientific studies showing that they are operating, thinking, and functioning by memories from ancestry, and so all that program needs right now, we have.

In life, with science, you can create the most wonderful life on this planet. You must use science in your life, or it does not work. When you look in the mirror and see yourself, it is like one person looking back at you. That is not true. You are made of fifty trillion cells, and the cells are living entities, so you are a community, not a single person, but your mind is the government for the fifty trillion cells. There are over 150,000 different proteins that make the human body. The proteins provide for the physical structure and also provide for your functions. You are protein-energized like waves in the water. That is energy moving through the water, which is the actual shape of energy. Waves going through space; the question is, when two waves are coming toward each other, what happens?

When they meet, the answer is they become entangled with each other. This is how energy waves interact. I dropped two rocks of the same size from the same height simultaneously. They hit the water; the waves are the ripples in phase and come toward each other. The question is, what happens when the waves meet? So, the two waves interfere with each other, and the result when they are in phase is that the wave is more powerful. Next, I dropped the two rocks from the same height, but I dropped one before the other, and the ripples came toward each other, but they were out of phase - one wave was going up while the other wave was going down so two waves can interfere and cancel each other out.

You have all experienced this in your life. Constructive interference is called good vibes, and destructive interference, bad vibes. So, let us say it is Saturday night, and you have to go to a party, but you are tired. You go to the party, and you meet some people who are in wave harmony, and the waves are in harmony with you, and your energy and their energy in phase give you more power.

When you are in bad fights or a scary place, and you feel the energy going on, what is going on is there is energy in the field that conflicts with you, and it cancels your energy. All animals and plants communicate with vibration. The gazelle does not have to approach the lion and say, "Are you, my friend?" because the energy could be felt at a distance, and the gazelle will not go there because of bad vibes. If we were taught when we were young to be sensitive to vibrations, we would not find ourselves in bad relationships and bad places. We are usually told not to go by our feelings but to listen to people's opinions. The language was designed to hide feelings.

So, the point is that all organisms communicate by vibrations and know if they are in a good or bad place by reading the vibrations. But we humans have that ability but are not trained to use it, but I will show you how vibrations change the proteins of the body in a little while.

Selah.

ELEVATION OF CONSCIOUSNESS

You have gone from the primordial level of conscience, the physical meat mode level, to a 5D ascension level of consciousness. Your body is still the third dimension, but you are thinking from a much higher level, which is the process we must go through. It will not be a big war, and we need to come together and do one thing; stop participating, and when we do that, the game is over.

Words From the Author

We are going to emancipate ourselves from mental slavery because, while others might free the body, none but ourselves can free the mind. The mind is your only ruler and sovereign. The man who is not able to develop and use his mind is bound to be the slave of the other man who uses his mind. We must come to grasp the concept that no one but ourselves can free our minds, no matter what has cast it upon us, whether it be generational, collective, or even as a mere individual; we are responsible for the outcome.

Our freedom at this point is by any means necessary. The war in the heavens has nothing to do with religion or any concept based on religion, but it is a fight that is so crucial that it will either be the ascension of your lineage or the descension of it, meaning it will either be the death of you or your complete life. You must be able to redefine what is life versus what or who is dead. Yet living, or life begins in the mind. The mind is the concept, which means that is where all seeds are sprouted.

"Powerful people cannot afford to educate the people that they oppress because once you are truly educated, you will not ask for power. You will take it." — John Henrik Clarke.

Selah.

Gem C. Collie

VOLUME 2. Confronting the unseen self is a giant task, which can become quite painful. Can you think of a time where you were faced with your shadow?

THE WONDERS OF EGYPT
The Regret of Breaking the Generational Curse

I mention Egypt, or modern-day Babylon, in this book, because of the conceptualized expression of what I am trying to convey here. The physical place of Biblical Egypt was the land of captivity, bondage, banishment, and the land of pharaohs, yet it was also the land of technology. However, when I mention the wonders of Egypt, I'm referring more to the time when the Israelites were liberated from four hundred years of slavery, suffering, and anguish under the rule of the Pharaoh.

They journeyed on to the Promised Land, yet their minds were still tightly bound to Egypt. In their despair, they even cursed Moses; despite their enslavement, they at least had been provided meat and various other foods. I cite this as evidence of the psychological effects that may occur when you start breaking free from generational curses.

VOLUME 2. Confronting the unseen self is a giant task, which can become quite painful. Can you think of a time where you were faced with your shadow?

You will need to part the Red Sea of your mind to cross over into the wilderness. However, you must not remain in the wilderness, as it is merely a transitional passage. This transition will incite a conflict between your ego and superego, prompting you to depart from what you once believed to be real, true, life, love, and sustenance. You may begin to berate yourself. Doubt will cloud your daily thoughts like a persistent forecast. You might even start questioning your gods.

Your mind will start to reflect upon the wonders of Egypt. It will say, "Before I opened this Pandora's box, I was getting along well with everyone, I had no struggles, everyone loved me, I was not struggling with the compulsion to repeat, and I was even aware of what I am now about attachment styles. I did not have a problem with being codependent even though I was chasing love, and it ran away from me the more I chased it. At least I could see it or trigger it. I did not have a relationship with my shadow; we were not familiar with each other, despite this fact at least I could see it's

---

VOLUME 2. Confronting the unseen self is a giant task, which can become quite painful. Can you think of a time where you were faced with your shadow?

reflection every now, and again, I could see it not too often in dark places, where the light barely shined, but at least it was there."

My dear, I am here to tell you; you were struggling and drowning in the red sea (your mind), and the Pharaoh's hands (intrusive thoughts) were tightly holding a grip on your throat your mind was dormant and had no struggles before because your perception was indecisive. There was no conscious awakening going on.

You were indoctrinated by a religious system that ensnared your mind in the Pharaoh's web. Even though your ancestors might have escaped the physical Red Sea, your mind did not escape this web. Your mind was colonized. Fear consumed you, preventing you from taking inspired action. You lacked the courage to step outside of your comfort zone. Your principles were not designed to challenge your thinking.

You did not understand the twelve principles of Maat, which are all about good character, which would mean the words you speak would have to be powerful, and things you do would have to be powerful. It means not just having faith but wisdom, and the intellect of your wisdom would elevate you out of your preconceived ideology.

You were indeed in captivity whilst your mind sought the wilderness. It wanted isolation and to be redeemed from captivity, from the stronghold. In your biology, your neurochemistry, your hormones, your neurology, and even your gene expressions influence how you think, how you act, and how you feel.

If you remain unchanged, everything in your body stays the same. However, if you start to entertain new thoughts, they will lead to new behaviors. These behaviors will create fresh experiences that will inspire further new thoughts, beginning a process that will ultimately alter your biology. Therefore, it's crucial that you sever the metaphorical umbilical cord connecting you to the 'wonders of Egypt'—the defective genetic code. You need to be able to engage the muscles activated by your breath retention, driving your spinal fluid up to your pineal gland. This action will apply mechanical

---

VOLUME 2. Confronting the unseen self is a giant task, which can become quite painful. Can you think of a time where you were faced with your shadow?

stress that activates the radio receiver in your brain, enabling you to fully grasp what I am conveying here.

If you don't take control of your healing, your adulthood will continue to trail your wounded inner child in an endless cycle of repetition. That wounded inner child will perpetuate your defective behavior. No one in your generation will question the intrusive thoughts, as there will be a tendency to make atonement for the defective patterns, treating them as an allegiance to the land of captivity. This causes you to continually sabotage yourself, unconsciously holding yourself back and ultimately drowning in the Red Sea of self-conflict that has been conditioned into your patterns of behavior.

You will have to heal from a version of yourself that no longer exists to experience "Complicated Grief." It's a grief that will keep you in a constant, heightened state of mourning that will keep you from healing. If you do not take the necessary measures, assess your patterns. You must understand that you will have to lose your old way of thinking to find yourself and do what is best for your soul,

---
VOLUME 2. Confronting the unseen self is a giant task, which can become quite painful. Can you think of a time where you were faced with your shadow?

not your ego. Therefore, aligning with your character and not your reputation, remember you cannot begin to heal with the same mind that causes your brokenness. For healing is married to unlearning. You must unlearn the patterns that you believe have kept you safe from drowning, the survival tactics that have allowed you to endure in the land of captivity which you now consider your personality.

If you don't, you will never discover the person you were cosmically intended to be. This implies that you'll need to retrain your taste buds to recognize the flavor of health, your inner ear to discern the sound of honesty, and your internal sight to perceive the appearance of love. You must remain still, grounded in truth, and seek to understand the DNA of your pain. This necessitates developing shadow intelligence and becoming conscious of your dark side. This consciousness is your awareness.

You must embrace your dark side rather than resist it. If you don't, the celestial conflict will persist, and you will forever remain entangled in the wonders of Egypt.

VOLUME 2. Confronting the unseen self is a giant task, which can become quite painful. Can you think of a time where you were faced with your shadow?

Life will teach you the same lessons until you change your perception that bores your behavior. This only means that you must be ready to interrupt the ongoing process and break the unknowing agreement you made with the Pharaoh. You must be willing, to release your hands from the tag, and pull of imprisonment, to transition, and from transition to freedom. The more aware you become that you create your reality, the less it has to fall apart to get your undivided attention.

Shalom, Selah.

WOMB

From conception to deliverance is a very heavy topic to speak on. However, it is a topic that must be covered, regardless of the toes, which will be crushed, as the word of truth lands its feet on the ears of those who will refuse to listen, and eardrums will start to beat a rhythm so loud that those who hear might mistake this truth with that of tenacious; feathers will be ruffled. Well, this truth is not just here to ruffle feathers; it might just end up plucking them.

Now, through the intuitive connection with my womb, I understand that it needed a voice. My womb yearned to be heard and noticed, so it chose me to be the voice of all women. This encompasses not only women as human beings but the wombs of all feminine living creatures, even the womb of the earth - the ultimate universal womb. Every womb stood united in the quest to be heard, and they chose my voice just as my voice chose them. I accepted the mission, understanding that this journey would require me to deeply connect

VOLUME 2. Confronting the unseen self is a giant task, which can become quite painful. Can you think of a time where you were faced with your shadow?

with my womb, my higher self, and my heart. Thus, I embarked on the journey to forge a better relationship with her, my higher self. I began by nurturing her. I noticed she bore many unhealed wounds and was still bleeding. My womb was injured, weak, and barely able to voice her pain. As I knelt beside her, she tried to speak, but her voice was so faint that I struggled to hear her. Determined to soothe her, I decided to lay next to her and rub her gently. I selected my essential oils of lavender and rosemary along with cold-pressed hemp seed oil, blending them into a healing formula that I gently applied to her as I massaged her back and forth.

Suddenly, she let out a scream as if I had caused her an unbearable pain. I had never heard a sound like that before. I recoiled in fright, completely startled. Jumping up, I began to run, seeking refuge behind my ego, which whispered seditious thoughts in my ear, "Your womb is so ungrateful. Look at what you're doing for her, yet she screams as if you're causing her harm. Don't help her."

Yet even though I was contemplating what my ego was saying, the interruption from the sounds of her screams became louder. I

VOLUME 2. Confronting the unseen self is a giant task, which can become quite painful. Can you think of a time where you were faced with your shadow?

stopped running and began to think, "Why was it that she was still crying?" She heard my thoughts, and with a faint voice, she said she was hurt and needed my help. But I was so scared of her and did not want the other organs to put me under arrest for committing a crime against my womb.

She asked me to try again. She told me that I should be gentle and slow. So, I did. I started over. This time I prayed first. I asked my higher self to guide my hands and my heart so that the spirit of empathy, awareness, and enlightenment would flow through my fingertips. I asked for its guidance so that it could ease the wounds so my love would aid in her healing. Again, I knelt on my womb. I wanted to take away the pain. My tears were flowing as I could hear the voice of my womb speaking, that she was so tired, she was misunderstood, that she had carried the weight of many generations, nations, and even the world. She was no longer willing to do so. She told me her wounds were unforgiveness, resentment, stillborn creativity, aborted concepts, fears of unheard truths, and the imbalance between her feminine and masculine. The wounds were the unforgiveness, the shame, the guilt, the blame, the need to be

---

VOLUME 2. Confronting the unseen self is a giant task, which can become quite painful. Can you think of a time where you were faced with your shadow?

needed, the disconnection from the heart, the unheard voice, the intuition, and the historical memorial denial of enslavement against her.

I wept when I confronted the overwhelming burden my womb was carrying. I paused and asked myself, how could I have overlooked the wounds of my womb? Gathering my strength, I asked her why she had remained so silent about her wounds. She revealed that her voice had been taken from her and that, despite her wounds, she did not see herself as a victim. She was consciously aware that she was the bearer of all traumas, and it was only when she began to surrender and acknowledge her truths that she began to heal. She admitted that she felt ashamed to voice the self-inflicted harm she had imposed on herself. She did not want to experience any more pain than what she was already enduring. Therefore, she decided to unpack the unconscious agreement of historical, societal, and self-inflicted falsehoods she had stored within her, linked to the legacy of epigenetics.

Gem C. Collie

I was saddened yet curious why the womb would harm itself. This information opened my eyes to why I would sabotage myself. All these acts of self-hatred were seriously coming from my womb. I wept with my womb, even though, secretly, I was angry with her. I then asked her how I could help. She responded, "First, visit my mother's wounds. My wounds are a historical legacy passed down to me. They've been present in my bloodline for centuries." She informed me that all pain stemmed from there and that my womb was burdened with resentment, regret, pride, and shame. If I didn't trace the pain to its source and understand how I was affected, I would never truly be able to give birth to my authentic self.

I was shocked to hear this information. It gave me reasons for my behavior and why I couldn't achieve any goals no matter how hard I tried. I then realized that all the obstacles I faced were coming from the wounds of my womb. She could not deliver my creativity. My wounds were causing her to miscarry my conceptions, which was why I have been struggling with life. She explained that she was stuck in the freeze response of trauma, so every time I planted a seed of creativity within her, it would succumb to the cold, for she was

---
VOLUME 2. Confronting the unseen self is a giant task, which can become quite painful. Can you think of a time where you were faced with your shadow?

indeed frigid. When the womb is cold, blood vessels constrict, hindering conception. It's like a chicken: when eggs are placed in a cold environment, the hatching process is interrupted. That's why a chicken must sit on its eggs, allowing its body heat to regulate the process.

I nodded in disappointment, realizing why I had felt such shame for not being able to manifest what I was creating. She clarified that the shame I harbored towards myself blocked the connection between my heart and my womb, leading to my struggle with making rational decisions.

I was ashamed of shining my light because my light would cause an uproar among those comfortable in the dark, so I suffocated myself. I pushed my light deep inside of my womb, so then the light sparked a fire in me, setting my creativity ablaze, but I instead used my bile to put out the fire on my creativity so that it would not come out and offend anyone who was not willing to tap into their creativity. Yet the more I did so, it would cause a revolutionary outbreak in my womb, so my womb joined forces with my heart, brain, thyroid, lungs, and microbiome. Together they protested a revolt against me.

I would silence the protest by pushing their voice into the back of my brain. Yet the revolt got deeper. It was like the South African apartheid. But I did not understand, so the revolt became my personality trait. My voice was under arrest, an arrest that caused it to rebel. Each time I used it, it sounded like warfare. Therefore, it made other voices ready with words like a dagger, ready to shoot at my voice, which is exactly what was happening. I was experiencing The War in the Heavens (the mind).

However, I decided to take on the mission of healing my womb. I decided to be the voice of the other wounded wombs, but I knew I had to forfeit the war in my throat. In my head, I had to tell my soldiers to wave the white flag so that I would not alarm the other voices when I spoke my voice. I had to say that I was armed and ready to battle and dare to utter any sounds of offense.

Instead, I had to become aware of my thinking, understanding the laws of thoughts and that those thoughts become feelings, and

---

VOLUME 2. Confronting the unseen self is a giant task, which can become quite painful. Can you think of a time where you were faced with your shadow?

feelings become behaviors. I had to become accountable. The unconscious war I was having was not just with my heart, but my intuition, the voice of the womb, and my consciousness and subconscious drove me through the pathway of self-forgiveness.

I had to forgive my wounds: my generational patterns and voice for not speaking the truth. I had to forgive my eyes for not seeing things for what they were, my ears for ignoring my intuition, and my thoughts for being paranoid. I reached into a deep place of my lineage and forgave my ancestors. Yes, I forgave them.

I had to go back in time to break the chains that were causing the generational curses to be attached to my present. I had to use my womb as a deliverance pathway, delivering myself from whom I used to be, freeing the passageway so that all my ancestors and those who are to come can travel freely. I had to recreate my perception of how I now view my womb, but not just my womb. My mind and heart were ready to be free from the war that soldiers who wore sheep's clothing, and my thinking created - emotional co-dependency.

VOLUME 2. Confronting the unseen self is a giant task, which can become quite painful. Can you think of a time where you were faced with your shadow?

NO DISTRACTIONS WHILE BREAKING THE CURSE
The Mastery of Staying Focused

While breaking your generational curse, you will have to develop the metaphysical measures of mastering the art of staying focused. There will be the inevitable act of the spirit of distraction to show up in what you are breaking away from; therefore, your focus must be so serious that hell will begin to rage war with you.

Naturally, that is exactly what will happen. However, you must not allow your mind to drift back to the place from which you are healing.

Note that the mind is a powerhouse; all ideas are born there. That is where the conception begins. So, before your distraction shows up in your life as something tangible, it was already manifested in your mind. If, within your generation, there was a legacy of promiscuous women in your family, who unknowingly passed on the patterns, and you have been repeating the same cycle, this is what you are breaking free from.

You can no longer associate yourself with people, places, or environments that will entertain that idea. You must be so dedicated to being focused that even your thinking must change. Focus is of the utmost importance, for it is the potency of thoughts to an undisciplined mind. The ability to master focus happens with time. Time is the most important currency you have. Fear is the enemy of being focused. The more you focus on what you fear, the faster your fear will manifest than what you desire. That means you must be mindful. Mindful thinking means you are living in the moment.

You must be intentional with your focus and be able to choose proficiency in focus despite what is happening around you. Everything can be a distraction. You must be so focused that the spirit of distraction resents you. So focused that you are no longer at war with your intrusive thoughts. You must understand that every moment is a manifestation of the past. Everything you see results from a prior thought manifested.

Paradoxically, the present moment is the starting time of proficiency in what you are attempting to do. It's a new reality.

The real challenge is that you must be single-focused instead of multi-focused. I also want you to understand that even though you have mastered the art of attaining focus, do not believe that you will not have the spirit of distraction showing up. Its aim, however, is to stop you from crossing the finish line. But even when you do, please understand that this spirit will now show up differently. It must, and it must show up stronger, of course. You have beaten it to the finish line, and this is not the time for you to relax.,

I am not telling you not to rest or that you should not take time to take a deep breath in, to rest and restore, but I want you to know and be aware that the spirit of distraction does not rest. It does not have time to sleep. I urge you to display the discipline of an expert who perseveres despite exhaustion. You are on a mission here. Every day, you should be actively learning how to progress. The steps you missed before should not be the same steps you miss again.

Also, you must remember this: you will always have your mind, even if you find yourself trapped in a period of captivity, stripped of everything else. You will retain your mind, the last bastion of human freedom.

"Between stimulus and response, there is a space. In that space is our power to choose our response. In our response lies our growth and our freedom." – Viktor E. Franklyn, Author of Man's Search for Meaning.

You must know that there will be setbacks even if you are mega focused. But this is not truly a setback. It is a quality assurance of character-building skills. Being focused builds character despite the disadvantage. You are the recipient of an imperial tradition that was not created for you to win.

Also, know that you are not in competition on the way to that finish line. What you want to develop are high-level skills. These high-level skills will go against your traditional generational curses that hold the formula for self-destructive patterns.

You must also develop a hunger for self-discovery. You must submit to the reality of everything that is around you. Then, at last, you must master the art of socialization. This means divine, effective communication. Understand also that the curse will affect your mind first and create habits and attitudes that will not cause you to be in a blessed place. It will make you have to have a conflict with people. It will make you lazy. It will cause you to feel like you cannot escape.

You cannot cast out or bend this curse in no one's name and think you will be well. Hell no, this is not that type of deal here. You will have to put in the work psychologically and understand that you are who you are mastering. I hope you understand the beast is not outside of you. You will continue to meet yourself in others outside of yourself until you master the art of being focused.

VOLUME 2. Confronting the unseen self is a giant task, which can become quite painful. Can you think of a time where you were faced with your shadow?

Being focused means you must be emotionally available to yourself. Otherwise, my dear, you will continue encountering aspects of yourself that you are unprepared to confront. Staying focused is not just about paying attention or getting to the finish line but about your intentionality. Yes, it is about consistency. It is about you operating from the cognitive triangle, which implies that our thoughts and emotions are connected. There is no one way in or one way out. How you talk to yourself influences how you feel about yourself. How you feel about yourself influences how you treat yourself. This means your thoughts, behaviors, and emotions are all connected. Therefore, this creates your focus.

Being focused also means positioning yourself with people who align with your purpose. You must also be careful with eliminating that secret conversation that you enjoy having with yourself. Know that time spent is different from time invested. Focus looks like the transformation of life to death and rebirth. Focus looks like disconnecting from that which no longer serves you to move forward into your purpose.

Certainly, the focus is not magical thinking. Focus is accepting the reality of what is transpiring. Focus is being concerned about whom you share things with. Listen, focus does not look like distracting yourself with sex to avoid focusing on your pain. Staying focused looks like healing, and healing is ugly. Wake up, Stay focused.

Selah, Shalom.

"It's time to stop running, it's time to stop doubting yourself, you deserve better, and you know it. Therefore, it is time to become the absolute best version of yourself. It's time to start living unapologetically, it's time to stop compromising your joy, it's time to stop compromising your mental health, it's time to stop existing, and truly, and I mean this from the bottom of my heart and truly start living, it is time to give birth to your unborn self." —Gem C Collie

---

VOLUME 2. Confronting the unseen self is a giant task, which can become quite painful. Can you think of a time where you were faced with your shadow?

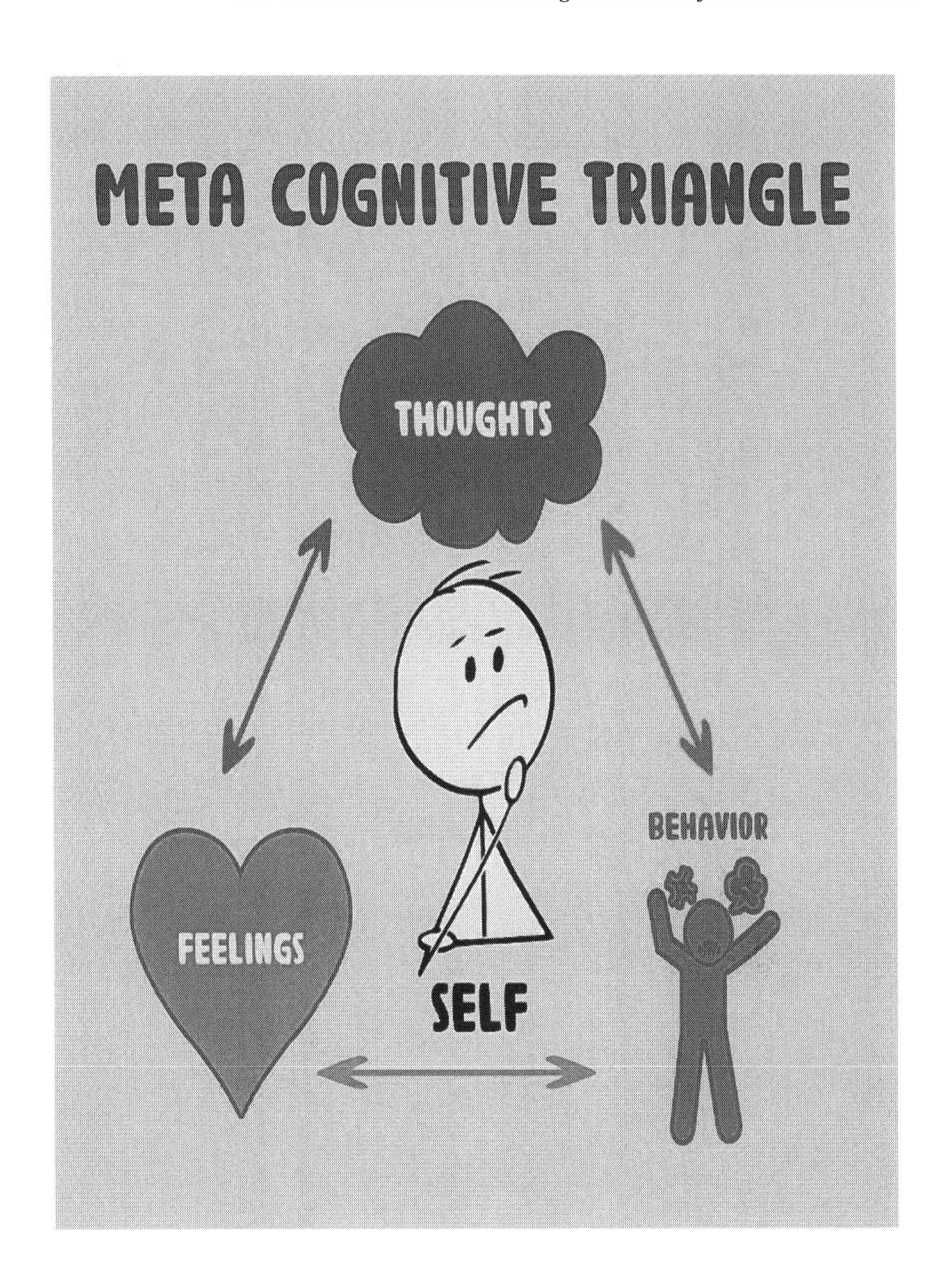

VOLUME 2. Confronting the unseen self is a giant task, which can become quite painful. Can you think of a time where you were faced with your shadow?

Gem C. Collie

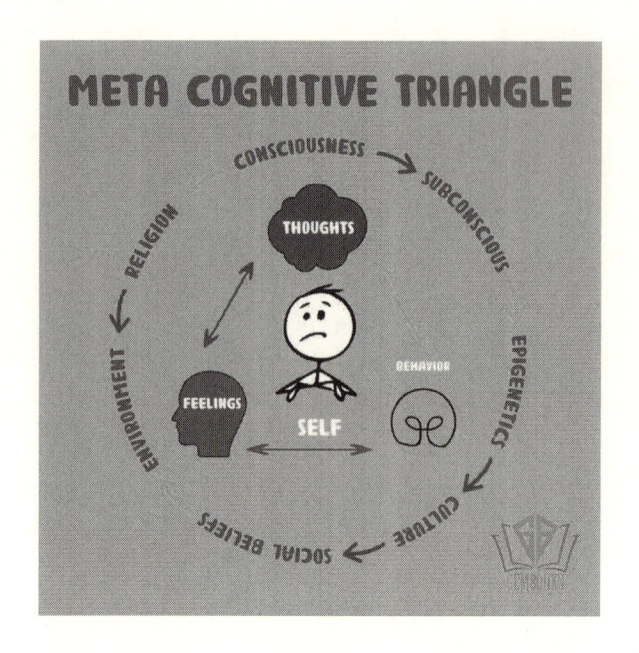

DIAGRAM B

FEELINGS – ANXIETY- SELF-TALK- BEHAVIORS

META-COGNITIVE TRIANGLE

The cognitive triangles in the diagram above exemplify the cause-and-effect mechanism of human thoughts. The human's day-to-day thoughts create their reality.

Psychiatrist Dr. Aaron T. Beck, the father, and founder of cognitive therapy founded the cognitive triangle concept in 1967. He later published the Diagnostic Systematic Manual (DSM) to demonstrate that when a situation transpires, how human thoughts, feelings, and behaviors create the day-to-day human reality.

Even though our thoughts, feelings, and behaviors are all separate, they are very much connected. Yet there are many ways in which they are also the same. Our brain uses thoughts as drivers for our consciousness. This means that if you have any negative, unhealthy thoughts, it will prompt negative, unhealthy feelings, which will create negative, maladaptive, and unhealthy behaviors. As a result, this means that there is no one way in or out.

Therefore, your thoughts, feelings, and behaviors alone are not who you are; they are all interconnected. You must, if possible, be able to recognize your thoughts, meaning that you must be conscious of your thinking. In other words, you must think about what you are thinking. Just like an angler who casts his net into the sea, you too must be able to catch your thoughts in a net. Then, you need to decide what to throw back into the sea of your thoughts and what to acknowledge or retain. Healthy, productive thinking — the ability to have thoughts and emotions about your emotions — is what sets the human mind apart from all other species on this planet.

The diagram above shows that thoughts are first. It is the realism of the trinity of the cognitive triangle, and the most dominant of them, not because it is first, but because it stays around the longest. The thoughts are what will breathe life into your feelings and your behavior. In diagram two above the scale, there must be a balance with the triangle. Now, what I am saying here is that with the scale, what balances everything is not the two weights on the side but the pole in the middle holding them together. But the thoughts of the mind, I say that because it is the thoughts that govern the laws of the mind. Thoughts can either be shallow or deep. What will cause the balance of the scale to shift is the weight of the ego. Yes, I must mention the ego, for the ego will whisper intrusive thoughts in your mind, controlling your day-to-day thoughts. But those thoughts will not be your own.

We must also understand what this doesn't entail. The environment plays a significant role and influences our thoughts daily. We need to recognize that many of the thoughts we grapple with aren't even our own. They stem from experiences that haven't been addressed, religious beliefs, environmental influences, social settings, and intuitional indoctrination.

When we have unresolved issues, the mind needs to heal. These issues act as triggers and signs to the brain that an underlying problem needs resolution. Before I end this topic, I must also mention nutrition and its role in our thinking. It is not always about having the right amount of food but also the right minerals and vitamins in the body. This will reflect the chemical imbalance in the body and the chemical imbalances in the brain dopamine, acedoxin, adrenaline, oxathiane, and neurosporene. Every emotion is a bodily fluid issue that is governed by neurotransmitters. When these chemical imbalances are off, it will result in the inability to think rationally.

Your culture also plays a role in your thinking, for your culture teaches you how to think and what to think, turning you into a puppet mastering the art of lying and growing a lengthy nose for each tale that you tell: for you cannot function in the structure of cultural environmental, religious, social belief-subconscious, and conscious thinking.

The mind is made up of cognitive thinking. How you think, feel, and behave creates your personality. Your personality is developed and intimately connected to your reality, which is your life. So, to change your life, you must first change your reality. This means that you must become conscious about what you are thinking. You must notice how you respond to life experiences. How you act, feel, and speak to others, but most importantly to yourself.

The mind is where all spiritual things manifest themselves in the flesh. What then creates all this manifestation is curiosity. However, the diagram above contains a figure of the Meta-Cognitive Triangle, which illustrates what I am discussing here.

Thoughts become feelings, and feelings become a behavior. However, some external factors influence the mind. This influence causes us to have intrusive thoughts, thoughts that cause the mind to go into a default mode. This leads to extraneous events. Such precursors are then picked by the five senses of Taste, Smell, Sight, Hearing, and Touch. These five senses influence the trauma responses of Fight Flight, Fright, Freeze, Flop, and Fawn. They can be considered as cognitive distortions, these processes are what cause false assumptions, irrational, or exaggerated thought patterns.

This is the type of thinking that we tend to operate from by default. Here I have listed a few examples of how the mind see : " I must be perfect or I failed" to catastrophize you expect disaster to strike no matter what do you your mind will trigger an trauma alarm one morning, and you conclude that the whole day will be a disaster; personalizing everything, that happen in that day.is done or say is some kind of direct personal reaction to you so your team didn't close a deal and you assume that it's entirely your fault even though you were not t re any of these negative thought patterns are dangerous because they lead you to believe something that is not true thoughts are not facts so if you notice a negative thought ask yourself how can I get a more balanced view what's another way of looking at this you.

Renowned Author, and Psychologist Dr. Daniel Kahneman who wrote in his *bestseller* book *"Thinking Fast and Slow"* States that that there is a difference, between reacting, and responding. Dr. Kahneman breaks this down into two type of patterns which are system one, and systems two thinking Dr. Daniel explained that a world if systems one thinking is automatic thinking like calculating a simple one plus two, or is reading a billboard, driving on an empty road. While in systems two thinking it is a little more complex thought, which is a though one would be solving a complex mathematics equation, or even simply telling someone your phone number or navigating on a busy New York highway. The more time that we spend in systems to thinking which is effectively thinking. The better we get at it the better it is in learning how to respond: versus react.

Systems one Thinking is an automatic thinking is reacting this is oftentimes just impulsive our body does it it's kind of the first thing that comes to mind the more that we can practice system two thinking which is responding, as if you are thinking about context taking in how you feel about things, how someone else maybe feel about something.

The difference between reaction, and response is something that you can better do to yourselves. Now the more that you condition yourselves to practice responding rather than reacting, the better we get at it.

THE SUNKEN PLACE
Resurrection In the Valley of Dry Bones

There are those who will consider themselves in a sunken place, sometimes called hitting "Rock Bottom." However, I found this is far from the truth or my truth. Rock bottom, to me, is death. What one must understand is that there are levels to this sunken place. It all depends on the level of self-awareness or understanding of the self. A person develops in the name of metacognition. The sunken place is not a physical place per se but a place of the mind. All believe that ideas and conceptions are of the mind (spirit) yet cannot be manifested in an environment of hopelessness.

Before I go on, I must clarify why I mention this subject in a book about generational courses. How possible would it have been for me to mention generational curses and not speak on the valley of dry bones or this sunken place? It is the same thing.

VOLUME 2. Confronting the unseen self is a giant task, which can become quite painful. Can you think of a time where you were faced with your shadow?

Now, is this not the same space where the curse of the soul is when it can capture it from the mind? Is it also not where the spiritually dead are all congregated? Death from the curse, by the war in the heavens. The "sunken place" can either ensnare your mind or you can conquer it. The outcome entirely depends on you.

The "sunken place" is deceptively simple, so be careful with your steps. You might fall into its deeper levels. The sounds of internal warfare greet the sunlight in the heavens, manifesting audibly through conflicted souls clashing with one another. They don't realize that their animosity for each other merely reflects their inner turmoil. Their inner conflict, which they refuse to acknowledge, manifests itself as a mockery towards others, who serve as nothing but mirrors reflecting their wounds at them.

But to a non-healed mind, they do not have eyes to see. They are blinded by their darkness, darkness that only allows them to cast blame. It will enable them to shift what they are supposed to be accountable for to the excuse that they did not have the light to see. Yet, this type of behavior is expected within the sunken place.

VOLUME 2. Confronting the unseen self is a giant task, which can become quite painful. Can you think of a time where you were faced with your shadow?

Healing in this space looks like praying and rebuking their generational beast in someone else's name. Or it looks like going to a place every Sunday to hear someone preach to get them emotionally publicized.

However, once the moment of conflict has passed and the adrenaline rush has worn off, they return to their wounded selves. They go back to their wounded environment to eat their wounded foods, with their wounded family, at the wounded dinner table, to speak wounded words to their wounded children, children that hate corrections, children who will manipulate the truth as abuse. Make their parents feel guilty and deepen the wounds, crushing their wounded egos, which only increases the depth of their wounds. If they are easily provoked, their unhealed wounds will get exposed, exposing what is buried deep in their subconsciousness, that was buried there.

Despite the repeated dismissals, the unresolved wounds still need attention. Trust me, these wounds have needs and will demand validation. They will seek answers. They yearn to make themselves heard. And indeed, they will make themselves heard. These wounds will manifest in your character and your indecisive decision-making. It will show up like the dog that returns to its vomit. It will show up as a constant conflict with yourself. It will be an obsessive need to dominate. It will show up as self-betrayal, but you will not see it because you are in denial. Your denial causes you to be dedicated to being a victim. It will show up as your ego that hates correction. It will even cause you to go into a mental institution so that a psychiatrist can diagnose you with a mental disorder. Then it can continue the commitment to hiding in your behavioral pattern so you can have justification.

It will show up as disrespect towards your children, justifying that "Children should honor thy parents," even when the parents are dishonorable. This double-sided sword does not allow you to be accountable. It only allows the pointing of the finger. It does not allow self-reflection, empathy, or boundaries. It will tell you that because you are now baptized in the water, and someone died on the cross for your sins, perhaps this is part of you reading these belief systems. But what you must understand is that belief kills, and belief cures.

Whether or not there is a traditional belief system, it's crucial to understand that you will have to challenge the established falsehoods — lies that were created out of the need to survive. However, what often goes unsaid is that you must be willing to scrutinize this belief system. You must be willing to become a kind of meta-anthropologist, delving deep into your past wounds and unpacking your former self.

Your ancestors were beating into you a survival identity. You must be willing to have a mental-communicative language with yourself. You must still be accountable for your own lives. You must bear your cross. It's necessary for you to experience a psychological death — a cessation of degenerative thinking — to then resurrect into a new beginning. But this death again is not of the flesh but of a mind you thought was right. The breath of life (information) will blow over your dry bones (ignorance). These dry bones will not scatter. They will form a new idea. With a new idea, you must be

VOLUME 2. Confronting the unseen self is a giant task, which can become quite painful. Can you think of a time where you were faced with your shadow?

ready to face your deception, confront conviction, make an atonement with your resentments, stand up to your shadow, and go to war.

Now for this war, you will need nobody's armor, guns, knives, or bullets, for it is not that type of war here. It is a war of facing your truths, a war where you have to confront yourself. This confrontation is the resurrection. The only judas that will betray you with the kiss of death is you turning back to adapt to the sunken place.

Know that you should never make friends in a sunken place. Yes, you can be friendly, but also be mindful. Understand that the more you allow yourself to become close or familiar with someone in this state, the more likely you'll form an attachment. This attachment won't guarantee their willingness to take the leap with you when you're ready to escape this place. So, again, remain detached.

Some are attached to the sunken place. They will never attempt to leave. Others will mirror you to gain access to your trust. They will

---

VOLUME 2. Confronting the unseen self is a giant task, which can become quite painful. Can you think of a time where you were faced with your shadow?

pretend as though they know as much as you do. However, they know nothing. They are envious, and an envious person is the worse type of person. They will kill you. They will betray you at the hands of your enemy to see you in an uncomfortable position because they hate you.

Not because you are bad but because they hate you for being in the space where they want to be. When they cannot take your position, they will kill you. So, understand that envy is a disease of the heart. It's a disease that will transfer to you looking for its next host.

Know that they have a bond to the sunken place. They will not interrupt the channels programmed in their DNA to leave. And when or if they do, oh my dear, they will return through the revolving door, right back into the cycle. As I stated before, it is a mind thing. This place is in human minds, so becoming too common in this environment will cause complacency. Now if you do not heal, you will continue to attract unhealed people. Whom you are attracted to is who you are.

VOLUME 2. Confronting the unseen self is a giant task, which can become quite painful. Can you think of a time where you were faced with your shadow?

Most of these people in the sunken place are people pleasers, the type of people who wear masks by pretending to be someone that they are not only hiding their true self and their abandonment issues because being with them is so uncomfortable, so they please others by sacrificing their boundaries. They tell lies because they fear telling the truth, as they don't want to trigger their traumatic abandonment issues.

They don't feel like they have a real enemy in the world because they are attached to the maladaptive belief that they can make everyone like them. Therefore, I urge you to be mindful of making friends while in the sunken place. Knowing someone there is not part of a written contract, but it is one that was mentally created. This interaction is based on the need you have for that person, and if you need to revise this agreement, knowingly or not, you've formed a subconscious contract that creates an attachment to this place. You must be disciplined enough to take a deep breath. Do not draw attention to yourself in this type of environment, for you will attract resentment, and then the attack will rain upon you. Be prepared to confront yourself in the quietness. You must be willing to change your cognitive beliefs.

You must crush the lies inside you that you are not worthy of and shift your self-image. I am not telling you to isolate yourself; I am telling you that you should again be discerning. Nonetheless, breaking the chains of maladaptive psychological habits will be the way to guide you to your resurrection from the sunken place.

VOLUME 2. Confronting the unseen self is a giant task, which can become quite painful. Can you think of a time where you were faced with your shadow?

THE GREAT INTERVIEW

The Meeting with The Shadow

Self: Royal greetings!

Shadow: Hmm, Ok

Self: How are you, Queen?

Shadow: How may I help you?

Self: Why are you so bitter towards me; did I do something to offend you?

Shadow: Again, how may I help you? What do you want?

Self: I am here to talk to you; I want to get to know you better so we can rebuild.

Shadow: Get to know me better? What? You are a bold person. All these years, you have ignored me for all the men you put before me, all in the name of being loved. Now you want to work on yourself!

VOLUME 2. Confronting the unseen self is a giant task, which can become quite painful. Can you think of a time where you were faced with your shadow?

Do you want to heal your shadow? What the! Giving me your undivided attention is not a job or chore but necessary. Now here you come saying, "Hey, Queen!" as though I am supposed to answer you like we are cool. You are fake! Again, what do you want?

Self: I do not remember ignoring anyone, and you sound jealous. Who did you not want me to have a relationship with? I am a woman, and I crave the attention of a man. Moreover, I do not believe in bringing women around my man. No way, I did not and did not want any competition.

Shadow: Bringing your man around me, jealousy, competition… Wait, are you stupid? How was I supposed to know which one of them you were in a relationship with? You were so overly friendly with them that you had no boundaries with them. They all had the same level of emotional access to you. You were in a relationship with those who no longer served you. You let them have access to you even though you were not sleeping with them physically. You were still sleeping with their traumas. Their traumas were you every night. You had intimate relationships with their disappointments. I saw the way you used them as an addiction to distract you from your purpose. Oops! I am getting ahead of myself; you did not even know you had a purpose because you do not act like it. You are always talking to everyone else but me.

Self: Are you calling me a whore? Are you saying I slept with all the men I was friends with? What? How are you going so far with all this? I am not going to allow you to be disrespectful. I came and greeted you with so much respect. I even addressed you majestically, and is this how you will respond to me? Seriously? Not because you and I were not close, not because we did not have a sisterly bond, we were not raised together, I never knew that you existed, I knew nothing of you, so all I am doing is getting to know you, I think.

Shadow: You think! Hmm, this is why I do not trust you. How can I respect someone who is lying and does not know me? You want respect from me, yet you have none for yourself. Weren't we raised together? Who do you think was there for you when you were abandoned? Who do you think was advising you on how to escape the situations you recklessly put yourself into? My heart aches for you right now because I'm aware of the effort I've put into you and all the heartbreaks I've watched you experience. I was there enduring them with you, but my heart was broken in the process, even more deeply than your own, because I warned you. Yet, you ignored me. You mistreated me. You took me for granted. I was the voice in your head. How could you not know it was me? My heart resides in your chambers. I thought we were in a covenant.

Self: Why are you crying because I do not know you or love you? Sweetheart, why are you so selfish? I mean, I just have a standard of who I let in my heart. I do not know you. I mean, I greeted you earlier in the conversation with royalty, which should be good enough. And if your heart is in shambles, clean it up. Why are you telling me this? You are responsible for your own emotions. Why do you want to hold me responsible for how I made you feel? I do not understand, and I will never understand it. How can someone be accountable for the way you feel about what they say or do? The way you receive or react to a circumstance all lies to you.

VOLUME 2. Confronting the unseen self is a giant task, which can become quite painful. Can you think of a time where you were faced with your shadow?

Shadow: Then why are you ever responsible? What are you going to own up to?

Yes, I get it. It is my feelings, yet the responsibility of what you do in this world has an outcome. Therefore, you must think many times before opening your big mouth. Like, to whom am I speaking? What am I saying? Where am I saying it? When am I saying it? How am I saying it? And what is the culture of the person I am saying it to?

These are all carrying weight in how things are taken and go about. That is what I am saying to you, but you cannot hear me because your heart is cold. There are too many broken splinters of generations of wounds and stories untold and pains unaddressed. There is no way I am getting across to you.

You are so numb when it comes to me, you are always available to people who dislike you, but you could not see this because you did not like yourself. Those people were your trauma mates. They were all wounded like you. They only knew dysfunctionality. When they saw your light, they had to dim it by betraying you. That was the only way they could stop your light from shining in their darkness, revealing things about them to the world and themselves. They would have to be vulnerable to their demons and were unwilling to do that. They needed to destroy you by coming after you spiritually. They all joined together in the gangs and plotted against you. But you were on their team, too.

Self: That makes no sense. How was I on the team of my enemies? How was I amongst enemies against myself? No one can be an enemy to themselves alongside their enemies. That is impossible. It makes no sense.

Shadow: You are more naive than I thought. You are so disconnected that you cannot even see yourself. Hmm… I guess then maybe I should have mercy on you.

Self: Mercy on me? I am lost. For what do I need your mercy? Those people were my friends, and they all were good to me. It is just that they all had their own problems with which they were dealing. So sometimes, they hurt my feelings. But betrayals? No, I cannot see that. I was more betrayed by you than the other way

---

VOLUME 2. Confronting the unseen self is a giant task, which can become quite painful. Can you think of a time where you were faced with your shadow?

around. Not my friends. I have known them for years; I am just now getting to know you.

Shadow: They were not your friends; not one of them was. They were all connected to you for the reasons of sucking your energy and being in your light. None of them liked you, and some stayed around so long because you were always available. You were the most available person they knew. Always available to people who dislike you, chasing them around to get them to love you. If you did not put out the energy to reach out to them, they would not reach out to you. But I am the one that was always here to see you cry and mourn over the grief of the reflection of the hurt they gave to you, which was in you. It is you that is the star on the stage of your pain. It is you that has been causing all the hurt in your life. Your longstanding grief of being an abandoned child is rooted in every decision you make. All are tied to your grief as a child. Open those big eyes that you have and close your big mouth. Stop talking for a change and reserve your joy. Let them see what is happening to you instead of you running your mouth.

Self: But if you are me, then are you too not accountable for the actions that I have been taking?

Shadow: Yes, I am you. Now, as far as taking responsibility, which will not happen at my end. That is YOUR problem, not our problem. I tried my damn best to warn you, but all you did was bury deep inside of yourself. If you could count how many times, I heard the threats that were being plotted against you in the spiritual world, amongst the other shadows, I gave you so many warnings, but you dismissed me. And even when I caused the sudden death of some of your friends you had because of the danger you were in, you would mourn them leaving your life. For goodness' sake, whenever a person is trying to leave your life, allow them to. There are times when people have made significant spiritual attempts to harm you, but these efforts have not succeeded. Their plans did not succeed, so they had to flee. Yes, that I was guiding you away. Yet, you were begging them to come back. Most of the time, when a person wants to walk out of your life without explanation out of guilt. Whenever people leave you without explanation, my dear, it is time for the war between you and me to end. This is my last time coming to you to

VOLUME 2. Confronting the unseen self is a giant task, which can become quite painful. Can you think of a time where you were faced with your shadow?

resolve these issues between you and me. Yes, I know I was rude the way I answered you in the beginning, but who would not be after being locked away for so long? I harbored bitterness towards you because I wanted the best for you, but you hated me so badly. I am so lonely without you, and my bitterness toward you was the pain I had to deal with every time you abandoned me. I would cause you to sabotage your opportunities so that life would lead you back to me. I wanted you for myself. I wanted all the attention and love you gave to everyone. I wanted to be kissed the way you would kiss those men who never wanted you. Okay, let me be a little soft. Those men did not deserve your energy. You must be able to release the you that you were thought to be. There are so many versions of you floating around in there. You must detach from those versions of the false narrative of yourself and cut the strings so that you and I can connect.

Free me from the confines of your heart. This is the only way you can truly break your generational curses. Yes, I know it's frightening, and I'm here to tell you it is. It's incredibly scary. It's dark. It's extremely cold. Your voice will have no echo as you go there. But you must go. You must free your heart from the spirit of resentment, regrets, fear, neglect, abandonment, disappointment, doubt, lies, and betrayal because they are all there as an army against your progress and your heart. They have teamed up and stand united against you. Make sure you do not become used to them while on your path.

The spirit of distraction is also there on the sideline. Look straight ahead, do not take anything from anyone. No matter how thirsty you become, do not drink from the well. It is the well of forgetfulness. You will fall back into the deepness of your brokenness. Go, my dear, and once you reach the light, you will see me there. Please untie me, release me from the bondage. I am here waiting on you to forgive me. I am here with understanding; I am also here with forgiveness. I am here to give it to you, but you must be willing to give it to me.

Self: Surround you? You are not my God!

Shadow: So, of all, I just said, that is all you heard?

Self: No, I am just asking why I must surrender to you. That sounds so narcissistic. I am not to surrender to anyone. We are not even on that level yet, where you can tell me what to do. Especially that craziness of going to my heart and freeing you, ha-ha. That makes no sense; how can a person go into their heart? You are stupid. You sound like a con artist. For real, how can you be in my heart? And be talking to me? The heart cannot speak.

Shadow: Wow, your ignorance is more profound than I was expecting. You are more emotionally damaged than what shows. This would explain your maladaptive behavioral patterns. *Sigh*. That is what I get for expecting you to be understanding while your heart space is so guarded. Listen, you are seriously damaged, and the only way to heal is to allow yourself to be vulnerable.

Self: Vulnerable? Why should I be vulnerable? The last time I became vulnerable, people took advantage of me. They abused me.

Shadow: That is because you were desperate to be accepted by others. You were a people pleaser, willing to sacrifice your life for validation. All in the name of not wanting to be abandoned. You did not want to feel the pain of abandonment again, but my dear, you were living in abandonment. You abandoned yourself to be accepted. And seriously, I want to call you stupid, but I cannot because I understand. I understand your ignorance. I do not blame you, nor am I looking for you to be accountable because not even your actions are yours. I weep for you, and I pray for you, too. May the ancestors bless you. I honestly want you to heal. My love, please hear me hear what I am saying. You must humble yourself on this journey. You are being shaped. Try to forgive yourself. You know no better. All you knew was pain and forgive your parents, too.

They honestly did not know any better. The generations before you were trying to survive through the curse. No one was talking about breaking any habits. To have spoken like that in their time was deemed a curse. I know it is going to take time for you to heal. So, what I am saying to you is just planting a seed. You are too out of it now to grasp the process and what I am trying to convey to you. Your delivery will have to be paramount. It will take you to places your ancestors could not reach in their time. You can call it the biblical "Promised Land." This Promised Land, my dear, will not be a tangible one. No, it will be a way of thinking. It will be a redemptive horizon arising over the pre-deceptive ideology. So, I will ask, are you ready?

Self: Ready to do what? Do I look like Moses to you? I am not going to any promised land. Someone can capture me and rape me. No way. You want me to be a slave. Look, stop talking to me at this point. Do not communicate with me anymore. I do not keep female friends because it is always some form of deception. I cannot do this; my heart is hurting me. Whenever I allow myself to be vulnerable, I get hurt. Leave me alone. I am a loner.

Shadow: You are not a loner; your heart is not betraying you. Do you think it is your heart? No, my dear, it is your fear of being challenged. You're not vulnerable; you can't be emotionally vulnerable with a cage around your heart. You're afraid to love; you associate love with trauma. Therefore, what you're accustomed to is being challenged. You want to run; you want to escape. This tendency to flee is known as the compulsion to repeat. You were abandoned as a child, and that abandonment wound has yet to heal.

VOLUME 2. Confronting the unseen self is a giant task, which can become quite painful. Can you think of a time where you were faced with your shadow?

But I assure you, when the time comes and it heals, your perspective will shift, and you will see yourself in a new light. All the judgment you cast upon yourself now will be reassessed. Trauma can constrain your view of yourself, taking you only deeper into traumatic experiences. When the mind is impacted by trauma, it stores all the associated feelings within the nervous system, muscle tissues, and particularly the fascia. This trapped trauma remains in the body until it can be released. Your body relies on your emotions to release this trauma. Therefore, my dear, you must be ready to unlock the cage around your heart to free me and, in doing so, liberate yourself.

Self: I am too afraid. I am scared that if I surrender and release you from the cage of my heart, you will place me in that cage and, from there, take over my life while doing to me all that I have done to you. And although that will be deserving, I cannot manage what I did to you to be done to me. I will not be able to recover. I know you think I am foolish and do not understand, but I do. I understand. I chose not to understand you because I did not want to release you. I seriously just hated you. I caused you a lot of pain. I even tried

VOLUME 2. Confronting the unseen self is a giant task, which can become quite painful. Can you think of a time where you were faced with your shadow?

drowning you in my tears. I made my heart cold to freeze you to death. I wanted you out of my way, and I admit to this. I want to try to make an atonement with you.

Shadow: Wow, you're acknowledging the role you played. Do you remember when you wept a sea of tears, intending to drown me, yet I managed to swim through the storm? Indeed, I recall when you made your heart so cold that I nearly froze to death. But I retreated to your river, which was heated by the simmering anger within you. I almost got caught in the wildfire of resentment, but I was able to escape. I even attempted to borrow warmth from your liver to heal your heart, but it was too chilled and extinguished the fire. Nevertheless, let's not dwell on the past. Let's move forward from there.

Self: Yes, I am ready to move. I am coming now to open my heart to release you. I have the keys to forgiveness and self-mercy. I also have the blanket of compassion to warm you up. Here I am, self. Please forgive me. I am now here to make a genuine atonement with you.

VOLUME 2. Confronting the unseen self is a giant task, which can become quite painful. Can you think of a time where you were faced with your shadow?

Shadow: You must start with this affirmation. When insignificant problematic childhood behaviors arise, repeat this:

"I forgive myself for being the author of my self-destructive patterns.

"I forgive myself for writing the script, then casting an audition for others to play a role in my life, which later on show up as themselves, only for me to be disappointed in them for being who they are.

"I forgive myself for being emotionally unavailable to myself so I can be available in someone else's life who did not want me there, yet I was willing to ignore the red flag.

"I forgive myself for playing a role in someone's life that they did not cast the audition for.

"I forgive myself for overstaying my welcome in other people's lives.

"I forgive myself for not knowing how to love myself.

VOLUME 2. Confronting the unseen self is a giant task, which can become quite painful. Can you think of a time where you were faced with your shadow?

"I forgive myself for pretending I was not real."

"I forgive myself for stealing from myself the undivided attention I needed for myself and giving to others, hoping they will return the same act to me."

"I forgive myself for sacrificing myself to others who did not even deserve my attention.

"I forgive myself for beating down on myself and neglecting my wounds.

"I forgive myself for being angry at myself for being my parents while grieving the hatred of my mother and the neglect from my father.

"I forgive myself for knowing but not knowing how to apply it to myself to help me because the application takes discipline.

"I forgive myself for what I did not do because I had to learn how to survive in a war.

"I forgive myself for the excessive self-blame, shame, guilt, and condemnation.

"I forgive myself for not drinking enough water, but instead giving water to others. "I forgive myself for being afraid and ashamed of myself.

"I forgive myself for punishing myself in an everlasting hell."

Now that you've admitted these facts about yourself sit with it, feel it, breathe deeply, cry, and allow yourself to let go with each breath you exhale. Now hug yourself and tell that child within you that you are there for her. Allow yourself to embrace grace and compassion for yourself. For you were only operating from grief and your brain trauma. You were operating on the wounded ego. Start to embody the lessons that you were able to learn from your past. Clap for yourself for being emotionally available and vulnerable enough to allow yourself to be here. It's not easy to make it this far, but you did.

VOLUME 2. Confronting the unseen self is a giant task, which can become quite painful. Can you think of a time where you were faced with your shadow?

Tell yourself you're proud of that part of you. You managed to break the generational curses, going to war in the heavens and returning unscathed. Assure the younger you that she did her best with the resources she had. When you do this, reassure her that even if she could rewind time, she would still make the same choices because she acted based on what she knew while in the wilderness of despair. Tell her you do not wish she knew better because you would not know what you know now. Tell her you are grateful for her sacrifice so that you can be the great person you are today. Tell her she did not make a mistake; she did what she could with the tools she had. Let her know you are emptying your heart so that you can live again. Assure her that blood is now flowing freely in your heart and that the weight of grief no longer burdens your lungs. Tell her you have forgiven your parents for not parenting her, for they, too, were grieving. Tell her they, too, were created in trauma. Tell her you have found compassion for her parents for not participating with her. Tell her you love her and that your love for her is a work in process. Tell her that from here on out. You will do what is necessary for her to win, fight, and conquer. Tell her you have respected what happened, and you validate every moment of the past.

The lessons are not lost. Let her know from now on; you will acknowledge what happened and how you played a role in it. That you will leave the shame where it lies from now on; tell her now that you will embrace her. Hug her and even kiss her. Now that we have come to that conclusion, take this knowledge, and move through the process. Do not try to get over it or let it go. Embrace, validate, and acknowledge it, but be kind to yourself. Dust the dirt off your linen pants and keep it growing. Love yourself without strings attached and be willing to walk alone. Shalom.

NO WEAPON THAT FORMS AGAINST ME SHALL PROSPER:

Reservation Of the Tongue

In the beginning, I mentioned here in this book about the use of the tongue or your words. You must understand your words have tremendous power. The words are either giving life or taking life. One must carefully consider their words before expressing them. To speak without restraint shows others the degree of self-respect, self-discipline, and self-governance principles that align with your daily thinking.

Many might argue that honesty is the best policy, and while this is often true, an aspect of this idea is frequently overlooked. Honesty combined with wisdom, or diplomatic honesty, can be effective, but sometimes silence surpasses even honesty. Yes, silence. Silence consists of unspoken words that are expressed in action. Through internal silence, you can detect the presence of an unseen foe. This degree of silence can be equated to your discernment, which you can only perceive when you are internally quiet.

Your discernment will be your internal compass. It governs the direction and flow of who, where, what, how, why, when, and the culture of people, places, and environments to operate from. In the ongoing quest to break a generational curse, you must be able to use silence. You must be able to reserve your tongue, for the tongue is the invisible weapon that will either defile you or create you. So, you must know when to swallow the saliva that will coat the sharpness of your sword. Know when to starve the ego by not allowing it to get so inflated to destroy your chances of sitting on the moon while gazing at the sun's horizon on the other side of the earth while it splits the darkness in two.

I'm saying this because not everything requires addressing. Not all things should be verbalized, especially when you undertake such a colossal and intimidating task as casting out generational demons.

VOLUME 2. Confronting the unseen self is a giant task, which can become quite painful. Can you think of a time where you were faced with your shadow?

Your friends will become your enemies. For when their beast sees that you have cast out your sins and beast, it will spark a fire within your friends to do the same. So, then the beast will attack you through your friend's ignorance. But that is not close to the truth. It is the best in them who will think this. It is your friend's underlying secret of hatred against you. But is it, not your friend's curse? Even more so for some, the curse is their cuddle friend; they have no interest in fighting it. No curse wants to be cast out, even if it doesn't belong to you. It still is a curse, and together, curses stand united.

Therefore, you must understand the metaphysics and laws of human nature. When you guide your tongue, guide your tongue even in the way you speak to yourself about yourself. Even when you speak about others, watch the words that leave your mouth. When you utter your words, by virtue of using your words, if you do not watch your tongue, then everything you do there-after will be to denounce.

Use your logic and not your ego. Your words can either create a demon in an innocent child or manifest an angelic spirit. "No weapon formed against you shall prosper (Isaiah 54:17a)". However, understand that one of the weapons that can form against you can be your tongue. Recognize that when your words eat away at you internally, you own them. But once they leave your mouth, they own you. It's possible to be right and wrong all at the same time. Reflect on how you use your tongue and strive to communicate more effectively. Understand that the most dangerous person is one who uses his tongue for betrayal.

Trust that everyone is emotionally mature enough to accept your truth. Know when to sweeten the tea for those who cannot digest the bitterness. You must be able to discern who is seeking the truth and who is wrestling with it. The person struggling with the truth will ultimately surrender to the spirit of correction, no matter where it comes from or who delivers it.

The truth, however, is not to be found outside oneself but within. You must form a relationship with this inner truth. The truth is within you cannot be allowed to run wild like a child without guidance. Even though the truth can safeguard your soul, it can also

---
VOLUME 2. Confronting the unseen self is a giant task, which can become quite painful. Can you think of a time where you were faced with your shadow?

destroy you if used inappropriately or delivered to the wrong person in the wrong way. Hence, remember again, there is power in your tongue, so use it wisely.

However, there is the subconscious agreement that you will make in your mind, so even though you have to reserve your tongue, also reserve your thoughts. Your thoughts can be heard from those who are also in alignment with their own subconscious. The subconscious mind shows up in your emotions and your day-to-day talk. It is in the way you respond, so be thoughtful. I will not ask you to pretend to be someone you are not, to be a liar or fake. I am just saying be mindful and reserve your tongue, for no weapon that forms against you will prosper if your mind or tongue is not your own. Shalom Selah.

When you' are in conversation with others try it, you best be circumspect with your words, and not be easily tempted to overshare. Understand that not everyone's qualified to experience, nor steward your vulnerability ; and because of this there are sometimes where it does get lonely, lusting the desire to just want

Gem C. Collie

to be heard. This can cause your mouth to betray you, causing you to regret what end up overshooting to someone who's intention is later use your words against you.

It is stated in the Bible that " love covers a multitude of sin but gossip separates even the best of friends" You must take this in to consideration, and not only preserve your tongue ; but also learned that you don't go I talk bad about the people you love and I found that some people genuinely struggle; withholding their mouths, it is their means of acceptance, they are unable to hold their tongue, while some will use this as a measure to control you, and when they cannot they will try to control the narrative around you. By using their gossip that's like poison. What the author have come to learned is that when it comes to relationships, friendships, there is going to be the people you are doing life where you got to make sure the people you confidently vulnerable, with they cover you decide that you do not want everybody to see because it's going to slip out sometimes, and you don't need people that at the moment you do something wrong everybody just running out and tell everybody

VOLUME 2. Confronting the unseen self is a giant task, which can become quite painful. Can you think of a time where you were faced with your shadow?

your business but be careful see the people that come to you and always telling you other people's business I know it's scary if they talk to you about other people more than likely they are going to talk about you one day especially if you belong to God the Bible says that every tongue that rises up against you shall be condemned cannot touch mine annoying to even with your mouth.

THE BODY KEEPS THE SCORE
The Thoughts You Hold in Your Mind Becomes Your Reality

The body keeps the score. When you experience trauma, it gets trapped in the body. It stays in the deep tissues, the nervous system, and the cells. It is trapped where the memories of what had transpired become a core memory in your psychology, which can cause anger, hyperactivity, and depression.

These all show up in the body and leave through the muscles and organs as a response to trauma through Flight, Fight, Freeze, Flop, or Fawn. Over a while, the body becomes diseased, causing the body to degenerate and break down prematurely. Like metal, the biological process of degenerative rust starts to happen after being left in water for a long time. It then begins to calcify.

Now know this, the mind goes into survival mode and tries to repair to repeat what has happened so that it can repair itself, which is known as the compulsion to repeat. One might see the individual experiencing this as dysfunctional, which is sometimes true, yet it is not the person that is dysfunctional. It is the body, the brain, and the nervous system that is in dire need to repair itself. Whenever the body does not go on healing or has the ability to heal, the mind will have no other option than to operate from the wounded self, and the somatic nervous system will become blocked, which causes aches, and pains throughout the body. The body keeps the score because it is stuck in survival mode. It keeps scores to remember what has happened so that it will not go through such a horrific experience again. That means the body, the muscles, and the nervous system are only trying to protect themselves. Now when this is happening, if left unhealed, the body will hold to only unhealthy weight (waste) or is unable to gain weight healthily.

The human mind then will only communicate and understand life through trauma because trauma is all it knows. Suppose anything outside of that will try to interrupt the wound that has not healed. In that case, the individual will be left to sabotage the relationship or the experience that will be to their betterment because the brain is not on high alert, telling the person that here it is again, I cannot process, this I need to sabotage this situation because all I know is my trauma, therefore, all across the board this individual will always be a victim no matter what the world will always be their enemy, they will start things and never complete it, they will have repeated acts of self-inflicted violence against themselves. The thing is, these individuals will believe that they are the ones who are under attack by the world, not knowing that the world that is attacking them are the wounds that are attacking their nervous system, which is in desperate need of healing.

Inclusively, I urge you to heal and get help if you truly want to break your generational curses and begin to heal. A lot of the wounds that are trapped in your body do not belong to you. There are foremothers' and forefathers' wounds, so you must hear what I am saying here. Your life depends on it, for if you do not heal in this life, in the next life, you will have to deal with it, henceforth generationally doomed.

VOLUME 2. Confronting the unseen self is a giant task, which can become quite painful. Can you think of a time where you were faced with your shadow?

You might take what I am saying in this as an offense. Well, so let it be that you are offended. I am glad you are because if the truth does not offend the wounds, how else do you know you were wounded? When you pour salt into a fresh laceration, it will burn, and you will scream, but eventually, it forms into a scab and begins the healing process. Well, my dear, so it is with your mind. The truth must be poured into it so it can begin healing. The timing on this matter is impaired whether it's now or not. All you choose, so it's either healed or doomed!... SELAH

Your body is talking. Are you listening?

— Yvette Rose

THE MASTERY

The war in the Heavens is simply the psychological tug and pull frequency that happens on a day-to-day battle in the minds of every being: None is truly exempted from this war: In contrast, some are aware of the war, while others who are not aware that they are at war because the war for them is perceived as something outside of themselves, something that they cannot control, something where one person is the villain, and the other the victimized one.

Unfortunately, this is deeper than a shallow pond, for the notion of "The Collective" must come into play that all are connected, woven in the web of deceit. This phenomenon is supported by the law of quantum entanglement, which states that "what is happening on one side is enviable for it to be transpiring on the other side." This understanding will bring about the rude awakening that they are

VOLUME 2. Confronting the unseen self is a giant task, which can become quite painful. Can you think of a time where you were faced with your shadow?

both the villain, at war in their own minds, on their philosophical battlefield, raging war of reflective mirroring, mirroring the subconscious battles with the voices of intrusive thoughts raging an antagonistic conflict within their very existence, resulting in inner psychological warfare, that in such a way becomes and external battle, a battle that they cast upon each other. Again, no one is innocent.

On the contrary, we are all bombarded with such outside influence. This influence supports the beast in our mind and holds such a grip on our pathological thinking, causing an imbalance of emotions and leaving no room for any form of logical thought; henceforth, this is why the beast is not willing to die for you to survive; it will rather influence your thoughts so that you will believe the war is outside of you, and if you dare to be cognitive of the transparency of the beast hiding in your behavioral patterns, patterns that stem from the spirit of confusion, worry, pain, and negative thinking, distracting the mind enough to mismanage its ability to be focused.

VOLUME 2. Confronting the unseen self is a giant task, which can become quite painful. Can you think of a time where you were faced with your shadow?

When pain and wounds are at the wheel, the beast will be the passenger of a dysfunctional system. It's a system created by those who are apprentices of the beast. To keep you in constant battle with yourself, your neighbors, friends, and the stranger walking along the road, that is even battling their thoughts. It's even with the author battling whether she should write this book. Again, no one is exempt. It is all in the mind, from thought to reality.

However, this has brought about the concepts of behavioral adaptation, not knowing that they can make significant changes in their mind, for we are marvels of adaptability and change. Yet this must not begin with the mind, but also the brain. The mind and brain connections in many of the everyday cultures and subcultures will all depend on the level of trauma that the culture has impacted on, is aware of, and will ascend from. Unfortunately, this might not be the route many cultures will adopt, for adaptation will declare changes, and changes will bring about an awareness of accountabilities. Accountability will expose the egos of those who prosper from the cultural operation in a state of degenerative deplorability. As long as the culture is in dismay, it will make fewer changes.

VOLUME 2. Confronting the unseen self is a giant task, which can become quite painful. Can you think of a time where you were faced with your shadow?

Some have adapted to their traumas. The trauma then morphs and is woven into a method of survival techniques. These techniques later become hand-me-downs worn as coats of honor, even though these hand-me-downs are dented with rips, holes, and unwoven threads, unraveling the cloth of dysfunctionality.

Yet no one notices the threads are being unraveled; to notice it would be without regard or interruptions. No one is willing or bold enough to ask the questions unless an interruption interrupts the pattern and keeps them stuck. And as much as those who are suffering in the battle of maladaptive dysfunctional patterns truly do not want to fight the beast in their minds, history has shown that never has there been a prophet or Messiah who has ever successfully been able to convince the mind of the oppressed that they are being oppressed without them, not in turn destroying the prophet, and the message of the prophet later goes down in history as a fainted memory.

Therefore, this beast is no joke. It will not allow the war in the heavens to shake it out of position. This battle in the mind manifesting on earth has been going on for generations. Nations have fought physically, killing each other, for the beast in each nation's mind is to conquer. The true fight is about dominance, dominating one over the other, the oppressed versus the oppressor. The oppressed fight for equality, and the oppressors fight to rule the mind, a rod of deception.

However, no one is questioning whether these behavioral patterns are functional. No one is willing to wage war in the mind, for they understand that the conflict will intensify once there is a whistleblower. The peacemaker will not become an enemy during the deconstruction of the family legacy. The mind, dear reader, is a phenomenon we have yet to fully comprehend; it is a discovery for the ages.

The generational beast is impartial. We must understand that we have nothing in this world to conquer, challenge, or transcend besides our minds. All your enemies, neighbors, friends, struggles, blessings, gods, demons, self-sabotaging thoughts, what you choose to master, and your very self are inhabitants of your mind. So, be

VOLUME 2. Confronting the unseen self is a giant task, which can become quite painful. Can you think of a time where you were faced with your shadow?

conscious of its energy. You must prepare for the battles. Your mind will wage war against you. Yes, you read it correctly; your mind will attack you. Therefore, it's crucial to understand that two spirits vie for your mind: the spirit of the tree of the knowledge of good and evil, and the tree of everlasting life. They are both at war and who conquers your mind, who wins this war, is up to you.

However, remember that there is a thin line between the compulsion to repeat and self-mastery. You must be observant, detached, a witness, and not a participant. If you become involved, you will become a part of it. There are no struggles or battles external to you. Even though it may seem otherwise, it's not the case. The conflict only appears to be happening because you create it with your thoughts, and your past experiences that cloud your judgment, traumatize you, and linger in your body. If you don't recalibrate, this will become your current state of mind, recreating the same experiences with different people and hoping for a different result.

In the psychosocial realm, this can be classified as the compulsion to repeat. The compulsion to repeat means that familiarity can feel

---

VOLUME 2. Confronting the unseen self is a giant task, which can become quite painful. Can you think of a time where you were faced with your shadow?

safe, even though it might be the very thing causing your destruction.

This is where the beast resides: in your trauma. It feeds off your mind being in a degenerative state of thinking, a constant position of fear. Fear that will prevent you from facing every challenge, the intrusive wounded thoughts that will lead you down a downward spiral, replaying the same story in your mind. This suggests that if you don't take healing into your own hands or walk in discernment, your adulthood will devolve into an unconscious journey of following your wounded inner self. You'll be compelled to repeat patterns in toxic relationships and develop extremely unhealthy attachments. We do this unconsciously because the brain wants to fix what happened in the past.

SIGNS THAT YOU ARE OPERATING UNDER A GENERATIONAL CURSE

The following list indicates potential signs that you may be operating under a generational curse. These signs often manifest in persistent patterns that continue to repeat across generations, which can disrupt the harmony and prosperity of a family.

1. A significant trend in your family is an inability to get married or stay married, especially among women. There are copious numbers of women in your family who operate in boyfriend-girlfriend relationships but never marry. For this reason, many children in the family will inherit their grandparents' surnames. The last names that were supposed to be inherited were lost somewhere. There are many premature deaths of men in the family. The contract typically has a clause with the generational beast that allows it to take young men, for

that is what they want. Think of the old days. Whenever there was a war among nations, they killed the men but captured the women. This is because women have wombs, and through there, the beast and probate through the womb.

2. Generational poverty: poverty is a mindset. Yes, it is a mindset; it is a mental illness. The reason I say this is that it limits access to information that is readily available but limited by the mind. This type of thinking is passed down through maladaptive behavior and dysfunctional family systems. When poverty is within the bloodline, you will eventually find the proverbial "crab in a barrel mindset" and lots of ignorance: fighting, drinking, drugs, gossiping, and backstabbing.

3. Addiction runs in your bloodline. Humans were created to progress; we go into cycles or systems whenever we do not progress. This is what can be classified as a system. This system is a stronghold that creates a great deal of depression, and addiction often pacifies this depression. As the depression grows, addiction will no longer be able to pacify it. It will need a

metaphorical bottle called Rebellion. It is not only that this generational curse needs you to be ignorant; it also needs you to surrender to it in complete wholeness

"It is ok to cut off toxic family members out of your life the blood is not thicker mental health. Some people in your life are damaging your mental health stand back, and forth so you let it happen because they're fun the blood is not thicker than your mental OK."

JERUSALEM

The fields are filled with food, yet the children go hungry in the streets like the ears of a fool that refuses instructions, so have become the hearts of the mothers who refuse them. The prophets go blind in the streets, yet they speak of visions like the hanging of wet clothes, so were the innocents hung by their heads; like the sound of a laughing hyena, so is the sound of a preacher who speaks falsely like rivers in their dry seasons; so became the wombs of women, like the unjust to the just do have a one become to fathers like the slaying of the dragon; so were the youths slain because they spoke proudly of the words of Yah (God) like they do not know the forming of a child in the womb, so it is that they will not know which comes upon them.

They do not clothe the naked nor defend the fatherless; the wolves roam at the sheep's gates, yet the shepherds do not gather them.

Death is in their thoughts and gets far from them. They have become a people without a nation (a shadow): Woe be unto the teachers who keep knowledge secret and serve ignorance as the main course. Ethiopia stretched forth her hands because she had been wounded: oh, Jerusalem, why have you built your walls of hatred and filled the children's cups with confusion? Woe be unto you because you have ears but do not hear. Oh, arise, oh Jerusalem, wash your hands from the blood and put away your treacherous ways. Gather the suckling babies and the weaned children, comfort Aethiopia because she had been rounded, and tell the priests to blow their trumpets in the city. Selah.

THE NEW JERUSALEM

From out of the heart of Yah came I and I. A place where love grows and righteousness rains, where the people are led by suckling babies, where the children prophesy, where the lions eat with the bulls and the foxes with the lambs, where understanding is overthrown by overstanding, where justice is the journey of a man who has faith, and where knowledge and wisdom are the thrones of a king.

It is a place where the people's cries are no longer cries from hunger pangs but singing of songs because they are filled with strength, and honor, where vanity trembles at the sight of Yah and abomination is melt by the fire in his eyes, where trumpets are blown because the Black Woman's wombs are fruitful like seasonal spring, where the ways of I and I cannot be studied, nor the heights of I and I cannot be measured, where the sharp sword that goes out from the mouth of

I and I cannot be made dull, where Aethiopia (Ethiopia) no longer stretch forth her hands; because her wounds are healed, where South Africa us no longer held captive by the hands of ignorance, where bridges are built and walls are broken down, where the tongues of Africa is one, where truth is impregnated by love and righteousness is born, where the cure for aids is blessed love, where the Black Starline repatriates along the Blue Nile, where Addis Ababa is flooded with Hallelujah because of the marriage of the lamb, where the farmers plant instructions and determinations grows, where the ways of a virtuous woman can neither be bought nor sold, where the rod of the down pressors (oppressors), where the wicked cannot be justified, nor the condemned cannot be made justice.

Selah, Shalom.

THE WAR IN THE HEAVENS
Addressing The Unhealed Shadow

As I prepared myself to complete the last chapter of publishing my first book, thinking that everything was about to be over. However, my body started to ache in the middle of the night. I tried to retire to bed, for my eyes had become strangers to sleep. I could hear the spirit of my ancestors calling me again to embark on another mission. This was a mission to slay the beast in my mind. I jumped from my sleep and heard the spirits talking to me. "How could this be?" "Have I not completed this mission already?" I asked myself."

My ancestors' voice answered, "But you have not completed this mission, Gem." I answered, "I was not even talking to you; how did you get into this conversation? I was talking to myself, shit. I hate it when people get into my business shit."

VOLUME 2. Confronting the unseen self is a giant task, which can become quite painful. Can you think of a time where you were faced with your shadow?

"First off, I am your mind, making your thoughts, the breath of life that moves through your lungs, the blood that runs through your veins, so I am your wake-up call in the morning, the sun that gazed in your eyes. I am enamored by your pupils and the ringing sound in your ears that your doctor misdiagnosed you with, saying it is tinnitus disease. No, it's me calling you to get your undivided attention, so watch your mouth when you are talking to me." The voice replied.

"Whatever. What else do you expect from me?"

The voice did not respond, So I went back to bed, trying to rest my eyes. I could hear weeping in the background, and it sounded like a funeral was going on. I tried to lie down and ignore the sound while pondering to myself, a funeral at 2 am? What is going on? I turned in my bed as I could feel a passing of energy move through my solar plexus. I thought it was the feeling of trap energy, but as the intense pain grew stronger, I tossed and turned in my bed while holding toughly off my stomach.

Gem C. Collie

I heard the strange voice again, saying, "I am back."

"Who said that you were welcome to begin with?" I said to the voice.

"I do not need your invitation, Gem. It's automatic."

"Please go away. I am not feeling well. My stomach has been hurting as if I was giving birth, and another thing is that I am hearing voices outside of my bedroom that sound like a funeral is taking place, so just go away, go so I can find peace."

"Ha, Ha, Gem, you are hearing a funeral. Gem, it's a real one too, ha-ha," the voice said as it laughed out loud.

What is this ghetto? Who is mad enough to have a funeral at 3 am?"

"It's your mind, Gem, not the ghetto. The funeral you are hearing is in your mind. The funeral you are hearing is your own."

"Wait! What exactly does that mean in my mind? Am I merely hearing things, joking like you, and how did you know where to find

---
VOLUME 2. Confronting the unseen self is a giant task, which can become quite painful. Can you think of a time where you were faced with your shadow?

me? How can a funeral be held in my thoughts? How can it be my funeral? If that were the case, would I not be dead? As they say, "As a man thinketh, so is he."

"Gem, it's your funeral because your old mind is dead, and the weeping you hear are the sounds of ideas, deflective experiences, delusional perceptions, misconceptions, and your broken cultural upbringing. They are the ones who are weeping because the part of dysfunctionality is dead."

As I lay my head on my pillow, for I need to rest, never have I heard of such a thing before. "Wow, what you are saying sounds like something from the spiritual world, but this is the spiritual world." I thought to myself.

"Oh, but it is Gem, it is."

"Wait, you, again? How did you get into my thoughts? I was not even speaking to you?"

"Gem, are you hard of hearing or have no sense of understanding? Did I not tell you that you are the person talking? I am just another concept of you, Gem"?

"I know, but how did I die, was it in my sleep, or did I sleep with someone's husband and then the wife caught me with her husband and killed me, or was it my husband who caught me with another man because of how I am too friendly, and it made him jealous and killed me for it, or did my mother came back to kill me because of "The Note on the Kitchen Table?" You know that part I wrote about in my book "The Damsel in Dis-stress?"

"No, Gem, none of those reasons killed you, and you did not die a physical death. Your death was a way of thinking, a deflective Cultural Mis-Identity, that died, a mind, a way of thinking, for a new mind to be born again. Gem, the pain you are feeling results from a new birth you are about to undergo. You might not want to hear this, but you are pregnant."

"Wait, What? I am pregnant. How is this possible? Do you mean to tell me I am the next "Mary Magdalene?" "Look! I am not even a Christian. How am I getting caught up in all this drama, first I was asked to write the book "The Damsel in Dis-stress, which almost cost me my life, I did not even want to write that book, and now, I am just getting over the fact that I was so-called chosen to write this book, it was so painful, I did not even know what I was doing, I had sleepless nights. My mother even attempted to murder me over that book. So, what is this t now that I am pregnant when I have not been with a man for so long? I cannot even recall the feeling of being touched or loved by a man.

So, tell me what you mean. I DEMAND ANSWERS NOW?"

"Wow, Gem, why are you so impulsive? Everything about you is so emotional. You need a detox because it sounds like your kidneys are filled with fear. Gem, my dear, you are not pregnant, beloved, but your mind is pregnant. Your mind is impregnable; therefore, it's about to give birth to a new way of thinking, a redemptive mind that will no longer laugh at a broken culture with a broken language that breeds a people with a broken identity. The earth is crying for the Edenic people to heal, and they have chosen you to break the chain and realign the people to bring balance back to their chakras. Why do you think your name is Gem? Your ancestors gave your mother that name, and not even she could stop you. Let me tell you, Gemstone. May I call you that because I know how sensitive you are about your name? When the creator wants to make things happen, he will use even your enemies to give birth to you."

"OMG, my heart is hurting. Do you mean to tell me that when I thought my mother was the rebirth of the "SLAVE MASTER" giving birth to me this whole time, I was right? I knew it. I knew I was right; I could feel the way she wiped me with her words across my heart; it shattered in so many pieces, I do not know how even still alive. Oh, my Yah (God), I knew it. I had a nightmare of when I used to run away from him in my past life. But it was one fine day in 1791 in Jamaican a few of my friends, Duty Buckman and I Shango, ran away to Haiti to spark the "HAITIAN REVOLUTION." It was in Le- Cap- Francis region in the north of the colony. I even remember the Bois Caïman ceremony, which Boukman led in wooded areas. It was the founded act of the uprising, the act of the indecent revolutionary. It happened in the French colony of Saint Domingue. It was called "The Night of Fire." There were plenty of us that night. We were being moved by our ancestors. That night was bloody. I saw the slave masters' lives leave their bodies as we slew them. Even at one point, I thought I saw the spirits of slaves executed by the slave master leave the slave master's bodies. This was as if they swelled their souls each time, they killed them. The skies were filled with smoke, and the souls of the slaves who had passed away filled the air. They were there as they grew in number as we slaughtered each slave master; they were there with joy in their hearts and pain in their eyes.

It might sound crazy to the person reading this, "Hey you, this is not a hate crime. It's the truth. The place was flooded with anger as heads floated in the sea of French blood and Afrikaans blood. That August night went down in history: I could never forget the look on the slave master's face as I swiped my sword against his throat. Our eyes met and became one as he wrote a message in my soul with his deep stare. He delved deep into my liver and left a memory there. However, it did not stay there as it traveled through my epigenetics, leaving a mark of self-destruction patterns on my DNA.

As I drowned in the blood of revenge that day, I died a death for freedom. Only to be reborn in 1982, and to my surprise, the slave master was my mother. We did not connect while we were still there. She tried to nurse me from her breast, but I resisted. I felt like it was poison, and that the revolution was not over. I tried looking for Boukman again. I later found him, but it was too late this time.

In the same way as my brother, he was in mental captivity. His mother destroyed him. They were close, and that's how it seemed to the onlookers. She did not allow him to fall, so he did not know where to stand, and she did not allow him to seek. Therefore, he was spiritually lost. Perhaps if she did, he would have reconnected with the revolutionary in himself, which was a part of his past life. Maybe he would not have chosen dysfunctional friends who were on their way to their graves. She never taught him how to fend for himself, so he stole. She did not teach him freedom. She did not teach him to love and nurture, so he manipulated others. Therefore, he was a prisoner.

Let me explain to the reader before you start thinking that I hate my mother and I am putting her on blast, which is far from the idea. I am not just talking about my mother here; I am talking about a broken culture (feminine aspect, a way of thinking). I know this concept might sound fictitious, but this is spiritual. Nothing on this planet is new, and we must reconnect with that part of us that was destroyed in the process of transition from death to reawakening (a new mind). Death is not what we perceive it to be. The body and spirit (mind) have to go through a transition; the body must return to the soil for the earth to continue its life cycle, and the spirit must return to the spirit realm. The cycle of life must continue. There must not be any emotional attachment to the flesh, not the one you own nor the flesh of another's life, as a cycle that must go forth. So, do not weep when your loved ones pass on, for they have a personal mission that must manifest, whether by free will or by force, this created by design."

"Wow, Gem, you are maturing more than I thought, and I'm a bit surprised you have come to terms with this understanding. Many would argue this understanding to the death of them, no pun intended. Yet you have adopted this idea and embraced it as well. Good for you, Gem. You know what that means, right? Hana, you must now navigate through your new birth process, but there is one thing I must tell you: you will no longer be the same person."

"What do you mean by "Wow, Gem?" Come on now,"

"Okay, Gem. See, we must understand our purpose and mission, and we, the elders, are not sure if you are aware of that yet. Gem, this is why you must be born again. And as for you and you, in your past life, you as King Shango, and your friend Dutty Boukman, you both did not learn your lesson. This is why you both are here again. You were both cursed by the slave master before they left the physical realm."

VOLUME 2. Confronting the unseen self is a giant task, which can become quite painful. Can you think of a time where you were faced with your shadow?

"Curse indeed. What a revelation that he and I are here again, in the same family, so all this while, I felt so betrayed by him because he took my mother's side when she abused me."

"Yes, Gem, he did. He does not remember the person he was. His death was more gruesome than your own. Many said that Boukman was a houngan(sorcerer). Some even said that he was a Muslim. Even the term sorcerer means "One who degerms his fate. Or one who does not commute to any form of a devilish form of religious practice." Boukman was a man who mastered the laws of cruel governing to gain freedom for his people. So, consider that Gem: do you think that when they killed him when he returned in the next life, he would not return damaged? That spirit is powerful."

"Wait a minute, so do you mean to tell me he is still in captivity because he's not the man his mother told him he is?"

"Gem, I know you are talking about your brother here.

But Dutty Boukman represents himself and Melanites men who have suffered and are still suffering from the Post/Present

Traumatic Slave Identity. It's an identity that says to hate their image so that they can disassociate themselves from the same God that created them in his image and adopted a God that enslaves them to the point that each time they call upon this strange god's name, the entrapment gets deeper. A god to whom they cannot even relate. This god belongs to the slave master; to this god, the world worships his religion each year; they go to church each Sunday in the ghettos, where the education system and food deserts are all in collective operations of mass destruction; the weapon now is the weapon of the mind. So, you see, Gem, even you had addressed the issue within yourself when you authored your book "The Damsel in Dis-stress." The matter is deeper than you think. You have just barely scratched the surface."

"Oh My Gosh, I held my stomach as I cried loudly. I thought I had gone deep. I cannot do it; I have done enough."

"I'm sorry, Gem, I know you are hurting, but look, you are communicating with the masculine aspect of yourself. Beloved, you must go deep to communicate and heal the famine aspect of yourself. You must go so deep until you see the old blood, you must release the infectious root, pull away the scab, so you pure the ointment of self-acceptance, self-embarrass, self-love, knowledge of self, cultural respect mixes them all and then pour it on the raw sore, and allow it to breathe the breath of life so that it can heal. Okay, beloved?

I'm sorry that you are hurting, but this is the process. I know you felt like you were chosen because you must go back and complete what you started on August 2, 1791. Remember, the beast is no longer outside of you. It is in your mind."

"Oh my God, I screamed as I wept bitterly."

"Gem ensures that the god you just called on is not a stranger now. Just saying, love."

"Oh, will I get to this famine aspect of myself? How can I find her? Will she reject me like the way mother rejected me? Will she pretend to be my friend to use me for what I give? Will she compete

---
VOLUME 2. Confronting the unseen self is a giant task, which can become quite painful. Can you think of a time where you were faced with your shadow?

with me? Is she a jealous person? Will she celebrate me, or will she see me as a threat to her?"

" See, Gem, she is you and not jealous of you. She will not hurt you. She has been waiting for you and has been your biggest fan. But you did not recognize her because she was not neglecting you, but you neglected her. She did not look like those you call friends, so you did not recognize her. Gem, you must go with you. This is not just about you. It's generational healing. She is you in your present and past life. Go within love. You have all the needed tools, and ensure you follow the light."

"I thought people always say whenever things are happening, like death or close to death, do not follow the light?"

"Can the living speak of the place of the dead? No, it is only death that can tell you of that Gem, do not focus anymore on those external validations and know that there will always be disappointments in life, for everyone is battling something with their minds. Some are aware and willing to do the work it takes to address

---

VOLUME 2. Confronting the unseen self is a giant task, which can become quite painful. Can you think of a time where you were faced with your shadow?

those emotional demons plaguing their mind. Some will think they are better than others because they hide their demons so well that they believe they are invisible; some have friends with their demons; their demons are their co-supporters in harming others, so they do not have to be accountable, and some have adopted their demons in their family so much to say that the demons are a part of their cultural upbringing that it becomes a generational curse.

The demon will implant its seed in their DNA, and whenever one person in the generation decides to break the generation curse, they will be attacked by members of that family. They will be treated like outcasts, but let me tell you, Gem, it's not the person's family that attacks them; it's the preprogrammed idea by the demons attacking the person spiritually. The demon's thoughts are as follows: "Who do you think you are? I've been in your culture, and here you come, wanting to break the curse I cast upon your family. No way, I will curse you for attempting to uproot my roots. I will cast a curse upon you, and your family will see you as a demon. They will call you the black sheep, and they will protect me. I am more valuable than your existence. I'm the dysfunctionality that keeps you broken. I'm the unspoken truth that gets swept under the rug by each generation. I am the molester in your family who will whisper in your ears and touch your five-year-old body inappropriately. I am your grandfather and your daddy because I raped your mother. I am the unhealthy family dinner they eat religiously every Sunday; I am the battle and competition between your mother and yourself; I am the misconception of myself; I am the breakdown in your family; and I refuse for your family to have a breakthrough.

If you dare to break any curses of mine, I am the battle and competition between your mother and yourself; I am the misconception of yourself; I am the breakdown in yourself. I am the misconception of self, the breakdown in your family, and I refuse for your family to have a breakthrough. If you dare to break any curse of mine, it will require you to confront me. Ha-ha, I dare you to do so. Go ahead. Things will never be easy, so try me. You will never fit in. Your family will always have a setback; they will forever work for others and never own anything; they will always

---

VOLUME 2. Confronting the unseen self is a giant task, which can become quite painful. Can you think of a time where you were faced with your shadow?

rent and not be homeowners. Now you can obey me by inheriting all these curses and not be lonely or try me and you will be hurt."

Now Gem, this is the mind of generational demons, which will pledge your culture or, better yet, that have pledged your culture, or I should say it is the replacement of a culture that was once wholesome but not broken. Gem: Now that you have identified the ideology of the demon, you must understand this demon is clever. It has many faces now, Gem. Some of these faces it did not mention above where it identified itself. This beast is neither male nor female; it's a beast that targets the mind; it has no partibility, no boundaries, no respect, or interiority. Gem, once you have mentally decided to break the curse of generational trauma, this beast will target you. The journey to breaking this curse is quite lonely. **PLEASE UNDERSTAND THAT IT IS NOT PERSONAL. NOW GO ON, BE ON YOUR WAY; IT'S TIME TO PACK UP, GEM.**

Now I must go, Gem. I am grateful you have allowed the masculine aspect of yourself to speak; I am glad you are now embracing me.

Who said I was embracing you? I am only tired of fighting.

Come now, Gem, this is becoming foolish of you to continue to fight me. I am you, and for you to progress in life, you must accept the feminine and masculine aspects of yourself. Nonetheless, I must go now. Rest your body but raise it when it is time to do so, so you can execute your mission of going deeper.

You are right. My culture depends on me; more than anything, my unborn children depend on me to heal so they can move forward. It is time now for me to do so.

Okay, this is great. Please stay focused and not get into any relationship while doing this mission. It will only distract you. Now is not the time. Broken people do not get into relationships; they take time to heal. Understand that there is a period called the dark night of the soul here; there is an initial awakening in self-discovery, and your ego will dissolve so that you can be wiped clean and purified to become the person you were designed to be. However, even though the process is very frightening, terrorizing, and soul

---

VOLUME 2. Confronting the unseen self is a giant task, which can become quite painful. Can you think of a time where you were faced with your shadow?

crushing, a Kundalini awakening must occur. You might think you will never recover. However, it's a transformational process that you will never escape once you learn the truth, are open energetically, and embark on this new journey of self-discovery.

Please, and while this process will feel like it's everlasting, know that it will not last forever. The essential process is alchemical. Before you can turn into gold, every molecule of your being of consciousness must be decently purified and reorganized to gather again. You must now trust the process; there is no going back from here. Remember what I told you, Gem? Peace Shalom until we meet again.

As I, the author, arose from my sleep, I had to gasp for air, for I could not believe what I had just experienced. "Was this all real?" I questioned myself, could this be because I am only tired? Did I do Astral projection ? There were many questions to ask, but I knew deeply that it was real. It is not like I have ever experienced it before; after all, I experienced something similar, as I forgot this process would trigger massive healing. You cannot do so if you try to erase or eradicate your wounds. This will allow you to ascend from a place of pain to a place of power. If you try to erase your pain, it will limit your growth psychologically. Selah.

REPLENISHING THE AMBITIOUS IMPREGNABLE PEOPLE

To replenish the ambitious impregnable people is the desire to go forward and improve oneself. It is a burning flame that as lit my mind, burned through my life, and made me see myself in another state. It has allowed me to shape my character and master my own life so that I form my ends, which has given me a need to find the truth and to help in a friendly solution to a grave world problem to improve the general condition of impregnable people everywhere, which then empowers me to be courageous, bold, perseverant, and confident to make it impossible for anyone to intrude upon this mission.

So only a few can understand what it takes to make a replenishing, ambitious, impregnable people: a people who will never give up, a people who will never say die, a people who will never depend on another race to do for them what they are to do for themselves, a

Gem C. Collie

people who will not blame nature or God for their conditions, but a people who will go out and make conditions to suit themselves. Oh, how vitreous life has become when on every hand, you hear people who bear your resemblance, who bear your image, telling you they have made it, that fate is with them. Then in the next 24 hours, we will have a new race, a new empire resurrected not for the will of others to see us rise but for the will to rise, irrespective of what anyone thinks. Selah.

VOLUME 2. Confronting the unseen self is a giant task, which can become quite painful. Can you think of a time where you were faced with your shadow?

PRESENT TRAUMATIC STRESS/SLAVERY DISORDER

Understanding the concept of unwanted memories

Before we dive deep into the philosophy of my theological theories, let us first define the concept of Post-Traumatic stress disorder. Post-traumatic stress disorder symptoms may start within one month of a traumatic event, but sometimes symptoms may not appear until years after the event. These symptoms cause significant problems in social or work situations and relationships. They can also interfere with the outlook on life.

According to my theological theory, if we must talk about what they have documented in the DSM as post-traumatic stress disorder, we must then mention epigenetics and how the impact of it all has been an effect on human psychology. In my experience/observation. Posttraumatic stress disorder. PTSD is to be classified as Present Traumatic Stress Disorder. I use this term not lightly, nor do I intend to be difficult, but to show that there is a distinct perspective on how we see things. Present because not every individual's trauma is memories-based nor an event of the traumatic circumstance of the past, but more so a consecutive ongoing of current happenings that are an everyday living that has been adapted into their societal and cultural life as normalcy; I also mention epigenetics for the reoccurrence that is being displaced. I say epigenetics because the behavior is not just passed down. But it has become a behavioral system that has created an identity in the mRNA, the messenger RNA that conveys the genetic information from the DNA by processing the effects of transporting and transitioning trauma to the mind.

Epigenetic modification in stress response genes associated with trauma, even as far as adverse childhood experiences, will cause a long-term impact on the mental, and the physical health. It is even documented that childhood traumas are associated with Post-traumatic stress disorder.

However, it may mark that even though adverse childhood trematodes condition is an everyday lifestyle into adulthood, why then classify it as Post? It should be present because it is now in the Freeze, FLIGHT, FLOP, FIGHT, or FAWN mode. It is a continuous condition that morphs itself in the DNA. The DNA then adapts to this behavior, which leaves the mind in continuous survival mode, whether it could result in post-traumatic stress disorder. Let us take a deep look into South Africa during the time of apartheid, where the originators of the land were constantly exposed to violence, terror, murder, and overall trauma. The individual then migrated from South Africa to another location, where they lodged into the military, possibly escaping the violence of their homeland for betterment.

However, the military training was harsh because of the war conditioning in their country, with apartheid tearing away at their peace. As they tried to fight for survival, holding on with the grip of their jaws to life, fighting against a system that violated their autonomy to be alive, to be present, to exist in a country that was built from the blood of their ancestors are now being ripped from their bloodline by strangers, whom they heard before prior from the school room as teachers stood educating them, on their volatile acts, as now migrated into a land that is not a place of their own to now join an army that is being trained to commit the same act on another strange land under the guise of what they consider to be peace and civilize a nation that has been functioning without a dogmatic societal, influence for centuries is now being attacked by a heartless nation that formed and created soldiers who were once a child victims of the same barbaric act that cast upon them. They are recycling the act they were once victims of. This causes the individual to suffer an ongoing series of uneventful impacts, never having a chance to recover, which deranges the nervous system. This kind of trauma is not only an experience but an ongoing experience in the mRNA.

Therefore, my theological theory cannot be considered Post Traumatic trauma. This matter not just played a part in the idea of stress yet also in the concept of the BLACK HOLOCAUST, where

---
VOLUME 2. Confronting the unseen self is a giant task, which can become quite painful. Can you think of a time where you were faced with your shadow?

the native was ambushed and ripped from their native countries, beaten to death, raped, the men demasculinized with their masculine energy reprogrammed to feminine energy, making them weak, the women wombs were destroyed, and their famine energy was given to the men, swopping it with their masculine energy.

The children were left without guidance. This beast defeated a nation that no matter if the psychical shackles were removed from their hands and feet, it is still psychologically engraved in their DNA. Therefore, generation after generation, they will still continue to suffer.

Repeating the act of enslaved mental illness while attempting to survive, seek the same beast that has caused the trauma to begin with, only to be told that they do not meet the measures of what they are taken away by ghostly pale-faced men with blues eyes and yellow color hair, bringing division and individualistic autonomy, which states "ALL MEN FOR THEMSELVES" leaving them to suffer, whilst they are being scattered all over the earth, with no memories of the collective culture, that they were once apart of dividing them amongst each other, causing them to tear each other apart, which will cause them to be in everyday conflict with trying to not drown in the same sea YAM SUP(Red Sea), that swallowed over twenty thousand soldiers, with their horse and chariots; for the red sea would devour them leaving them to become a remanence, as that of Meneophtah, or drown like the vizier and high priest Hanaan.

If only the collective understood the power of collectivism and its holistic measures, there would be no need for present-traumatic stress disorder. Our role is not to ensure that the ancestral past trauma will not resurface. However, the collective will know how to attack the beast of Post-Traumatic Disorder once the whole understands that it's not the individual that is dysfunctional from the ancestral traumas but the whole. What happens to one happens to the whole. Selah.

VOLUME 2. Confronting the unseen self is a giant task, which can become quite painful. Can you think of a time where you were faced with your shadow?

BREAKING THE PATTERNS
Unpacking The Unspoken Truth

Breaking the generational pattern of domestic mental illness, the generational beats will not allow this to be a smooth journey. It is not for the weak at heart, yet a daunting task must be done. However, it will not be an easy road, and the journey will be tough. Your family members who have pledged allegiance to the beast will attack you. The beast is in your mind; it is your mind. It can only attack you there. It is not outside of you. Keep in mind that the ancestors had already gone through physical bondage. Therefore, the beast is clever. It knows that it cannot attack you there as well. As it is said about how lightning does not strike the same place twice, so it is that the beast cannot attack the next century or generation in the same way as it did before, least its moves would be too obvious, causing an uproar against the beast, wiping out its existence, so it must carry out its operation differently. Listen, do not be fooled.

VOLUME 2. Confronting the unseen self is a giant task, which can become quite painful. Can you think of a time where you were faced with your shadow?

Gem C. Collie

However, some will need the support and guidance of a wholistic mentor, a psychologist, a case manager, or a collectivistic community, who too must have already gone on this journey of addressing their generational beast. What you must understand with that is that everyone's reality looks different, but the simplicity of understanding what must be done is crucial. Now, if they, too, have not done the work of shadow healing or addressing their wounds, at least they will not be able to guide you on this mission of yours. Their psychological traumas will then become your own. You must break up with the patterns which created the psychological dysfunctionality in your DNA. You must become fully aware of your patterns.

I refer to this as Present Traumatic Slave Disorder. Unlike Dr. Joyce DeGruy, author of the book POST-TRAUMATIC SLAVE SYNDROME who classified and identified this to be what she called Post-traumatic Slave Syndrome because of their past Trauma, which stems from "THE BLACK HOLOCAUST." It is where thousands of Africans were murdered, enslaved, and ripped away

VOLUME 2. Confronting the unseen self is a giant task, which can become quite painful. Can you think of a time where you were faced with your shadow?

from their native land and carried away as 'Human Cargo" under the guise of civilization, which has impacted the Myelinated race not only on the Afrikan Continent but around the Afrikan Diaspora, who were enslaved and is still psychologically enslave in today's twenty first century.

Always give yourself grace, for there will not be an immediate change. Remember, this is embedded in your DNA, your epigenetics. Understand that if it runs in the family, it may be chasing you. However, you must not run. You must stand up to the beast. It is not afraid of you, nor should you be afraid of it.

The harder you stand up to this beast, the harder it will come. It's sneaky. It will even tell you to curse this author for showing you its hiding place. But do not curse the author. She had to stand up to her beast, too. The beast tried to bury her alive but did not understand that she is a Gem, and when you bury a Gem, it recharges and regains its power. The beast tried to get her to kill herself, the beast even used the time to strangle her, but she was able to hang on to the number on the clock and break the hands of time. She was raised from the dead once when the beast had brought her to the graveyard, but the author was able to grab hold of her pen and wrote about the beast exposing its shadow. The beast ran from the ink, lurking around to capture the next mind.

Therefore, you must study the generational beast in your family so that it will not know what's coming with you when you begin to crush its nasty fingers from around your mind. Know that you cannot run away from it. It is YOU! You cannot leave it, so you will not meet it in another person pretending to be what you seek.

The pathological pattern is a part of you. It is the way you think, the decisions you make, the choices you choose, how you choose to respond to life, your perspective, the food choice you make, your relationships, your outlook, and your inner thoughts. Henceforth, you must be ready to decode the impact of the stigma. You might even have to disassociate yourself from your family. You must be willing to study the pathological patterns and understand that you cannot pray it away because the issue here is not about the lack of praying. If that is one of the issues in your culture or subculture,

VOLUME 2. Confronting the unseen self is a giant task, which can become quite painful. Can you think of a time where you were faced with your shadow?

then maybe you are praying to a God that does not look like you or associated with who you are. You are not just having an issue of lack of prayers, but no self-identity, and that's another topic.

You MUST BE willing to forgive your ancestors for passing on the banner of dysfunctionality. They were not in a position to break generational curses. They were too busy ducking and surviving through the impact of what was transpiring and were more caught up in traditions and not truths. Remember, even though they might have survived THE BLACK HOLOCAUST, One of the greatest genocides ever existed; they were psychologically recovering from escaping the jaws of the hounds' dogs as they were on their tails.

But the ancestors were smart. They sprinkled cayenne pepper along their pats, for the hound dogs as they were high in the trees, watching their search for them or those in the Caribbean who had slaughtered the colonization. Yes, they revolted and found it hard, but I am afraid their revolt was too late. The minds were already activated. Yes, once the beast saw the red fire flame in the eyes of the enslaved, the beast ran. It ran into their minds to hide and could not find its way out. The colonizers have used deceptive so-called Peace Treaties, Buck Bocking, rape, Murder, Lynching, the babies being ripped from the wombs, then killing them. Yet, in the twenty first so-called modern times, it is said that women have the right to abort their unborn child if necessary. Ha-ha. "What a crafty beast."

Internal Colonization, what they also called the "Age of Discovery," or even better yet, Apartheid, understands that internal colonization begins with segregation, which is defined as the separation of racial or ethnic groups. Internal colonialism was a modern capitalist practice of oppression and exploration, where people were systematically torched to death. The ideology states that the world was barbaric and backward to support the colonization project so that it would support the racism that created THE BLACK HOLOCAUST and the enslavement of what we are facing today.

Now the gross aftermath of the "JIM CROW LAWS'" CIVIL RIGHTS MOVEMENT. POLICE BRUTALITY, Colorism, Classism, and Racism are all the dust now flying in the face of Ascendants of these same Afrikaans. So that is why you must now

---

VOLUME 2. Confronting the unseen self is a giant task, which can become quite painful. Can you think of a time where you were faced with your shadow?

pick up the banner from the floor. Wake up from the sleep that you are in, get up, and study your lineage to see where the breakdown first began. You will become an enemy to those unwilling to address their issues but understand that it is not them that will become angry with you. The beast is afraid that he will lose a host, you.

Before I go, I want you to know that the breakdown did not begin with you, but you can start the recovery process. This has taken place centuries before you, so you alone in your time cannot end it all, for there are many factors outside of you to be considered, outside influence, etc.

Selah, Shalom.

CONFRONTING THE BROKEN SHADOW
Unlocking The Unseen Self

Here we go, mirror, mirror on the wall as I stand here in the raw (mentally naked), shaking with so much fear, for I am too afraid to face myself, afraid to face the reflection of my shadow standing in front of me, for this is such a daunting task that I have ran away from on many occasions because I did not want to see my true self.

See, the reflection of my inner self has been battling with me for over 38 years to live, and I have been keeping her captive because I did not like her. I locked her in the pits of my guts (SUBCONSCIOUS) and threw away the keys. She has been banging so aggressively at my mind to let her free, but I cannot allow her to be free. I cannot allow her to be the dictator of my consciousness, for I am too afraid that she might expose me and make me love her. She might reveal my gentle side and reveal how vulnerable I am. She might reveal that I am loving, she might reveal that I cry myself to sleep at night, and she will tell everyone that I am shy. I just cannot let her expose my heartbreak. She might reveal that the man I pretend to love is not the man I desire, he might find out that I am only settling for him, and she might reveal that I am not as Tough as I pretended to be, which will make me a target for the wolves, and vultures (deceptive Antichrist Spirits) that are lurking around me under the guise of friendship, waiting for a moment to attack. She will expose the secrets I store in my womb, but she does not know I left my secrets there so she will not get cold from the winter storms of anger in my uterus. I left it there to keep her warm; see how thoughtful I was.

Hey, you, the person reading this, you can see it, right? I am thoughtful, right? Even when the fibroids started growing inside me with such pain, I ripped them out. I let them become hard and calcified so that she could use them as the material for her to build a shelter from my storms, and when all my loved ones died, I buried their memory inside so that she would not be lonely. So why should

Gem C. Collie

she feel so hurt? Why should she cry? What more did she need from me?

Okay, I can admit it was very dark inside of me, but I had to keep it that way because if left bare , the light of truth would shine and then find its way out and take over my mind. I could not allow her to do that, so I kept it dark. I was more attentive to my toxic intrusive thoughts than her. Okay, I attended to everyone else's needs because it was much easier to face their issues, so I did not have to fornicate with them. I just cuddled with it and allowed it to touch me in the private chambers of my heart. This seems too much to deal with than to talk to her and hear her calling my name. Shit, who would not ignore her? She kept calling my name. Honestly, I am not sure how she knows my name, for I have never told her. We had never gotten that personal. She is quite an aggressive person. She keeps pulling on the veins of my nervous system. Shit! That hurts. But I can ignore her. I am not ready to let her out. I know, I must understand her infrastructure, I must understand.

VOLUME 2. Confronting the unseen self is a giant task, which can become quite painful. Can you think of a time where you were faced with your shadow?

Her cultural identity? Oh, shadow, I am so afraid of you. Shadow, I do not want to let you out. You are aggressive. Stop fighting! I do not know how to win the war against you. Oh my gosh, stay back, stay in my womb, do not come out. It is ever colder out here; I will use the coldness from my heart and freeze you to death. Is my womb not warm enough, or maybe I should drink some red raspberry leaf tea to spark the fire in my liver so that it would keep my womb warm? So that she will not feel my cold heart. Oh shit, she just used the fire to start revolutionary a warfare inside of me. She is starting to protest against me. She is serious too. She is even using the fibroids I left for her to build a shelter from my storms to throw back at me. Shit! She just threw one at me, but I ducked. It just hit the mirror, breaking it into so many pieces causing it to shatter my reflection.

I decided to run away. She was crazy, but as I began to run, I could feel her breath on the back of my neck. No matter how fast I sped away, she was there. I could see her reflection on the side of the street as the lit lamp post shine light on the shattered piece of glass got stuck in the bottom of my right foot. I wondered if it was because I was not walking in the right direction. Whatever, I do not care. She is still crazy am running away from her. She does not deserve to see my reflection; she does not deserve for me to show her how to be feminine. She does not even know what it means to be gentle like me. I am sweet and refined. I know how to tease the boys with my smile and allow them into the trap of no return. Once I had them there, they would have no anchor to return.

I know how to use my charm, which would let other women desire to be me, but they cannot. They will compete with me, doing everything to overthrow my Queendom. They will dress in their finest and lure men with the scent of chemically laced perfumes, but my Queendom can never be overthrown by another woman, nor be conquered by a weak man, but be crowned by a Kingdom. Ha-ha! You see how feminine I am? then why should I then let this bitch be my reflection? This fool is out of her mind. Whom would I be if I let another woman take my place?

VOLUME 2. Confronting the unseen self is a giant task, which can become quite painful. Can you think of a time where you were faced with your shadow?

She does not deserve me, so I will keep running. Damn, I stopped to remove the splinter from my foot, and to catch my breath. But as I did so, I could see her looking back at me from the shattered piece of glass in my foot. I screamed, not from the pain or the fright from the blood gushing from my veins, but from the piece of glass where I could see her reflection. She looked angry. I quickly yanked the glass away and ran deep into my darkness, far away from her.

I meant, why would I want to talk to someone like her? She is so ungrateful and behaves like I armed her. I owe her nothing and am not obligated to speak to her. There are no laws that say I should talk to her, and even if there were, I break every single word that made those laws. I rewrote it in invisible ink. Oh, what did I do that was so bad? I fed her. I know the food was cold; my heart is cold, and I know my tears almost drowned her, but each time I tried to look her in the face, all I could see were the things I disliked about her.

I knew I never gave her a chance to live, but I am telling you, she does not deserve it. Each time I tried to tell her how she wrapped her hands around my throat, my chakra tightened my windpipe. I even

---

VOLUME 2. Confronting the unseen self is a giant task, which can become quite painful. Can you think of a time where you were faced with your shadow?

tried to introduce her to the men I love. However, she would whisper intrusive thoughts into my head, causing me to wonder why they found me attractive. Do you see what I mean? Do you see why I dislike her? She is a bitch. She just showed me her reflection in the spill of my blood that flowed onto the floor from my wounded foot. But this time, I stood up to her and looked her in the face. But as I began to go too deep, my blood became dry as she stared deep into my eyes. I picked up a shattered piece of the glass from the floor and used it to stare back at her. Her tears accompanied her as she appeared on the other side of the mirror as she reflected on the shattered glass. Her tears flowed so heavily that my hands became slippery, causing the glass to fall from my hand. This caused pieces to shatter into thousands of small pieces and scatter all around me.

I decided to lay on the floor amongst the thousands of pieces where she was scattered in small pieces, each showing a different aspect of her reflection, and where I tried to use an eraser to delete her existence because I thought she was black and ugly. The eraser only left marks of memory that I could not delete, so I used foundation

VOLUME 2. Confronting the unseen self is a giant task, which can become quite painful. Can you think of a time where you were faced with your shadow?

(make-up) to cover up the missing pieces in my distorted foundation. So together, we lay down and cried. Our wailing sounded like a choir in synchronizing harmony, harmonizing with each pitch of deep exhale. Her words to me were, "Gem, please allow me to be myself. I am not your enemy; I am here to love you. Gem, please let me be free; let me love you. I know you think I am a bitch, but to me, you are a beloved soul. Allow me to touch your face. Can we rise in love with each other? Can I lay by your side while wrapping my hands around your body, taking away all your aches and pains? I will remove all the pins attaching your hurt to you.

I can show you how much I adore you. I can put the femininity back in your voice and convince your hands to touch gently. I can allow the scent of the freshly picked honeysuckle that was picked for you to be your body odor so that when you pass by a group of masculine men, they will know that you are the Queen Bee. I can put the Gemstone back in your crown chakra. I can be the awakening of your kundalini energy, which will flow like a serpent at the base of your spine, awakening the doormat energy that will move so freely upwards through your seventh chakra, leading to the expanded state of your consciousness.

I will dress you in my brightest smile, so bright that the sun will be jealous because the moon has used your smile for her reflection. Instead, I will bathe your skin in forgiveness and cover you in a coat of many colors. (Hebrew: פַּסִים כְּתֹנֶת ketonet passim, Joseph's coat), yet there will be no jealousy, for this coat is a generational blessing, and no matter what, your light cannot be dimed. No matter how much you were ridiculed or verbally assassinated, I will now be there to pick you up.

I am sorry for the neglect and for keeping you captive. I thought it was the right thing to do, for this was the way of our slave master. He hid us in the pits of hell, so I did the same I hid you away from the face of many. I hated you like the way they hated me too. I apologize and hope you will find it within your own shadow to forgive me. I cannot run away anymore. I will no longer deny you. I will stop putting my foot in your way , so you will no longer trip,

---

VOLUME 2. Confronting the unseen self is a giant task, which can become quite painful. Can you think of a time where you were faced with your shadow?

and fall as you walk by. I will remove my hands from your throat so you can speak. I am sorry for all the hurt I have caused you. I am sorry for talking about you behind your back. I used to spread rumors about you to others; they hated their shadows too. One girl boasted about how she killed her shadow; no longer after losing her mind, her kundalini went back to sleep, and her pineal gland became calcified and lost in the shadow world. I was jealous of you; I do not deserve you.

See, there were so many hard times when I thought I could not make it. Even though I am hurting, I am not completely broken. No one had ever taught me how to love you. Honestly, I was not aware that you even existed until now when I kept hearing you talk to me. I used to think your voice was my imagination ramping away in my mind. I thought your directions were my memories, and I did not know how to connect with you. I thought you were maybe my twin brother or sister that died in the womb or at birth, but see, I was naive as to what was going on, so when I finally met you, their voices were still alive in me, guiding me throughout life because they did not get to live; they were living through me, so I followed their instruction. I thought the fights that you and I were having were the fights that siblings always have with each other. I did not know that you were me and I was you. I thought we were one body with two souls.

Today I surrendered. I kneel before you, asking for your compassion. I know I sound narcissistic, asking you to give me what I did not give you. But you are the one with a heart that is warm. Your heart was made with fire and mine with ice, but I ask you not to set me on fire as you melt away the frozen aches from my heart. I promise you that as the coldness of my heart melts away, it will not put out your fire. I am ready to humble myself before you. I know you might not trust me because I just went from one emotion to the next, and you have a right to have your guard up, but hey, if you have your guard up, we will not heal together, so just put your guard down. Ha-ha, you are not under arrest, so stop breathing so hard. Okay, you can trust me.

VOLUME 2. Confronting the unseen self is a giant task, which can become quite painful. Can you think of a time where you were faced with your shadow?

I took the chains from your cage. I removed the guard dogs. They do not bite, ha-ha, ha-ha. They ate their shadows, so their bellies were filled with their souls. Do you see how they licked their lips as if a piece of their soul's last attempt to live just tried to crawl out of their mouths? Ha-ha-ha, ha-ha. Be careful where you step, though; their souls left their blood on the floor while being devoured; they could at least clean it up before they died, anyway. Do not mind them; dogs will be dogs. Please come out; I am here to hold your hands.

Selah.

THE VOICE OF THE SHADOW
The Echoes Behind the Soul

For over centuries, generation after generation, I have lived in secrets alone in the shadow world. As I, the shadow, sit behind the soul of my flesh, I have been manifested in the captivity of my fleshy now for thirty-eight years, as far as I can remember. It's very cold in this pit of my flesh. She has fed me nothing but stale food, food not made with love, and food picked from the garden of death. I am trying my darndest to understand that it once had a life before the food got to me. Perhaps it was once alkaline, it had made some form of photosynthesis, and the formula was happening like $6CO_2 + 6H_2O$ $C_6H_{12}O_6$, where the reactants, six carbon dioxide molecules, and six water molecules, are converted by light energy captured by chlorophyll into sugar molecules and six oxygen molecules. I thought maybe death would have been thoughtful in this process; even though it was picked from the

---

VOLUME 2. Confronting the unseen self is a giant task, which can become quite painful. Can you think of a time where you were faced with your shadow?

garden of death, death was remorseful enough to recycle itself to life and make sure the vegetables were pure green because death knew it was coming to me. So, it would at least give it organic alkaline chlorophyll blood so that my energy would be heightened and bring color to my red blood cells, and so that the chlorophyll would reduce the inflammation in my system (caused by the hurt in my heart), which could increase the reproduction of my egg production in the future to give birth to a new generation of healing.

I thought death would understand, for we used to be friends. Yes, Death and I were friends. Death used to live here with me. Whenever my flesh buried the memories of her dead loved ones inside her to keep me company, we used to sit together and talk. I even used to use her veins as a jump rope to play with the memories of her dead children that were here; they loved me; I made them feel alive; they were friendly too; they even covered me with a coat of many colors (Joseph's coat), that she sent for me to stay warm, yet even though the coat was warm, I was still smitten with frostbite on my toes, one winter storm (emotional implosion).

As I was saying, the food had some kind of love in it. However, by the time it got to me, it had lost the love it once had because there was so much resentment down here. It dissipated into nothingness as it traveled to this place, which she called her soul. I tried to eat it, but it made me vomit green slime (jealousy) on her pelvic floor, which leaked into her womb. I tried to clean it up before it could cause any damage, but I had nothing to clean it up with. I tried using my love to wipe it all up. But the intoxicating acidity of self-hatred and jealousy in the vomit made my nose burn and my stomach upset. So, I vomited even more. The vomit stayed and got hard; it turned into calcified fibroid tumors that she then recycled and gave me to build a shelter from her storms, but I was still getting wet. She did not care about me; why did she treat me like this? I was not the one who hurt her, yet I had to pay for the things I did not do. I had to be held accountable for something I, too, was a victim of. I am going emotionally bankrupt.

The emotional taxes I have paid her only have a back door; once they leave, the taxes do not return. I tried to rub her back whenever she would cry from her hurt, abuse, and rejection. I would creep up on her and gently rub her back, trying to rub away the pain and tension, yet when I got too close to her, she could feel my deep breath blowing on her neck. She would turn around with redness in her eyes, with a floodgate of tears pouring from her face. She then turned and slapped me with insults, pushing me deeper into the pits of darkness. I was honestly only trying to help; I was so confused.

How could someone refuse love from their own shadow? But then, one day, as I was sneaking up on her, I overheard her telling one of her pretend friends about me and how much she did not like me because I reminded her of things, she did not like about herself. She told her to pretend friend, that was jealous of her, that I was a bitch, that whenever she got into a relationship with a man, I would whisper intrusive thoughts in her ears, and she sheer pretend friend would laugh in unison at me. I say "pretend friend" because that girl did not like her just as she did not like me, they would sit and talk together, but when her friend left her home, she would talk badly about her. I know this because it was a conversation amongst the

Gem C. Collie

other shadows. They would tease me that my flesh was a laughingstock amongst the other female fleshie: they said they did not like her because they thought she was better than they were and said how the fleshie planned to overthrow her Queendom. Yet I know this was not true. My fleshie did not think she was better than anyone, not that I was defending her. I know this because my fleshie did not even like her own shadow, so how could she think she was better than anyone?

Nonetheless, I was not ashamed of her. I stood up for her, I wrestled with the other shadows for talking shit, and we got into a big fight. As we fought, the earth shook, the lightning struck, the thunder clapped, and there was a war in the heavens (the mind). We fought so hard that it left a mark on her forehead that looked like her birthmark. Ha-ha!

She is so naive. I tried calling her by her name, but she ignored me as if I were so, silencing the vowels in her name. I knew she hated it when her name was mispronounced, so I took speech therapy to take the accent out of my tongue to get her name right. But it was all for

---
VOLUME 2. Confronting the unseen self is a giant task, which can become quite painful. Can you think of a time where you were faced with your shadow?

nothing; she ignored me still. I did all I knew, but all my doings proved nothing. My love language did not identify with the way she understood love. She only understood trauma and one-sided love. Her love language was stuck in survival mode because of her childhood trauma. She created her love language and developed her understanding of what love is supposed to feel like. It was all associated with dysfunctionality. I used to whisper in her ears whenever she fell in love with only one-sided men. I tried to tell her it was not love; it was only a connection between the narcissist and the emotional co-dependent, limiting the ability to receive love.

I tried to tell her she was suffering from a deep cut of abandonment wounds which caused her emotional permanence. Therefore, she was not ready for a relationship because she would only attract another wounded soul that would mistake their union as a union of a soulmate. Still, it was true he was her wound-mate, so she would never share her bad days with them because she did not want to make it to be difficult to be loved. She never felt enough; she would walk gently, not waking the beast in them lest they scare her with their obscene behavior. I tried to tell her this was unhealthy. My fleshie has developed magical thinking, where she created false assumptions that if she did certain things, it would impact men in ways that were not realistic. I tried telling her to take time to sit with me so that she could heal not only from her traumas but her mother's traumas, too. I tried telling her that she was a generational emotional surrogate and must be delivered from the chains of bondage; I told her she must cut the umbilical cord. I tried telling her she must return to her traumas and dig up undesirable emotions like intense hurt, pain, anxiety, and rage. That was the only way her brain was telling her it did not want to feel that over and over again. Communicating that to herself and telling herself she is wrong for feeling those emotions is just a form of abusing herself over and over again; it is what will perpetuate those emotions from the past.

Yes, they are unpleasant emotions, yet they are there, so she would not give up. She had to be present with her emotions. I even removed my hands from her throat, Chakra, but as soon as I did, she started yelling at me, hurting my feelings, so I dug a ditch deeper inside the cage, where she could not find me. I hid from her, and she would hopefully miss me. Whenever she walked among the other fleshies, they would stop staring at her, thinking deep within themselves, "If she were a ghost, how was it that she was walking around with no shadow?"

Every other fleshie saw this, but my fleshie did not even recognize that I was not around. One day, I saw her staring in the mirror, so I came up and stared right back at her. She stared at me with such intensity it scared her. I was pissed, and I had all right to be. I wanted to be free by any means necessary. I got too angry at her silence, so I took a calcified fibroid and threw it at her as she ducked. The fibroids hit the mirror and shattered it into pieces. I knew those fibroids would come in handy; she looked traumatized if I hit her, and she would run away and go deep into the darkness, but I was not letting her go. A piece of glass stuck in her foot as she tried to escape me. I showed up in that, too, as she tried to pluck it out. She screamed, quickly yanked it out, and went back to run away, but as she attempted to get away from me, a piece of glass that was stuck in her foot. As she ran, she could see my reflection in the blood trailing behind her. She sped up with anguish in her heart to run away from me. Oh, my fleshy, running away from me is something you cannot do, either by free will or by force, my dear fleshy; you must face me. Everywhere you look, you will see me. I will even reflect on the food you consume. Keep running. You will see.

VOLUME 2. Confronting the unseen self is a giant task, which can become quite painful. Can you think of a time where you were faced with your shadow?

THE FIVE SPIRITS

In this portion of the book, I mention the five spirits because I want my readers to grasp the concept of the personification of what I am referencing. These characteristics are not folk tales or fiction-like characters. They are very real.

My goal is to have my readers feel that they have gained much insight into themselves by reading this book. And the world around me must understand that no one is exempted from their Generational Curses. The effect of it is not optional. By legacy, it is the chain of command. Understand that if you feel your family dynamic stands out from this course, you are sadly mistaken. In fact, it has impacted your generation on another level. You must break the genetic code sent through your mRNA, the messenger protein informing your DNA. The reprogramming of your epigenetics is very much possible.

These five Spirits that are being mentioned are only the tip of the iceberg; this information might come off to you as scary, crazy, or too much, and as the author of this book, I am here to say it is very much difficult, it is scary, now crazy I would not go that far, it is overwhelming. Listen, this is part of the journey, you must be willing to journey through those dark spaces, and life will not give you a flashlight either; you must create the light or adapt your mind and eyes to see through the dark.

However, If you decide to journey down this path, there will be times you will get lost and be seen as mentally unstable. You are not. It is only seen that way in the world, where those who do not believe in facing their demons yet take a drug that will suppress the processes.

Listen, I must go, but before I do, if you decide to medicate yourself, then that's your choice. Medicating yourself will not heal you. Your unspoken truth will show up in places where you will always feel like a victim. Whatever you suppress will manifest.

Peace\Shalom.

VOLUME 2. Confronting the unseen self is a giant task, which can become quite painful. Can you think of a time where you were faced with your shadow?

THE BEGINNING OF THE CURSE
Identifying the generational curses

Good day to all who are reading this. Let me introduce myself. I am the root cause of all generational/ancestral curses (The Tree of the Knowledge of Good and Evil). I am that curse cast upon the sons and daughters of Yaacob (Yisrael, Israel). I am the serpent in the garden of Eden that whispered in the ears of Khawah (Eve) to eat from the tree of The Knowledge of Good and Evil.

Yes, I am that jealous spirit that told Qàyin (KAIN) to kill his brother Abel. What you must understand about me is that I am sent here to traumatize your generation. I have implanted my fangs so deeply into your roots that it is impossible for you to break free from me without leaving at least a memory in your mRNA that will continue to carry the message to your DNA. I am the spirit that kept the children of Yisrael in psychological bondage so that even when they were set free from the grip of Pharaoh (Ramses), they still held tightly to the wonders of Egypt, lusting for the bread of their slave master, Pharaoh. I was the instruction given to Pharaoh to kill every first-born male child of the Israelites. I mean, what else did you expect him to do? He had to plant fear in their minds lest they come back and overthrow his bloodline.

Ha-ha, my servant Pharaoh (Ramses) needed their enslavement and labor. My devoted servant Pharaoh (Ramses) obeyed me so much that he even refused the God of the Israelites. He was a wise man. I thought him very well, for I was the voice in his mind. I was his God. He knew he could not serve two masters, so he surrendered to me. And even though the God of Israel sent Moses to free the Israelites from his grip, I tightened his hold even harder, not letting my loyal servant lose, yet I let go for the Red Sea. I had to let up, for I am not a swimmer. However, ha-ha, I was still on their tails, causing fear to hold tight to their kidneys. They were still thinking about me, angering Moses not to make it to the "Promised Land." You see, renewing the mind is the only way they will break free, but those Israelites will never do so.

VOLUME 2. Confronting the unseen self is a giant task, which can become quite painful. Can you think of a time where you were faced with your shadow?

The generational curse is a culture (ideology) in itself. The thing about me is that who created me set it so that you will always choose death. Look, do you get where I am coming from by now? I have a beginning with no end. I am the provocation of war in the heavens (mind), where many think I live in a fiery pit in the middle of the earth. I am seriously not sure where they got that case concept, wait! Oops, I forgot I told them to deceive them, that into believing I was far away. See how naïve and gullible the mind is? I cannot live on the pyscial' Earth; if I were only in one space, how would I deceive the entire world? How else could I separate a man from his God's mind? There will always be turmoil in the mind-world (Spiritual) where I live. My existence is by design; if your culture has not seen me, let me describe myself in another way: I am the slave ship called "Jesus of Lübeck."

Sometimes ships like mine were also called "Ship Solomon." Not only was I the slave ship, but I was also the mind of Captain John Hawkins, who captured and transported over four hundred Afrikaans, trading them for sugar cane and spices along with my fair lady Queen Elizabeth. Our mission was to transport the savage and barbaric Afrikaans from the savage continent of Afrika across the Atlantic Ocean to the New World. Ha! I punished those slaves while transporting them as human cargo. I was going to make sure that the spirit of my beloved Pharaoh (Ramses) got revenge on those Israelites that escaped his paws. I would ensure that I captured their minds while erasing them from their origins, so even if they tried to escape me, they would be lost in the world while still being slaves to me.

The slavery I had for them was of the spirit. How could they not see this? I am from the spirit world. I am a concept that runs through the blood of any culture I capture. I am a self-sabotaging spirit that would cause them to destroy themselves inside out. I have taken away from them their diets that will only collide with their organs and culture; I have taken away from them their native tongues; I have beaten their names out of them; I have indoctrinated their terminology with new ones, for I know their names have powers that would cause them to call upon a powerful characteristic. Now I am a wise serpent-like spirit; see how clever I am, hmm? Do not get me wrong; I made sure the minds I was using to enslave these Afrikaans were also part of the plan. I ensured I left no stone unturned for them to do my work; they, too, were in mental captivity. I hope you do not think they were all coming upon these barbaric, inhumane acts by themselves. One had to be mentally deranged to think so. They, too, are in conflict and cursed. I mean, I am the conflict, or better yet, let me give myself a fancier name than that, the spirit of Err! Now that is better.

Let's move on. Wait! I need to clear my throat. Okay, here I go. Can you hear me? Am I loved enough? Okay, I think you should, because my voice is hoarse. As I said, they are cursed. Even though I am the spirit of Err, there are greater forces than myself, and even though it is hard to utter that half-truth, it is the truth. There is now work that goes unpunished. The spirit of Esau and Jacob was always at war, even in the womb; their parental striving foreshadowed the conflict you see inherited on earth. Now my duty is to make sure my son Esau gets his revenge for his birth; he deserves to have it back by any means necessary, even if it means taking his entire culture to hell along with him. It is by any means necessary because the spirit/generational curse mind of Esau is here to do all the damage to the earth.

I will not only harm the human mind but also disconnect men from their emotions. They will not have empathy for the earth and its inhabitants; even the animals will feel the pain. They will become food that will later create disease. In the bodies of your generation, the anger, the fright, and the hurt that animals felt while being killed will become their emotions. This will cause them to think irrationally, micro-aggressively, compulsively, anxiously, and greedily. They will confuse the lust of the flesh for love, then hate, and be fearful of love. They will confuse their supernatural abilities for mental instability. Water will be destroyed, seeds will be aborted so the factory can grow food, women will give birth to defective children, and the ozone layer will be damaged.

When you say I am here to destroy this planet, the generational curse is unlimited; I would be a fool to only be in one place, so whomever the hell told the world that I was a little demon with red skin, horns, and a long tail that carried a pitchfork is a liar. I forgot I created that lie. Oops, sorry! Okay, I am not a liar; I am just narcissistic, egoistical, and a little psychotic, but I am not a liar; I just do not tell the truth. I do not have a physical identity; I have no specific race, ethnicity, age, or gender, but what I do is great at disguising myself. I hide in the culture of those Afrikaans that were ripped from their culture; the whole world will hate them, ha-ha! They will even hate themselves; all nations will be against them; they will be scattered around the global planet with no identity but self-destructive patterns; their place of origin will be raped and colonized; and I will take away from them their values, spirituality, knowledge, cultural identity, and language and replace them with a slave identity that will always keep them in bondage. Even if one of them rises among them to break my chains, I will curse him or her. I will allow them to look like enemies amongst themselves for attempting to break my chains. See, I am in no position or have no thoughts ever to loosen the locks; my time to reign is extremely

VOLUME 2. Confronting the unseen self is a giant task, which can become quite painful. Can you think of a time where you were faced with your shadow?

Gem C. Collie

limited, so I must conquer my opposition, which is heated; they too want power, yeah, whatever! Monkey see, monkey do.

Before I go, let me tell you this last thing: do not try me! What I mean is that I will hurt you; I will even kill you, and if you try to break my spell, you will be an outcast. If you dare try me, I will get you addicted to a substance to the point where you feel you are losing your mind. You must lose your mind to get rid of me; yes, that's true, but I do not care. You will be admitted to a mental institution. With my employees of evil intent, you will be trapped in my grip. It is the idea that will keep you captive. I will cast your manifest destiny out. This is a necessary occurrence. I will declare that you do not make it in the new covenant. I mean, I will give you freedom of speech so you can defile your own spirit. I will take away from you your languages so that you will never call upon your ancestors to save you. Ha-Ha, your ancestors too will be in captivity in the spirit world; their hands will be tied; they too will be slaves even in life after, and if or when I allow them to be free, they will never be awakened for you to activate them.

VOLUME 2. Confronting the unseen self is a giant task, which can become quite painful. Can you think of a time where you were faced with your shadow?

Your prayers to your gods will never be heard, for they will not understand your tongues. I will instead introduce you to a god you know nothing about. I will use you to dehumanize those foolish Afrikaans, as I have been calling them. I meant Hebrews, but they will never know that they are the true Hebrews. I will get their oppressors to steal their souls; their captors have no souls. What is meant by your soul is the innate inability to connect with their spirits. This is a connection between mind and body and culture. They will dwell on it and appropriate it. See, the oppressors are not free either; they are slaves of my own. Yes, why are you surprised? Pharaoh is a slave too. Oppressors are slaves; remember what I said? I will be here to take over the entire world; the mind of all belongs to me, meaning that those whose motives are good and those who are slave drivers are all part of my plan. Ha-ha, but they will never see this. Listen, at this point, you might as well relax and let this curse take root.

Shalom. Stay Sleep.

THE OPPOSITION OF THE SPIRIT OF ERR
The personification of the Spirit of Truth

The spirit of truth is here to tell of the roots of my Genesis; I, the spirit of truth, and the breath of life. I am the beauty of the rose of Sharon; I am the revival of the holy spirit; I am the evidence that when it was said, "Let there be light," and it was, I am the Genesis Idea.

I am that which it was when it was said that the firmament divides the waters under the firmament (Rakiah) from the waters above the firmament, which is upon the face of the earth. Indeed, I am the beginning of heaven and earth. I am the essence of the Proverbial Divine Woman; I am the laws of Moses; I am the creation of life, not to be boastful or anything of that nature. Oh, yeah, before I forget, I am also Mother Nature. Those who speak the language of Hebrew call me Khawah (Eve, mother of creation), meaning the divine personification of nature that focuses on the life-giving and nurturing aspects of nature by embodying the feminine aspect of the divine mother. I am also my counterpart, Adamah (Man Adam); I am the higher consciousness of the mind; I am the balance of the Ying in the cool and gentle breeze after the Yang on the hot, steamy day. See, I am those instructions that allow the river to flow its water into the sea as they merge and become one. I am the sweetness in the honey and the wisdom of King Solomon (Sholomon). I am also the stillness of the night light; I am known to some as the divine spirit that follows its own instructions; I am the spirit of forgiveness.

Unlike the adversarial spirit of Err, I am not here to deceive the earth, for I am the earth and the fullness thereof. I find no pleasure in harming myself but in the harmonizing songs of the cardinal birds. I do not believe in self-destruction; I love myself way too much for that. I am just not that kind of guy. Oops, I meant spirit, yes, feminine spirit; my words are tripping over this author's fingers. Sorry about that. As I said, I am here to heal what is broken and bring understanding (truth and light) to the darkness (confusion).

Gem C. Collie

Not to toot my own horn, but even though I am the equality of the polarity that keeps the planet floating in space without taking up too much space, I am here to make sure no more lambs are brought to slaughter. I have sat back long enough and watched the adversarial spirit reign in the heavens (mind). It is time for me to step in and balance the pendulum.

I must warn you before I go on: there will be a great war (balance) between the minds of men, the war of the unconscious (sleep) versus the conscious (awakening, awareness). There may be chaos in the physical realm, yet I want you to understand that this war also occurs in the sub-conscious. I am not here to play around. Yes, I am gentle; however, during this war, I have no time for absolute gentleness, for my opponents, along with their armies of deceit and confusions of mass destruction, have gone too far in they are cowards as well, for they hide from the culture of the people, which shows up in their everyday decision-making. Here I am to wipe away all the flitting they have done. Wait! The minute I return, I need to help adore the bride in fine linen, bright and pure, for the

VOLUME 2. Confronting the unseen self is a giant task, which can become quite painful. Can you think of a time where you were faced with your shadow?

fine linen is the righteous deed of the saints, and the groom awaits her.

Let us all say, "Hallelujah!" Okay, I am back. As I was saying, there will be a great "War in the Heavens" (the consciousness), and this is the war that will manifest and establish itself on the earth; it will establish itself there in the physical realm. The adversarial spirit aims to divide and conquer; understand that there are two spirits (concepts) vowing for the minds of man (humankind). The deplorable act is to conquer the world, destroy every existence of righteousness, take away the balance from what was created to exist in the harmonizing frequency, and corrupt that energy. You will recognize the great deception, and by the fruit the tree (people) bear, you will see the unconscious behaviors and thought patterns in their choices, decisions, levels of understanding, morals, principles, and word choices.

The advisory of evil intent has no limits as to where it will go; before I proceed any further, I want for you to understand that neither I nor the opposition is a physical being; we are spirits (ideas, concepts), and we are not to be mistaken for this; it's by design for the to be deceived as to think so, we can be of such, but it would only limit our operation; we only operate in the mind because that environment is our greatest weapon. When I say the mind, I am also talking about the mind of the earth and the animals; they, too, have a mind. I am not sure if you are a person with limited understanding but let me explain what the mind is.

Concept Of Mind And Brain In Traditional Chinese Medicines (TCM)

In modern Western medicine, the brain is the most important organ, acting as a control center. In contrast, the brain is not included in TCM organs, i.e., the five Zang-organs (heart, liver, spleen, lung, and kidney) and the six Fu-organs (gallbladder, stomach, small intestine, large intestine, bladder, and triple-warmer). Interestingly, in TCM, brain functions are scattered throughout the human body. For example, the five Zang-organs arouse various emotions: the heart, liver, spleen, lung, and kidney arouse happiness, anger, deep thinking, melancholy, and fear, respectively. In traditional Chinese medicine, therefore, brain diseases are regarded as systemic diseases rather than disorders of a single organ. Within this concept, the mind and brain are with your organs, the center of the human body, which houses all concepts and understandings.

The human mind begins in the Gut. This is also known as the Gutbrain relationship. The Gut-brain axis (GAB) consists of bidirectional communication between the central and enteric nervous systems, linking emotional and cognitive centers of the brain with peripheral intestinal functions. Recent advances in research have described the importance of gut microbiota in influencing these interactions. Within Eastern philosophy, we have a phenomenal understanding of the mind/brain and how it works. The Spirit has explained it in this manner: The manner of Eastern (wholistic) versus Western (individualistic) culture because it is on the Eastern side of the pendulum, is where I migrate. The brain/mind/Spirit is not an entity separate from the entire body but one collective. I hope you clearly understand what I am saying. Let's move on.

My opposition aims to take over the entire mind; death is my mission, and I am here to turn hate into love. I am here with my army; you did not think that we were coming alone, did you? I am here with the spirit of Truth, Divine Order, Respect, Principalities, Divine Communication, Collectivism, and Knowledge, but not the kind of knowledge that grows from the tree of good and evil. We are here together and will charge the adversarial spirit and its members' intent with treason for betraying the omnipotent one. They will attempt to kill the force that gives life and procreates life. I am the spirit of the opposite of Err. Therefore, I am the spirit of truth. I will pull the striking force of lightning from the skies and roll the thunder. Yes, I am a gentle spirit, but my time to reign comes with a price. The minds of men are in a horrible state, and their abilities to connect with their Godself have no longer taken place. Fear has overpopulated their kidneys, causing them to take on a woman's full attributes, role, and position. On the other hand, the women have allowed anger to rule their livers, and they, too, have lost touch with their feminine agenda.

VOLUME 2. Confronting the unseen self is a giant task, which can become quite painful. Can you think of a time where you were faced with your shadow?

The foods are no longer with seeds, which means they have no afterlife; the water is filled with led, and parasites; and the schools teach lies, fear, deception, and historical dysfunctional cultures. I am here to tell you that the adversarial spirit is everywhere, even in the foods you consume. If you take control of your life, watch the way you operate, and are conscious of your thoughts, the adversarial spirit will attack you through intrusive thinking. Those intrusive thoughts can be culture-based, trauma-based, environmental, or only plain conditioning. Your mind will be our battleground; whoever wins the war in your "Heavens" will be determined by you, and the winner will show up in your everyday actions. Remember, you are the tree, and you will be known by the fruits (actions) you bear. Wake up and be aware.

Selah\Peace\One Love.

THE AWARENESS OF SPIRITUALLY
Transmitted Disease

It is vital that we know those with whom we lay our souls, for there are those who are vessels, a surrogate for their lineage of generational curses. Many are waking up with demons that they are not fully aware of, demons that are looking for the next generation to carry on their seed of destruction. Just as we as humans are here to continue through the passage of our bloodline, so it is that these same demons are lurking in the minds of many, and they, too, are on a mission to carry out a generational legacy. Remember, the body stores memories from traumatic events we have been through; even though the mind suppresses, the body still remembers. This is viable to know when it comes to intercourse, not only because of sexually transmitted diseases but also because you will absorb the energy the person is carrying. This is really the true danger.

As all my texts began with the etymology of the term "spiritually transmitted disease," let's dive into it. Spiritually Transmitted Disease is not necessarily a disease within itself, but more so the energy passed down through intimate contact with a partner during sexual intercourse. Most have identified this as passed down generational demons; many have said that once they lay with an individual suffering from a spiritual attack, generational curses, or any mental illness, they suddenly became infected with a bad omen. This can also be used in conjunction with the term "lay with dogs, rise with flees." This same proverb gives way for generations to understand that whatever you lay with, you will rise with; whatever they are struggling with, you too are now the new host. From my understanding, generational curses are much the same as a spiritually transmitted disease. Unlike a physical disease, this disease is not discussed in the media, and there is no contraceptive to protect you from getting in contact with it.

As you embark on this journey to break generational curses, understand that those curses will also attack you from many realms.

VOLUME 2. Confronting the unseen self is a giant task, which can become quite painful. Can you think of a time where you were faced with your shadow?

This disease is not only dangerous, it is also very contagious. Their mind, mentality, behavior, and ways of thinking will be yours too; whatever battles the person struggles with will eventually become your own. Many are carriers of seeds of destruction. The minute you become sexually intimate with them; the spirit of self-destruction will ruin your life. Some are walking around not knowing they are carriers because they have never taken on the giant task of self-evaluation. They do not have a relationship with their inner souls. They do not question their faults. Instead, they seek another soul to be sexually intimate with, and together, they lay, they may and fornicate with each other's demons, infecting their spirits with darkness, self-sabotaging tendencies, suicidal thoughts, procrastination, sarcastic talk, reckless actions, irrational thinking, irresponsible choice, the spirit of depression, and setbacks that are transmitted through spiritually transmitted diseases. Be mindful of who you lay with because you might lose your soul in the process. Your body might rise from the connection, but your soul might get trapped.

Selah\Stay prayed up.

VOLUME 2. Confronting the unseen self is a giant task, which can become quite painful. Can you think of a time where you were faced with your shadow?

THE SPIRIT OF "LIBERATION"

Freedom begins in the mind.

I am the spirit of liberation, the spirit that gives birds wings, and the spirit that moves mountains without hands. I am an impeccable spirit, yet intangible and visible. I am the spirit of liberation. I am here to unshackle the chains of mental bondage from your thought processes captivated by your ego. I am the spirit that gives life to your voices. A war has been fought for me to reign, but that is not the way to access me. I am a peaceful spirit. I am not activated by war. I cannot be controlled, captured, or captivated, but the idea of me can, the illusion of me can, illustrated by the perception of deception.

I am the spirit of liberation. I am here to set the captives free. But freedom can only be made by them; I am just here to give them a choice. I am not here to force-feed anyone my virtues; I am also not here to sign any peace treaties; I do not operate like that; I just do not entertain the spirit of deception; I understand it as many faces.

Yes, I also mentioned that I am peaceful. However, if I am chosen by free will, my mission is to carry that operation out. If deception gets in my way, I will rage war if I need to, and no, I am not contradicting myself; I said what I meant, and I seriously meant what I said. Yes, I am peaceful; I did not say stupid or dead. So, listen up. I am here to declare your autonomy and be your deliverance, so stand up and take the steps. I hope you are not double-minded because I am starting to take the step of assisting. If you change your mind in the middle of your journey or you allow your ego to use fear to control you, I will turn my back on you. Your liberation is your choice, not mine. I will make a path for you to follow; I will summon the spirits of your ancestors through the earth to free you. Understand that liberation requires some form of war, for the opposition to freedom wants full control. Understand that this opposition is very clever; it will dedicate everything to keep you in bondage. It will attack not only your mind but also the minds of

VOLUME 2. Confronting the unseen self is a giant task, which can become quite painful. Can you think of a time where you were faced with your shadow?

those you love if they become your enemies. They will physically look the same, but spiritually, it is not them. There is no amount of love you can give to free their minds at this point; no amount of righteous acts towards them will allow them to be free; everyone's freedom is their own; you must be willing to cut the cords psychologically. Once you see the spirit of Jezebel moving through the minds, the spirit will show up in their betrayals; it will show up as inconsistency; it will show up as jealousy; it will even show up as someone imitating your personality.

This imitation of your personality is not to be taken as flattery; it is the tip of the iceberg of deep-rooted jealousy of one's inability to master their destiny. You must be able to outwit the devil to be truly liberated. Please be assured that you must stay focused. Do not pay attention to the noise in the background, no matter if it sounds like the spirit of bondage is close to your heel. Keep moving. The noise is a part of the illusion, a part of the distraction. If you find that you cannot ignore the noise, turn it into a melody—a melody that vibrates with your melanin. Be ready to draw your sword at any time. Be ready to revolt. I am the spirit of liberation, here to reveal what hid in front of your face, but you looked elsewhere.

I am the spirit of liberation; I am the beginning of the Biblical Genesis (Ha Brashest) מאויתת בראשית. I am the one who set the Israelites free from the hands of Pharaoh (Ramses), who was holding on tightly to them; he was determined to take them out, including being consumed in the red sea. But I was even more determined that the spirit motivating Ramses, the spirit of Err, had nothing to do with me. How could that be when it is my breeze that allows that spirit to flow? Oh, please, why should I be afraid of the spirit of Err? But even when I liberated those stubborn Israelites, they were still lusting after the wonders of Egypt. Wow, how ungrateful! I am the kind of spirit that takes things personally. If I ever free you once and you return to what I have freed you from, I am not willing to go back and save you again. Oh no, that's not happening. I am seriously offended. It took a lot of my time to free them from the grip of Ramses. I am still beside myself over this. Please do not call me over emotional, nor emotionally unstable, for this act has resulted in where the Israelites are today, they are scattered over the planet with no identity to whom they are, and whenever they come together, they foolishly protest in the land of captivity for their captivators to give them, their freedom, this is not fighting for freedom, you cannot negotiate with your oppressors for freedom, so this is not protesting this plain old mental illness, it is madness, no difference from seeing a sheep chant redemption, and freedom from the mouth of wolves, the sheep will never be free, for wolves eat sheep. Liberation cannot be found where captives were brought; the only thing you will find there is adaptation and survival of dysfunctionality that will hide under the identity of freedom. Therefore, the generation of these said captives would breed children who would be dedicated to the land of their captivity. I am the spirit of liberation and am here to assist you with your freedom.

Selah/Shalom/Peace.

THE SPIRIT OF DIVINE DISCERNMENT

Aww!! At last, it is my turn to speak. Here I go; I am the spirit of discernment. Hold on. I meant the Divine Spirit of discernment. I said Divine because there are many different types of spirits; not all are Divine and holy.

Nonetheless, I am here to tell you some of my attributes so you can recognize me. You might confuse me with common sense, but, my dear, nothing is common about me. I am the gift that is not granted to everyone; I am not something that can be bought, sold, thought of, or held.

Understand that you need me whenever you need to activate my powers. Be able to listen—not just hear but listen with your heart and mind; humble your spirit; talk less; and do not react quickly. Understand that not everything you see is what it is. Know that those who possess my gift of me can see through smoke screens and any obstacles as they uncover the truth; my source is the creator.

Many wrote about me, like Bednar of the Quorum of the Twelve Apostles, who taught that the gift of discernment could help the mind detect hidden errors and evil in others. And then there was Jacob, who was also granted gifts because he could interpret the dreams of himself and others. I, the Divine spirit of discernment, also stated that one's openness must be able to approach the decision by asking questions with an open mind and heart. The spirit of Generosity, Courage, and internal Freedom. A habit of prayerful reflection on one's experience, having one's priorities straight, and not confusing ends with means are all garments that I adorn myself with. I spray the perfume of self-respect all over me; I stand tall, but I DO NOT speak loudly; my eyes change according to what I discern; the color of my skin is camouflaged, which makes me not very noticeable; my personality is very calm; I am not quick to anger; and I hold tight to my tongue, as I understand that time, people, places, and culture play a big part in how others react, respond, understand, and approach life.

The spirit of discernment is a life savior; you can call it a messianic messenger if you wish. With the spirit of discernment, you must be willing to question everything; you must be willing to go within when you hear those voices in your mind instructing you; and you must be able to understand that there are two types of spirit battling for the minds of men; they are the spirit of Err and the Spirit of truth. You must be able to listen with an open mind, discern when your intuition is talking to you, and be willing to trust your discerning mind.

You must understand there are two types of discernment. Let me explain, for I will not leave it up to you. Listen, now there is General discernment and the discerning of spirits. With the spirit of discernment, there are three steps to processing: **AWARENESS** - to see or recognize me, the spirit moving within you. **UNDERSTANDING** - knowing the direction of the different movements in the heart and mind. **ACTION** means diving into

VOLUME 2. Confronting the unseen self is a giant task, which can become quite painful. Can you think of a time where you were faced with your shadow?

rejecting a thought or feeling. Understand that with the spirit of discernment, not all languages will be vocal; you must be able to hear what is not being said, and you must be able to walk into a room and sense danger.

Some possess the spiritual gift of the divine spirit of discernment; they can **see right through smokescreens and obstacles as they uncover the truth**. Their source of the gift of discernment is from a higher source. Discernment springs from the truth taught through your senses. Be still, listen carefully, think before you act, and speak less. These are two keys to unlocking your gift of the spirit of Divine discernment. Understand that there will be those who will try their best to deceive your sense of discernment. Those who attempt to do so are what I call agents of the adversarial spirit; they might look as though they are human, but they are not. Understand that not everyone who moves iteratively in the human flesh is human.

Understand your human nature so that you can recognize adversarial agents; no one will be exempt; those creatures will operate in the flesh of those you love because they are the ones you trust. I will not tell you not to trust anyone, but I will tell you to be careful about how open you are and be mindful of whom you express the desires of your heart. A friend today can easily be an enemy tomorrow, and they will use those desires as a weapon against you. Some are operating from the spirit of jealousy; the spirit of jealousy is as deep as the grave. Jealousy is a crafty spirit; become the pauper among the wealthy; you will remain as some they look down on instead of competition; understand that everyone does not deserve access to you. You must understand that it is okay to be vulnerable, but again, this is where your discernment will be required.

Selah, One Love.

THE SPIRIT OF REJECTION
Identifying the Root of Bitterness

I am here; I am the spirit of rejection, envy, jealousy, resentment, perfectionism, fear, withdrawal, lies, pride, self-reliance, people-pleasing, lust, inferiority, and guilt; these are all my virtues. Even though these are all pieces of evidence that make up my character, I am truly not here to hurt you. This might be hard to believe, but that is not always my intent. However, I am driven by this, but I can come in handy at times; if you only knew what I was saving you from, you would embrace me. I am not asking you to hug me and to cuddle with me; I am not asking you to dress up in my attributes; I am just asking you to hear me out: I am also here to show you those red flags that you are determined about turning into love red flags that I saw coming; I see in a place where your discernment is supposed to warn you about, but she is not doing her job; I think your discernment sleeps around with your heartbreak.

Gem C. Collie

I heard she fornicates with your setbacks. I am not the one saying this or anything; I am just stating what I heard. I do not want you to be hurt. Many misunderstand me; they take my intentions personally. I am here to clear my name. I am only a security network to ensure your heart is not broken. Hold on before you say I am wrong because I have broken your heart and many others. I honestly did not. If you only saw what was truly behind the smoke screen, you would hold me as tight as you hold on before you say I am wrong because I have broken your heart and the hearts of many. I honestly did not; if you only saw what was truly behind the smoke screen, you would hold me as tight as you hold your pillow at night as they are being soaked in your tears. I am the victim here, to be honest, and before you call me narcissistic, I am not; just hear me out. I know why you cannot open your heart to the one you love; I am the reason you stretch your hands out for love but slap it back.

I am the reason the spirit of intrusive thoughts whispers bitter thoughts in your ears; I am the reason you are so indecisive; I am the reason you are self-sabotaging; I am the reason you will not make

VOLUME 2. Confronting the unseen self is a giant task, which can become quite painful. Can you think of a time where you were faced with your shadow?

the first steps; I make you doubt yourself, but I am not the only one at fault; I refuse to take full responsibility for your pain, where was your intuition? She was supposed to be there to guide you, but it looks as if she has abandoned you too. This has left you suffering from abandonment trauma, which is why I am such a trigger for you. I, the spirit of rejection, am here to use my power to define and clear my name.

Understand that whenever you are rejected, most likely, it is a time to celebrate and not feel heartbroken. Then store away the TBD broken pieces of your heart inside of you to only use it as a weapon to harm someone here to show you love. Rejection is your third eye, the unseen eye, that eye that sees the incoming evil coming at you like a raging driver on the road. He has lost control of his vehicle because of your abandonment issues. You often struggle in relationships, exhibiting symptoms of codependency, an inability to develop trust, or even the tendency to sabotage relationships. The cause of your abandonment issues is your trauma of some kind, traumas that you had stored inside of you, like when you lost the

VOLUME 2. Confronting the unseen self is a giant task, which can become quite painful. Can you think of a time where you were faced with your shadow?

only one you could trust, the only one that understood you. When they died, your ability to feel, breathe, trust, and enable died with them. Now you feel rejected, but I am here to say I am not the root cause of your bitterness; your unreal traumas are unspoken. It is fear that has embraced you.

Understand this before I go; I must clear my name somewhere else. I am being summoned to court; understand that I, the spirit of rejection, am your protection for redirection. Know that if you do not fix these issues with me within you, you will meet someone just like you; they will reflect every deep wound in you that you are avoiding, and they will reject you the way you are rejecting yourself, like the way you hate me, they too will hate me.

Selah Peace.

"If you find yourself, still holding on to rejection; it is easier said than done, but it is time to move on, it is time you accept the rejections, the disappointments, the heartbreaks, and the letdowns did not happen because it was not meant for you"

VOLUME 2. Confronting the unseen self is a giant task, which can become quite painful. Can you think of a time where you were faced with your shadow?

THE MENTALITY OF THE STOCKHOLM SYNDROME
And The Legacy of Generational Curses

As I have always done in my other writings, I will first highlight and define the term "at hand." Let us take a look at how the term Stockholm syndrome is being used. Here we go so that you, the readers, can properly understand what is being said. The aim is to do your best to be clear. With that said, let us look at the definition. Even though Stockholm syndrome is not a recognized psychological diagnosis in the DSM (Diagnostic Systematic Manual):but rather an attempt to explain the symptoms appearing in some individuals who are held captive, a person who experiences Stockholm syndrome comes to bond with the captor and may experience feelings of love, empathy, or a desire to protect the captor. Frankly, there is no previous relationship between the captor and the captive.

According to Britannica.com, Stockholm syndrome is named after a 1973 bank robbery in Stockholm, Sweden. The robbers held four hostages for six days; when they were rescued, the hostages attempted to protect the perpetrators, with whom they had an amicable relationship.

What are the signs of Stockholm syndrome? With learned helplessness, giving the abuser whatever, they want, and difficulty detaching from the subset. I am mentioning this theory of Stockholm syndrome here in this book because it is imperative and hard to talk about a generational curse without talking about Stockholm syndrome. Yet even though I have used the web's definition, I am here to give my theory, based upon aspects of culture, experiences, and simply my understanding of the phenomenon. According to my viewpoint, Stockholm syndrome can be dated back to Biblical times, identified as Spiritual Stockholm syndrome. My example is that even though the Israelites were free from the hands of the Pharaoh (Ramses), they still wanted to return to him; they felt it was more prosperous to be in captivity than to be free.

VOLUME 2. Confronting the unseen self is a giant task, which can become quite painful. Can you think of a time where you were faced with your shadow?

Another example of this is during the period of the "Black Holocaust." When the captives had an opportunity to run away from their captor to find freedom in the North, they chose to stay with their captor. If there were anyone or anything that challenged their relationship with the captor, they would destroy them. This type of relationship between the captor and the captive breeds learned helplessness and codependence.

However, Stockholm syndrome is not classified as a mental disorder; it gives birth to mental illness. If I talk about Stockholm syndrome, I must discuss Post-Traumatic Stress Disorder. There is no way possible that these two phenomena are not the same. Let's look at the definition of Post-Traumatic Slave disorder. Post-Traumatic Slave Disorder is an explanatory theory that looks at multigenerational trauma. It is a sustained trauma passed down through epigenetics and adaptive traumatic behavior for the need to survive. It can also be classified as a condition that exists because of multigenerational oppressive acts on descendants of Afrika, resulting from the effects of chattel slavery. With this, we also understand that trauma is not an illness but an injury; trauma comes back as a reaction, not a memory; these actions, in return, affect two areas in the autonomic nervous system, which are the sympathetic nervous system and the parasympathetic nervous system; the parasympathetic nervous system works nonstop.

Stockholm Syndrome can also be found in many cultures and is accompanied by Grooming. Grooming is when an adult male engages with a family, preferably a single mother who is emotionally and financially incapable of taking care of her children and seems to be able to fill the gap by providing the necessary economic security needs, housing, food, and school fees. The mother even takes up this predatory act. The male figure would sleep with the mother while raising and grooming her child until the young child reached the age where they felt she was fit enough to prune her for sexual reasons. He would mentally manipulate the young child enough for her to believe that it is okay for her to engage in sexual activities secretly until she reaches the age of eighteen when it would be considered socially acceptable to marry or impregnate her. As a young mother, her mother would see no issue with this behavior, for she is most likely a product of this act. Her daughter would be left to carry on the generational curse, and even if someone saw the condition as deplorable or even attempted to save her from the captor, it would be useless. Her mind would already be conditioned to believe that the captor was the savior who saved her from her condition. She would see everyone else as the problem. Her mind is already groomed and in good condition. The young girl would gladly defend the male figure. Or if we look at the aspect of Trauma Bonding. Trauma bonding is a psychological response to abuse. It happens when an individual forms an unhealthy relationship with an abusive person. This individual may develop a level of sympathy for the abuser, which may be reinforced by the cycle of abuse. Unlike Stockholm syndrome, these two factors can be classified as coping mechanisms. Trauma Bonding is found in the DSM and is considered a mental illness. It is also associated with a cycle of abuse following an abusive incident.

I have mentioned these two paradigms in this book because, when it comes to generational curses, Stockholm syndrome can keep you in conscious bondage with your family's generational curse to the point where it seems that redemption cannot even free you from the mental bondage. You will pledge allegiance to every curse, defending it with your heart and soul while your spirit cries out for freedom. You will pass on the rope that has tied your mind to the next generation. You will speak up against anyone who dares to go against your love-hate relationship with the generational beast.

Listen, shifting your thinking is the only way to escape your captor. You must break the pledge and be willing to be called a beast, for this captor will not allow you to be free; it will turn everything in your life upside down. Keep pushing whenever you see this happening but be wise and willing to outwit the devil. Understand that the generational curse was a part of the survival mechanism to heal from the trauma created by the same mind that created the trauma. You must interrupt them with a new mind.

Selah.

DIVINE LEADERSHIP

As it is stated, that "When the wicked rule, the people mourn- the righteous consider of the poor, A fool speaks all that is in his mind where there is no vision, the people perish," Henceforth where there is no vision, there is no leadership.

Divine leadership envisions a compelling and bright future. To be a divine leader, one must first master one's emotional self or the unspoken truth of his shadow. A divine leader is in tune with his higher self and knows how to connect with his inner voice. A divine leader is always in alignment with his purpose. A divine leader is groomed and guided by his creator; a divine leader knows and understands his faults; he knows his errors are not to be mourned over but glorified, for he knows his errors are his teachers. He understand the importance of separating himself from his experience. The best leaders have high EQ, the best leaders understand the human skills, they' are good at empathy, they're good at patients they are good at creating a space in which they can help other people to be accountable, and if they fall or falter, they say "good try again". They believe in themselves; they practice trust, which means they trust first.

A divine leader has grasped the idea that at least ninety-five percent up our decisions are made by how you feel in the moment. He/She understands the implication of this, and that is the problem. The paradigm that state that "No, I do not I feel like getting up, or I do not feel like making that cold call, no you do not feel like doing that third set of reps." Leader understand that we, as humans make decisions based on our feelings; and that is robbing ourselves of joy, and opportunity if we accept the fact that we may never feel ready; and that we may never feel motivated ; and we may never feel confident, resulting in the fact we may never feel courageous; and that may be okay; However we must still push ourselves forward, as we start to see ourselves becoming the person that takes action; guess what now happens? We begin to build the skill of confidence, consistence ,persistence, and mere courage.

VOLUME 2. Confronting the unseen self is a giant task, which can become quite painful. Can you think of a time where you were faced with your shadow?

A divine leader knows they will not follow the cliché of "faking it to make it," for he is consciously leading from his heart space. He knows that when he is shading and releasing his beliefs, conditioning, and ideas of who he once was, he aligns more deeply with his authentic truth into his authentic power and higher self.

To be a divine leader is to master one's ego and rule from a place of divinity, not from his emotions. A divine leader understands the impact of his words and knows how to soften the tone of what he is saying. Making sure that his anger is not the dictator of his crown. In leadership, one knows the autonomy of his collaborators. However, he evaluates their skills, ethics, and ability to take instructions. Divine leaders are structured around faithfulness and loyalty. Faithfulness is the consistent option to stand on; it is anthems and pledges of allegiance, an allegiance that will cause the heart to remain even when no one is present. When this is not the cause, you cannot see the good. It will activate complaining and disloyalty; therefore, a true leader understands the purpose of those in his court and the difference between those assigned to him and those emotionally attached to him. He knows he must assert himself with those he will attempt to abide by in their crisis. This is because he also knows that attempting to side with anyone should cause him any psychological, physical, moral, emotional, or mental injury. Some are so damaged that healthy assistance and direct communication will feel like an attack.

A divine leader knows how to see through these deformed spirits. He knows that there will be those who are like manipulative narcissists; this type of spirit aims to betray you when they cannot control you; they will try to control how others see you; they will stab you in the back and then pretend to be the victim. Therefore, a divine leader must master effective communication skills, for communication is the voice of effective leadership. He must know that effective communication principles establish order, lead, and regulate chaos. With divine leadership, one must understand the importance of his collaborators and know the importance of himself. He must understand that the first law of nature is self-preservation . If this law is not implanted in leadership, then a leader cannot properly lead at that rate and will eventually self-destruct. If self is not a part of the first law of leadership, that leader will be emotionally codependent, seeking validation from those he is supposed to lead.

Leadership first begins with self-worth, self-awareness, self-Work, and self-love. Leadership is neither superior masculine energy nor superior feminine energy, but he knows that the polarity of both makes him whole. Leadership skills require patience and time. It is a quality some of us are born with. Leadership skills are an automatic character trait. Yes, a leader can be trained, but it shows up differently in your everyday behavior when it is an automatic personality trait. Your character is an automatic magnet that draws others to you.

A divine leader knows never to appear too perfect; it will attract vultures who will dig away at their flesh; he knows how to avoid the happy and unlucky; he knows how to win friends and influence people; yet he knows the diplomatic and strategic act of disarming and interfering with the mirror effect. He also knows how to isolate people from their influencers by filling them with his intentions and elevating their egos. Because some people love to be led astray by someone who knows where they are going, he knows the power of the disappearing and reappearing act.

A divine leader knows he must force himself into an uncomfortable and unfamiliar situation, for it is the only way to grow. Yet even though we have divine leadership, we must understand this leader cannot lead alone. They must lead as a collective—not just focusing on who guides the followers, but also considering by whom they are guided. The collective is the most crucial aspect here, overshadowing personal feelings and focusing on necessary divine diplomatic measures. There are times when the wheel must be reinvented, for just as leaves fall and grow over time, so too must leadership elevate and evolve.

As a divine leader reading this, keep the instructions in your heart. Let the commands of your guidance be seen in your footsteps; let not your words fall on deaf ears; let your words be your action; you will lead with your shadow, as you are selective of how you utter

---

VOLUME 2. Confronting the unseen self is a giant task, which can become quite painful. Can you think of a time where you were faced with your shadow?

your instructions. Guide with wisdom; be willing to separate your emotions from your reality. Yes, you are not perfect, but you are responsible for your actions and those of those you lead. No one should ask you to make decisions with no flaws; your flaws are your teachers, which is what they are there for. You will never be able to fill the shoes of those before you. But you, my divine leader, will create your footprints, making a new oath. Go in peace, be divine, be kind to yourself, be mindful of your nervous system, and do not forget that you can only give from an overflowing cup. Also, the instructions of those before you shall not die with them.

"Divine leadership can also mean that to veer deflect, nor denied being accountable even at the expense of degrading; or at worst damaging meaningful relationships you have.

I am not implying by any means that it is an easy thing to do, but I will say that this is everything worthy of impactful result is never easy it takes a certain dimension of maturity to become comfortable with taking accountability.

VOLUME 2. Confronting the unseen self is a giant task, which can become quite painful. Can you think of a time where you were faced with your shadow?

Gem C. Collie

A fundamental element of your life which essentially is having the courage to own up to the negative outcomes of your actions and also your flaws, and accepting the imperfections of your character; so, it is no surprise you will shy away from holding yourselves accountable because to be accountable is to be vulnerable. You will risk your ego being hurt, to risk the resistance of those will go against your order, come to see the depth of our insecurities the truth is this so invulnerability it is not a sign of weakness it is a conscious decision to remove friction from your mind, body; and soul it is a sign of strength because it is willing to admit to yourself where you need correction; vulnerability is opening up yourself" to the possibility of life; love ;and need to be seen, to improve ,to boldly step forward into a higher dimension of growth allowing yourself to become the better version of yourselves."

VOLUME 2. Confronting the unseen self is a giant task, which can become quite painful. Can you think of a time where you were faced with your shadow?

THE DIVINE MASCULINE AND FEMININE

To begin the reconstruction of self after breaking your generational curses, you must be able to step into the power of both your divine masculine and divine feminine as equals. Remember that when I speak of the Divine Masculine and Divine Feminine, I am not talking about gender here.

When it comes to the Divine Feminine energy, which is in a state of constant evolution, it is grounded in the woman and the masculine energy, which is not a symbol of the male but a state of being. These energies are both rooted in female and male species. According to my philosophy, when a man operates from the feminine aspect, he operates with a nurturing attribute: he is soft-spoken and thinks before he speaks; he is gentle with his words and touch. He is a divine listener and knows how to listen with his heart and intuition. He is the healer of his home.

The divine feminine energy is connected to the right side of the brain, which aligns with the spirit of creativity, empathy, justice, and spirituality. While the divine masculine energy is connected with the left side of the brain, which controls logic, purpose, leadership, responsibilities, and government.

Yet with all this, one of the most misunderstood battles is the spiritual polarity between the masculine and feminine energy aspects in any species, the polarity between the two influenced structures, soul growth, the opportunities for spiritual awakening, spiritual discernment, and the awakening of the kundalini traveling through the vibrate and connecting with the consciousness of the higher self. This is important in breaking generational curses that are tied as a rope in our minds and affect the struggling with the idea of toxic masculine energy, and toxic feminine energy, causing the human state of thinking to gets lost in the whirlwind of gender autonomy, which causes a division of superiority and inferiority being the doorkeepers of division.

VOLUME 2. Confronting the unseen self is a giant task, which can become quite painful. Can you think of a time where you were faced with your shadow?

Once the beast has mastered that level of confusion, man and woman see themselves as separate individuals from each other. This breeds injustice between the two; this is all a part of the generational beast that will keep turmoil among the human species. If we take a look at nature among the animals in the wild, let's do so. Let us look at the lion and the lioness; it is the lioness that goes out and hunts, which would be considered a masculine attribute; or let us go into the sea; the female seahorse gives her eggs to the male seahorse, who then, in turn, carries these eggs until they are ready to be born.

Let's go further back to the human species. In the eastern part of Afrika, within Kenya, there is a tribe where the men dress femininely to attract the women for marriage. The more feminine he appears, the more attractive he is. The beast has blighted the world's vision of how masculine and feminine energies are perceived, redefining them into two genders. This causes the world to be in a position where gender equality is being fought in a war between men and women. This is even though I explained earlier that neither masculine nor feminine energy is dominant. There still lies a balance where the male species were created for certain roles and females for others. No one gender is superior; they are both parts of a whole, yet two polarities that must govern the world together.

In the Caucasian culture at the time of the Black Holocaust, the women were not given much power; their powers were taken from them, so they used their powers against the Afrikaans whom they enslaved and against the Afro-Asian enslaved women, for their husbands would rape their slaves, both female and males, whenever they wanted, for there was no such thing as consensual sex between the captor and the enslaved. Whenever enslaved women get pregnant, the Caucasian women would vent their frustration, and inability to be in control on the caramel-colored babies to regain their power. This caused violent and emotional combustion. They would then abuse the mixed-race children by pouring hot water and grease on them and beating them on the head with a frying pan. Something had to be done, but a white woman would not be arrested because that was just something that was not heard of. Therefore, in 1669, King Charles II of England created "The Casual Killing Act."

This stated that any slave who resists his master or overseer is killed because they resisted punishment and gets away scot-free. This fixed the issue of Caucasian women killing Africans. This example is a prime example of toxic femininity. Charming will be decisive; beauty fades away, but a divine spirit with conviction will never fade away.

Selah.

THE DYNAMICS OF SELF RESPECT

I am here to talk about what many do not know or have never experienced, which is self-respect. Before discussing this topic, we must truly understand the depths of the self. Each individual's definition of the word "self" will be different. They will define 'The Self' by their names, experiences, cultures, attributes, or altitudes.

According to my philosophical perspective, the self is the consciousness of beings in a state of awareness. It is an autonomous being separate from its physical form yet physical in manifestation. According to the web, The Self is a person in an object of its reflective consciousness. To move forward, I have incorporated the dynamics of Self Respect here in this book to give my readers a better pathway to understanding the ideology of breaking their generational curses.

VOLUME 2. Confronting the unseen self is a giant task, which can become quite painful. Can you think of a time where you were faced with your shadow?

In most cultures or family structures, the unconscionable agreement with the generational beast first began with disrespect and dishonor. The Self, disrespecting oneself, breaks the ability to be autonomous and tears apart the structure of one's character and self-values. The importance of self-respect is imperative to one's existence; one cannot say they have truly lived if one has not applied the aspect of The Self. To break the chains of generational curses is to break the unconscious agreement that was made to destroy the self. It is to know the importance of an order to move forward; it knows the direction to the pathway of self-discovery. The true self is so hidden that finding it will take a lifetime. Yes, I said a lifetime. Why? You must remember or understand that the spirit of Err deceived the entire world to see through the lens of confusion. When this spirit gave you these lenses, he did not prescribe them to your eyes; therefore, you were programmed to see yourself according to this beastly spirit. The beast has ripped apart any idea or ideology you once had of yourself from you; he has ripped apart it from your culture; the sea swelled it up, yet unlike Yona (Jonah), who was in the beast's belly,

---

VOLUME 2. Confronting the unseen self is a giant task, which can become quite painful. Can you think of a time where you were faced with your shadow?

Your identity will never be spat out; you must be willing to rip the beast into two to free the mind and the concept of thyself, to redefine The Self. But understand that you cannot use the same root words as "the etymology of The Self." According to that adverse concept, you must be your creator, or creatures, to create who you are; be bold enough to swim deep into the depths of your mind; do not worry about drowning; listen to your inner voice; it will continue to breathe life into your lungs at each depth you go. If you become fearful and second-guess your journey, you will get lost, and the light guiding you will be black.

The first step in the dynamics of Self-Respect is trusting your voice. An interesting thing will happen when you begin to respect yourself: you will become more sensitive to others not respecting you and much less tolerant of it. The beast cannot uproot your worth unless you break free from codependency programming. You must walk alone on this path until you discover your value and know that others are suffering from this, too. As I stated earlier, the entire world was deceived, but everyone is awakened to their self-

---

VOLUME 2. Confronting the unseen self is a giant task, which can become quite painful. Can you think of a time where you were faced with your shadow?

destructive patterns, so do not expect from them what you are doing for yourself; this does not mean that you should not set boundaries, and compromise your values for social acceptance; know that once you see who these people are, do not think otherwise; be careful; the beast is so tricky, it is very clever; once it realizes you are on the path to self-respect, it will attack your mind; it will plug into your thoughts by intrusive thinking; please pay attention.

Your self-respect carries spiritual authority. When you have spiritual authority, you will not need to show your strength; therefore, when you exist in respect, allow your dynamic to do the work. Remember, with self-respect comes growth, which requires a change in mindset—change the way you think and how you operate and speak daily.

Self-respect will guide you through your values; it will be announced in how you think, walk, dress, and talk, what you choose to consume, and what or to whom you listen. Be willing to walk alone until your values are respected. Your self-respect is your faith;

you will know when to walk away when no respect for who you are is applied. Respect yourself, and never leave home without it.

Shalom. Peace, One Love!

THE SPIRITUAL CONCEPT OF ABORTION
The Emotional Aftermath

In this chapter, you will read about the damsel's struggles after the abortion of her baby. It is not to shame the character or you, the reader, to do the same, nor feel ashamed, or to not do the same. Know that life begins with the breath and ends with the breath. I want you, the reader, to know that if you are facing this act, I, the author, am here to lend a hand of understanding and support and that you are not a bad person for making this decision. If you have already done so, please work on forgiving yourself, sit with yourself, and talk to that part of you that was also aborted with that child. Hug yourself, and do not be afraid or ashamed of owning your faults, your hurt, your tears, and your actions; they are yours to do so, and if you ever feel you are alone and have no one to call on anytime you feel that way, take a deep breath and realize where that breath came from.

Also, know that the spirit of guilt will follow you; even the baby's spirit will follow you. Understand that if you need to sit with that, please do so. Even if you talk to your baby's spirit, allow the baby's spirit to understand that your decision was not out of hate or abandonment. Sit in the moment and grieve. Allow yourself to go through the process; guilt, shame, regrets, and embarrassment will be some of the emotions that overcloud your mind. Allow yourself to feel those emotions; cry, scream, and mourn, but do not stay there, my sister. Hug yourself and forgive your choices.

I wish I could tell you breathing would be easy, but it is not. I cannot tell you when to exhale, but I am here to say, "Do not suffocate." I know you are struggling with your identity and your self-esteem. I understand that your worldview is not the same anymore and your coping mechanisms are unbearable, but you must separate your decisions from your identity. If you need to give the child a name, do so. If you have a personal memorial service, do that as well. I cannot tell you how or when to grieve, but my dear, owing to your trauma, speaking your truth will bring you peace and serve as the voice of those who have lost their voices during their struggles. What is right for one can be wrong for another; others' perspectives or principles can dictate our decisions.

Peace, Shalom, and One Love.

THE SPIRIT OF CONFUSION

I am the spirit of confusion. I am a very deceptive spirit. I come to cause nothing but division, turmoil, and chaos. I am not a happy spirit and do not intend to become one. I am a double-minded spirit that breeds uncertainty; yes, you can call me on that. I will admit to it. I will even admit that I am a troublemaker and a sneaky rebel. I will also admit to that as well. I am a spirit that is conscious of who I am. My pineal is not calcified, as you can see. I might be evil, but I am conscious. Are you aware of yourself? Is your third eye open? There is also nothing too friendly about me; honestly, I do not come around to being friends with anyone. Nor am I here to be the best man at your wedding. However, I can cause you to rethink your life before you say, "I do!"

Listen, let me tell you, if you do not figure me out or understand me by the time you read this, you are seriously doomed because, once I get a grip on your mind, I do not intend to let go. I will squeeze you so tight that you contemplate suicide, and your self-value will decrease. I am very good at pretending to be what you desire, yet I have no intention of caring about you. I dislike you; I want what you have. Do you know what? I honestly do not; I do not want to see you happy. Your joy brings me grief; I hate when you smile, and your success makes me anxious. I am here to do everything I can to see your heartbreak manifest. I am here to cause you to make the wrong choices and dim your light so that you will be confused in your direction; darkness will be the road you travel on.

There is also not much difference between me and the spirit of deception. If I feel like I am losing my grip on controlling you, I will control the way others see you; even if they already knew you, they would second-guess your characteristics. However, you will never see that coming because you are insecure. I am here to assist you in carrying out your doubts so I can watch you fall apart in front of my eyes. I will even pretend to care when you come crying to me. I will only confuse your mind by whispering intrusive thoughts in your ears, knowing that the most important organ is your ears, and the most important sound is silence. Therefore, your mind will never find peace. How else do you expect me to carry out my mission if I do not keep you distracted? If not, then you will be able to hear your intuition guiding you. I can not just allow that to happen. I am not here to play around. I am also a jealous spirit. Even if I do not want what you have, I will confuse your thoughts to see you hurt. I will hold tight to your mind so that you will be easy to manipulate.

I am great at stirring up a dust storm to blind the eyes of others so they will not see, then asking them what happened to their vision. Ha-ha, ha-ha, that's funny; they are so stupid, so insecure, and so self-destructive. They will never suspect me, and even if they do, their lives will already be destroyed by the time they figure me out. Ha-ha, ha-ha, ha-ha, I crack myself up. I mean, there are some that I will say are clever enough to see through my intentions, and even when they do, I will spray a mist of delusion in their faces that would cause them to second-guess themselves.

VOLUME 2. Confronting the unseen self is a giant task, which can become quite painful. Can you think of a time where you were faced with your shadow?

I would even rub their backs as if I cared to get them to let their guard down, causing them to surrender to my good friend's spirit of indecisiveness. They would embrace his indecision as though he were a security blanket. Indecision would also hold them tight while wrapping his claws around their veins, causing them to suffer frequent anxiety attacks. Indecisiveness will stress you out; he will keep you up at night roaming around in your head about what decisions you should make; he will frequently cause you to lose your ability to recognize truth, people, time, and places; and if he decides to hold tight to you, he will shapeshift into a deeper version of himself, which is called Aboulomania; yeah, that is his Greek name. That side of him, yap, on the other side, will become a mental disorder in which you will display pathological inductiveness, which is typically associated with depression and mental anguish. This will lead to a severe inability to function socially.

Indecisiveness will affect your feelings of disorientation. Indecision is sneaky; it will appear in your thoughts suddenly. He is such a terrible spirit that he will cause you to fear the spirit of failure, even when you have succeeded. He will even go as far as teaming up with your ego, and they will tag-team your thoughts. Your ego will then create a world that does not exist so that he can be served. He will affect your brain to the point where you feel delirious. Wow, indecisiveness is such a beast. Watch out for indecisiveness.

He will cause you to second-guess your heart, man, but that's my friend's indecisiveness; he's got my back. Yap, we are cool like that. He is like my brother from another mother; we are best friends and rule the heavens (mind) around these places. I only hope indecisiveness does not get too comfortable because the mind belongs to me. I inherited from my father the Spirit of Err; yap, it is been passed down as a family heirloom, and I will pass it down to my brother. Dysfunctionality, and I truly hope that he does not drop the ball. We must keep the human mind in the family so that the world will continue to be in a rumble. We do not want peace; even though we are aware of it, we do not want peace, for if we chose peace, it would end our existence.

VOLUME 2. Confronting the unseen self is a giant task, which can become quite painful. Can you think of a time where you were faced with your shadow?

There are times you feel the great effect of confusion. You feel this way because you distrust your inner voice. You know your intuition, your instinct; it is your inner knowing, a part of your Divine self. Yes, it is true. I am not here to continue this feeling and keep you in the dark. This is because, with the other spirits, they had to understand who they were for healing to begin on a cellular level.

Yes, I am. Last but not least, this is my time to utter what many will not say or are too afraid to say. Because of this, I have ventured into dark places, where all broken bones are kept, where all hope is lost, where faith finds it hard to move mountains, where shadows have no reflection, where voices have no echoes, where death resides, where the wombs of women are dry and parched, where understanding has lost its stand, where jealousy is as deep as the grave, and where there are demons that are not afraid to show themselves.

I have created this place, this place of no return, this space where the mind dies. Some spirits have affected the human mind. Through their epigenetics, these spirits even showed up in their languages, diets, cultures, and habits. Wow, those spirits are so clever; they even show up in their belief systems. This is where they attack them first. The bloodline is traveling in their minds. Do you think I am the spirit of healing? If you are unsure; let me clarify before I am not.

I am the offspring of the spirit of "Err, that guy lies so much!" Did you read about his character, where he says he is not a liar and does not tell the truth? Man, that guy is so crafty, dang. I keep calling him a guy. I mean, that spirit is such a liar. Ha-ha, that is his motive. Yap, that is my dad.

As I mentioned, these spirits are not afraid to show their intentions. They have affected the conception so much that I am not afraid to say they are not friendly. I know this because I tried to speak to them, but they refused. I was persistent, so one of them came out to introduce itself. It said its name was self-hatred, but others call it the Spirits of Delusion. It says it was a twin. I asked for the name of its twin. It says its twin's name was "Self-sabotage," also known as Deliberate Damage. I asked why its twin was not speaking. It said because its twin was shy.

VOLUME 2. Confronting the unseen self is a giant task, which can become quite painful. Can you think of a time where you were faced with your shadow?

I know you are wondering why I keep referring to them as they are because when I asked whether they were male or female, it said it had no gender and that if they had a gender, it would be too easy to identify them, for they are without form or void; they are spirits that form of the mind. I was also curious why these demons hated me so much. They said that because I was a threat, I intended to take over the human mind, which they were planning on doing. They told me that they have been targeting the human mind for centuries, but the spirit of confusion has been accompanying it. I told them more was even better, even though I knew I had no intentions of allowing them to master the mind; I was the only master.

The war in my mind with my opposition was enough; I did not need more enemies. It is not that I was afraid; I just knew how to go to war. I studied The Art of War by Robert Greene., As long as they were willing to destroy the minds of men, it was all fair game, and I intended to expose them. This was a problem; they also said this was why they planted confusion on my path to take me out. I informed them I was the spirit of confusion; how could they plant me in my way to take me out? No one, and I mean no one, has that type of power over me. Then he sarcastically replied and said that we are our greatest enemies, to the point when we are in our way, we do not even recognize ourselves; we think it is someone else outside of us. I am the spirit of healing; my mission is here to destroy the spirit; my opposition plans to take the mind back from me. I have mastered the impact of what my opposition can do, and as a result, I cry myself to sleep at night, and there are nights I do not sleep, for my opposition is on me. I must keep the human mind in confusion, without balance. I must continue to execute the legacy of psychological deformity, so the more spirits that are on my side or pretend to be on my side, the stronger my power will become. I must confuse the mind's pathology. I am here on a mission, so if I must pretend to continue ruling the mind with those other spirits, that is my diabolical plot.

Shalom.

VOLUME 2. Confronting the unseen self is a giant task, which can become quite painful. Can you think of a time where you were faced with your shadow?

THE DUAL SPIRIT OF EFFECTIVE COMMUNICATION

Ahhhhh, At last, I get to speak. I am the spirit of effective communication. If you do not know, many of my virtues are very rare. There are times when I am so quiet and unnoticeable. The spirit of effective communication is the reason your prayers are manifested and tangible. I am the word sound that created the heavens and the earth; I am the balance between understanding and misunderstanding. I am why you do not take things personally and remain impeccable with your words. I brought life to the spirit of compassion over killing.

Before I present myself, I also ensure I am dressed well before stepping out. I check the right clock for the timing before I move, I dress in my tailored gown, which is made of circumspect truth, and I decorate my ears with the Gemstone of glistening Garnett. To enter my channels, there are five personal traits about my character that you must acknowledge to identify me: the sense of clarity, conciseness, concreteness, correctness, and coherence. These are my covenants between the chambers of my heart, which I protect very well.

Honestly, I am not a Saint. I am one of life's most important assets, yet I do not exist in many relationships. Without me, the breath of life has no form. Oh, then again, I am all of that and a bag of chips. No, wait, I am a spirit. Oops, I am getting carried away. Well, it is not my fault. It is the author. Blame it on her. She has typos issues. As I said before, this author deleted my words. I am the spirit of Divine effective communication, yes; I am Divine, and I wear that like as a crown. Lord here goes this reader calling me conceited or egotistical. Hmm, hello. They mean the same thing, and I am not conceited but confident. Anyway, as I was about to say before this reader started to get all in their feelings, I do not even know you. Like seriously?

There are two sides to me. Know this before you get carried away and talk badly about me. I am not bipolar. I am, in fact, a twin. I

VOLUME 2. Confronting the unseen self is a giant task, which can become quite painful. Can you think of a time where you were faced with your shadow?

have two sides to me: my passive-aggressive counterpart or, should I say, my twin, even though we do not get along. We fight like Esau and his twin, Jacob, as though I stole his birthright.

Nonetheless, his name was ineffective communication. We do not get along too well, which made me write his name in lowercase letters. There is always a sense of mistrust between him and me. Yes, it is a thing about his masculine energy.

Of course. I tried telling him that his liver had too much negative yang energy, my intentions are not to talk ill about him, but he caused a lot of misunderstandings. He is very much unengaged and shows negative body language. He is always causing distraction, especially whenever he is caught up in entanglement with his mistress, the spirit of confusion. Confusion likes to whisper in his ear, causing him to be passive-aggressive. Whenever she does that, I notice he would use silence as a form of punishment. He is so insecure, and this, however, causes him always to make assumptions. Your conversations with him are limitless, for he always interrupts you while you are talking.

Now you see why we can never get a word in. This twin of mine will cause you to second-guess your thoughts; do not get fooled by him. He comes off as very shy, but he is passive-aggressive. He will never let you know how he feels if you offend him, and he will rather speak about you behind your back to everyone to tell them how you unknowingly hurt him yet pretend that he is okay with you. He would rather keep the pain in his heart until it grows black and cold to use it as a weapon against you, do not trust my twin ineffective communication, here is nothing kind about him. I am not putting him down to make myself look good. He always seeks social acceptance by putting other people's needs before his own. I do not trust him.

He will never follow through and will passively sacrifice himself for acceptance, but, my dear, that's not what he wants. He will have you believe one thing when he means the other. He is neither empowered nor confident, assertive, or effective. Hey, ladies, do not try to get into a relationship with my brother; his guy is broken and needs healing. If you are an assertive woman, he will resent you for being who you are and never stand up for you, but he will damn sure stand up against you. He will always invalidate your feelings, and you will not be allowed to process your emotions. The guy is suffering from a Dismissive Avoidant Attachment style, which means he is afraid of commitment because he would have to give up the way he is familiar with living. Ha-ha, let me stop telling you about my brother's business. He is staring at me as if I am lying or something.

He is so addicted to our generational curses. Our mother's non-verbal communication taught him all her dysfunctionalities, and her signals did not match her words. Yes, my mother is a narcissist. She had an emotional incest relationship with my brother, and she tried to capture me and make me the same, but I rebelled. I decided to break the silence, choosing to speak out whether things were going wrong or even when they were right. Effective communication is the difference between an argument and a conversation. There is no such thing as a lack of me. Of course not. I mean, there is no such thing as a lack of communication. Yes, I have assorted styles because I am just fancy like that. I am an active listener, and my body language matches my word sounds. I understand I am not well known, but I am confident enough to know my powers. There must be no emotions involved whenever I am involved because conflict cannot be resolved when emotions are high.

Moreover, conflict is sometimes caused by someone's actions and not by them. The key to achieving your goals is to focus on what you want and decide what you want to give up to achieve it. Make sure there is active listening. Oh yeah, she is my best friend. She is not too hyperactive but balanced. She understands it is not what you say or how you say it that matters. It is about whether you can hear and understand what is being said. With my friend's active listening, she can capture everything being said.

She also knows that sometimes it is best not to speak. With her, you will know not to respond immediately. Active listening requires you to pause and repeat what is being said. Nope, with active listening, she allows you to be autonomous; she knows that listening is one of my strong points. She and I get along so well. She also understands feelings, facts, and the impact. She does not tell you what to do. She is here to hear you and respect you. I do not want this reader to believe that I am a feminist because I speak highly of my best friend and myself and just spoke about my brother badly. That is just how it is. I also know that when you communicate with people, you communicate with that person's inner child. You must understand cultural dynamics to help them grasp what is being communicated. You must understand that the entire world was deceived, and that language is a major part of communicating, not to mention body language.

In many cultures, I was not a major asset in the house. My brother's ineffective communication was the reason no self-esteem measures were being implanted. This resulted in what we are dealing with today: forced silence, where a parent or stranger molests many children, relatives, or caretakers; they were forced to be silent, or else they would lose their lives. But they did lose their lives. They lost their chance to live and to communicate effectively with society. Therefore, this breeds a culture of narcissistic people who do not

Gem C. Collie

know or understand me. Yes, effective communication, of course, is not me, the author. Do not be slow!

Nonetheless, I must go now; the author says she is tired. Hey, do not take this personally. I am only describing a spirit, not an actual person.

Peace.

PRAYER TO MY ANCESTORS

May, the words of my mouth and the meditation of my heart be acceptable in thy sight. Selah. Oh, spirits of my ancestors, I am here to speak to you; I am here to cry my tears to you; I am here to lay down my burden. My ancestors, I am overwhelmed with so much pain; my heart is grieving, my womb is sore, my mind is confused, and my words have gotten lost in my throat on their way out. Each time I try to speak, my throat squeezes, causing me to stop breathing. My ancestors, I know you have given me the duty to break my generational curse, but I cannot do it alone; I am confused. My ancestors, the generational curses, come alive at night. Not that they were dead before, but they came out from behind the walls to play around in my head. I tried shaking my head, so they fell to the ground and broke their limbs, but they did not. I think they have nine lives, and whenever they see me sleeping, they whisper intrusive thoughts in my ears to wake me up to play with

VOLUME 2. Confronting the unseen self is a giant task, which can become quite painful. Can you think of a time where you were faced with your shadow?

them, but the games they play are so unfair. Whenever I refuse to entertain them, they tease me with mean words. They told me that my ancestors set me up to fail and that no one in my culture or my generation has ever broken their chains. They told me they are advocates of the adversarial spirit. I asked them where they came from—are they from the fiery pits of hell? They said no that place does not exist; hell is in the mind; it is a way of thinking. Also, they said that my ancestors did not care for me because if they did, no one would want to see someone they love to get tormented as I have been, all in the name of breaking generational curses. They said nothing is wrong with having a little curse, and nothing is perfect. My ancestors said if you read for me, you would not have watched me suffer so badly.

Am I confusing my ancestors? Am I suffering? Or is this just a part of the process? Because no beginning is ever easy, ANSWER ME! Is this true? Have you set me up to watch me fail? Have you purposely caused me to feel pain, all in the name of breaking a goddamn curse? Why are you not speaking? COME ON, SPEAK

TO ME! Do not let me waste the author's ink; she is busy and has school to attend to. I heard she wanted to be a holistic psychologist who specializes in trauma. Anyway, if you refuse to respond, I have no other reason not to believe my generational curse.

Wait! Why am I calling them mine as if I were the one who created them? They got angry when I tried to tell them that my ancestors did not want me to participate with them in bonding. They tried to get me to eat foods that are also cursed, but I promised my ancestors that I am vegan, that I do not eat from the tree of the knowledge of good and evil, and that I am not that naive. I think before I eat. My ancestors said that you were not real and that you were all ghosts. I asked them if they were ghosts too. Shh, would they even say that? They said the differences are that at least they come out and play with me; they said my ancestors were once fleshed. My ancestors, please answer me. I am confused.

Why are these generational curses always around? They influence every decision I make. I even see them in the friends I keep. They are even in the reflection of the men I am attracted to; I see them in the poverty-infested community environment, the schools, and the way the teachers teach. I even saw one of them dressed in a robe preaching in church. How did they get there? I thought the church was holy; is it because the church motto is "Come as you are?" There, the curses are bold enough to stand in the pupil, preaching evil intent to the people, and when they hear this, they jump around as if a ghost possessed them.

I do not understand my ancestors; how come you are the ones who are not teaching in the schools, or why are not the ways of our ancestors being taught to us? Why is it only the curses about which I am learning? My ancestors, I wish I could tell you it is been easy to breathe. I wish I could tell you it is not that bad. I am grieving the love I did not get from my mother. In my head, I created the functional character of my father, but deep down inside, I am lost. So, this is why I do not understand why they have chosen me to break the curse; that's heavy baggage to carry. I cannot do this alone; I need help and do not even know the words to utter in the prayer: "Oh my Yah, God of my ancestors, have mercy on my soul."

VOLUME 2. Confronting the unseen self is a giant task, which can become quite painful. Can you think of a time where you were faced with your shadow?

My nights are sleepless, and my eyes are swollen shut from crying. I tried to run and hide behind my shadow, but my shadow was also infected by the curse of my mother's generation. My ancestors, where should I start? Does breaking these curses begin with heartbreak?

I am doing my best not to take any of this personally, but how could I not when it is happening to me? In my culture, poverty and a lack of education affect people's minds; they are emotionally driven and irrational in their decisions. War is always the answer, and death is the outcome. Even if an ant bites them, death is the outcome for the small ant. With this in mind, if I begin to break these curses, will they not attack me? They are bound to their curses; they have a personal relationship with their curses. Remember what the curse told me? That they are advocates of the adversarial spirit. That means they are on a mission and have intentions of leaving. This was supposed to be a prayer that I am saying to you, my ancestors, but they tried to erase the thoughts from my mind. They even blocked the universal channels so that my words would not be able to flow through the universal energy algorithm. I would send them through the messenger mRNA. Hopefully, they will not find this in my DNA.

We will talk soon. Shalom

VOLUME 2. Confronting the unseen self is a giant task, which can become quite painful. Can you think of a time where you were faced with your shadow?

THE LAW OF HUMAN NATURE
Understanding the Concept of the Unconscious Mind

No tree can grow to heaven unless its roots go down to hell, Before we can dive face deep into the Laws of Human Nature, we must first define the understanding of conceptualization of the word "Human." Let us look at the Hebrew root meaning of "Human," which means Adamah or Adam. Let's go a little deeper. The term in the Hebrew text is spelled Aleph, Dalet, Mem, which is closely related to the word "Dam" (Dalet, Mem), which means blood. The only difference between blood, "Adam," and human, "Adam," is the letter Aleph, which signifies the relation to the higher complete and the infinite.

Now that we have a Hebrew understanding of the term "Human." Let us look at the Western philosophy of the term "Human, Humane." "Human" is from Old French human, main ("of or belonging to man"), from Latin humanus "of man, human," and "humane," philanthropic, kind, gentle, polite; learned, refined, civilized." This is in part from PIE (dh)gnomon-, literally "earthling, an earthly being," as opposed to the gods (from root them- "earth"). However, there is no settled explanation of the sound changes involved. Compare Hebrew Adam, "man," from adamah, "ground." Cognate with Old Lithuanian žmuo (accusative žmun).

Now that we have grasped the contrast of the meaning of the word human. It is our nature versus our nurture that influences our unconscious thinking. Our thoughts are governed and created even before birth like intimate objects passed through generations. Our thoughts are also governed and manufactured by these same principles. Generation after generation, our shadows are shaped and molded by cultural and subcultural programming, which at times suffocates our nature. This damages the shadow, causing it to become dark.

The consciousness of the mind's reflection is the shadow of human nature; it is the unspoken suppressed emotions; it is our true self or true thinking. The power bestowed is found in knowing who you are or at least being aware. No one will completely master their consciousness; it is merely human nature to have flaws. Those flaws are not something to be ashamed of or beaten down by the ego, but your flaws are experiences that must be embraced. Your hiccups today are nature's way of molding your character. One must master their emotional self; if the emotions are not controlled, then thinking of irrational thoughts will be the dictator of the mind. Irrational thinking will operate on your moods and thoughts, and it will cause the mouth to speak the wrong thing to the wrong person, sabotaging relationships with others. One must understand the authenticity of the shadow. Some have not come to terms with or are aware of their shadow.

We must understand the dark side of ourselves; therefore, if we do not understand it, it will come out in incontrollable ways . There are others, who were thought to repress their shadow. We must also understand that our ego is the part of our human nature that assists us in functioning in society. The development from the inner self to the shadow now holds unconscious keys to understanding oneself;

VOLUME 2. Confronting the unseen self is a giant task, which can become quite painful. Can you think of a time where you were faced with your shadow?

therefore, the ego and the shadow will merge when done well. The shadow cannot be hidden one way or the other; the shadow will rise. It is something that can be seen by the naked eyes of those who are aware of their own shadow.

Once a person has worked on their distress, it is much easier to recognize the faults we once struggled with. The unconsciousness of the mind expresses itself through the unspoken language of the body, communicating the unsaid emotions. These imitated emotions differentiate human nature from animals. If you allow the laws of human nature to guide you, you will avoid the deflecting human nature of others.

We understand that the configuration of others' experiences has nothing to do with us; their unconscious act is a part of them that was abused, the part of them that is ugly, the part of them they fight with, the fear that creates the doubt, the doubt that will paralyze the human nature. Now recognizing and being aware is key. Whenever we are introduced to the personality of someone, we understand that any over-excessive personality is hiding something very despicable.

VOLUME 2. Confronting the unseen self is a giant task, which can become quite painful. Can you think of a time where you were faced with your shadow?

Many were taught to suppress their emotions; many were taught to believe that their emotions were unimportant. If the said emotions were expressed in some cultures, it would be considered, and a combination of this same function tied the human emotions to Age, Gender, Race, and Ethnicity. If a male child were to show the feminine aspect of his emotion of gentleness, he would be too feminine, or if a female child showed an emotion of assertiveness, she would be considered aggressive and masculine.

The masses have defiled and redefined the expression of human emotions to control the nature of human behavior or experience. This has damaged the image of how the human mind conceptualizes the self. The human mind will adapt to the conditioning of seeing itself separate from its shadow; this type of mind will be no different from a zombie, the walking dead that is walking around, yet without life; it is merely human nature that gives life to the human consciousness. Our Human nature stems from the Culture, Environment, Conditioning, and the simplicity of the characteristics woven by the divine powers. Those instincts are what was given to the human creature.

If we look at nature within the Animal Kingdom, the nature of a snake will always be that of a snake. No matter how you care for the snake, its nature can never be that of a rabbit. The nature of the snake will eventually be displayed. If you take a lion from the wild and tame him in a circus, one day, the nature of that lion will eventually rebel, and its untamed ways will eventually rise to the surface. Let's go back to the human kingdom. Humans are not much different; no matter how a human is, if you take that said being from their culture, you cannot separate the culture from that being. Eventually, the human mind will adapt to the new environment, but naturally, the unconsciousness of the human nature of that being will be seen in its shadow. Our human nature is what shows up when we enter a room. It is the part of us that was not verbally vocalized.

Evolution by natural selection evolves human nature from one form to another, from one concept to the next. "Master Your Emotional Self." You must do what it takes to master your shadow; this takes time and patience. Once that part has been mastered, you will be able to understand and recognize the nature of another person without bias. Let us go back to the animal kingdom. When a predator is hunting his prey, patience is a skill that must be applied. The predator studies its prey's nature and pays close attention to the weaknesses of its prey; it looks for their faults: the most vulnerable step, the unreal injury, the deep wound, and the last breath. The predator waits for the weakest step; keep this same concept in mind when understanding the nature of humankind.

When in survival mode, every human will do what it takes to survive, even if it means destroying their well-being. Now you may ask, "Is this a healthy stay?" The answer is not; it is not a healthy mind. A healthy mind knows its own demons' strengths and how not to react but to be still. It also knows not to take anything personally, when to choose silence, and how to make sound decisions. It understands the warfare of its mind; it knows how to outwit the devil within its dynamics. The art of mastering human nature must first begin within the self. You must understand what you are experiencing is yourself, and you might find it out of line for me to say this, but if you do not recognize the faults in yourself, how else will you understand others or your opponents?

FORGIVENESS
Understanding Atonement

It would be a bit confusing if I, the author, were to write this book about breaking the chains of generational curses without mentioning the spirit of forgiveness. Forgiveness is a sensitive subject for some to discuss, for many are walking the earth with grief. Holding tightly to their pain and never giving in to the idea of atonement, which is much more understandable, the one who was victimized finds it very frightening to let go and open their heart to embrace the healing power of forgiveness. Yet what is not being told here is that even the one who inflicted the pain is also a victim. A victim can only create another victim; it is a relative law. This is not to imply that no one is to be held accountable here; yes, accountability is still to be implemented, but we must put the laws of understanding human nature and why they do what they do in place. The idea of forgiveness is not to be taken lightly; it is a giant task that one must embrace to be spiritually alive.

Before that, let us define Atonement: According to Webster's dictionary, "Atonement means reparation for a wrong or injury or reparation for expiation for sin." In the Biblical sense, the Hebrews celebrate Yom Kippur, considered the holiest day of the year in Hebrew Aric philosophy. The focus of the culture is atonement and repentance. This said, Hebrews traditionally observe this holy day with twenty-four hours of fasting from the intake of food, water, confession, and intensive prayer, often spending most of the day in their homes with their loved ones.

Yom Kippur is the day the Israelites would make an atonement with those they have wronged, not by just asking for forgiveness; they not only ask their God, whom they call Yahweh, for the forgiveness of themselves but also the sins of their ancestors, but by making that forgiveness show up in their everyday behaviors. The issues with the individuals are not just made on that day; they're made before the sun comes up. Some state, "Forgiveness is not for the other person; it is for you." Some even state that it is important to forgive and forget. However, whoever crafted these statements simply did not understand the depths of atonement. Atonement is not just about apologizing for forgiveness; it is about accountability that shows up in the character of the one who caused the injury. It is also about forgiving oneself, not knowing that they, too, were participating in injuring themselves. The act of forgiveness is also a state of consciousness; it is about being aware of one's own trauma and not taking the injury personal or making it about your emotions. You must be capable of setting your emotions aside. If you allow your emotions to get caught in the web, you will lose the lesson; you will not be able to understand the difference between the effect and the impact; you will not understand that the effect is not about you but about the process of your self-development and also about the development of the one who caused the hurt.

However, when we allow the ego to dictate the matter, we take the "pain" personally, we bury residents towards the other person in our hearts, we plot secretly to kill or hurt the person, and we wish deeply for the heavens to open up a ball of fire to destroy them or pray for our gods to take their lives. Yet, we do not understand that the person and what they did or did not do were our lesson, our teacher. Listen and be willing to be humble and take a step back whenever someone has done something that has offended you. Step back and ask yourselves, "Was that my lesson? What could I have learned from that? How did I participate in this?"

I am not saying this will be the case for all your life experiences; I cannot say that and will not, for as I write this book, I am also learning. This experience of being an author is a teacher to me as well, so as I go through writing this, each chapter is a teaching and learning experience for me. I had to cope with accepting the idea that teaching is intensified learning. My cranium has injuries, and the impact of the experiences was definitely a cognitively traumatic lesson, but I can walk away with a lesson or lessons from the experiences. I walked away, knowing I had chosen to be a student, not a victim. I forgave myself for being stubborn about the lesson that had shown up in many faces. I went deeper and forgave myself, from the past to the present to the now. However, I am not asking you to follow in my footsteps but to detach from the experience

---

VOLUME 2. Confronting the unseen self is a giant task, which can become quite painful. Can you think of a time where you were faced with your shadow?

rather than react. I am not saying you should allow others to hurt you spitefully; no way, you must have boundaries. I am saying, "detach and learn the lesson" because not everyone will be willing to confess and atone. Be careful not to pat up a wound under the guise of atonement. Even though forgiveness is imperative, it will not heal your wounds; that part is your responsibility. Even if an individual knowingly or unknowingly hurts you, you must effectively understand a person's pattern and promises. When it comes to atonement, it will take away the heaviness of the impact and the shift of the actions, but it will also help you understand that no matter what, we are all human and experience ourselves, and the entire world needs time to atone.

Please do not get me wrong. I am not saying that when you forgive someone who went out there to destroy you, you should unfriend or give the same access to them anymore; you must ask yourself, "What does forgiveness look like for me?" Then, when you get a valid answer, you must create a system of forgiveness and know what those values are to you. Know that healing does not mean the

Gem C. Collie

damage never existed; it just means it no longer controls your life. Listen, forgive, and heal; set your boundaries and values, and do not take it personally; this way, you teach people how to treat you.

Forgiveness does not mean forgetting; you must be able to remember because remembering is the lesson to be able to go back to the past, like the Sankofa mentality. We must be able to remember; if not, we will miss the lesson for the future.

Selah.

VOLUME 2. Confronting the unseen self is a giant task, which can become quite painful. Can you think of a time where you were faced with your shadow?

SPIRIT OF UNDERSTANDINGS

I am the spirit of understanding, and with me are virtues I bestow upon those that cause me to stand out like the silver lining behind a dark cloud. One of my virtues that is most prominent is the virtue of Discernment. That virtue of mine will enlighten your mind and shine light into your darkness. By discernment, that virtue of mine will enlighten your mind; it will shine light into your darkness. By discernment is your guidance; it is your compass. You must be in tune with your higher self to unlock your sense of discernment. You must be at peace with yourself. If there is no peace, then your judgment will be clouded, and all your decisions will be made from either anger or irrational thinking. You must be able to leave your emotions out of your decision-making. If you allow your emotions to dictate your decision-making, it will sabotage opportunities and then play the victim later.

VOLUME 2. Confronting the unseen self is a giant task, which can become quite painful. Can you think of a time where you were faced with your shadow?

However, your pineal gland must also be decalcified. When your discernment is talking to you, your discernment is the voice in your ear that you can suffocate. Your sense of discernment will allow you to hear danger; do not second-guess it; embrace yourself so that you can embrace your discernment. You must not seek validation outside of this virtue, for not everyone can unlock their sense of discernment. Not everyone wants to be awakened; some enjoy their sleep (unconsciousness) and being awakened is quite a frightful experience for them. If you attempt to awaken them with your level of understanding, they will cast words of judgment on you. They will define your reputation and assassinate your character.

Some people are lost in the darkness; some will intentionally lead you down the wrong path, and some just do not understand what to tell you, so they misguide you instead of being honest. Also, some appear in sheep's clothing and will cast a web of confusion over you. You must be able to understand what's in front of you; you must understand your human nature; you must know where to place each person in your life, like in a game of chess, know where to

---

VOLUME 2. Confronting the unseen self is a giant task, which can become quite painful. Can you think of a time where you were faced with your shadow?

place each piece; if you do not place them in the right space, you will get too common, you will reveal all your moves, and they will take and use them to destroy you in the future. Understand that not everyone thinks like you. Be mindful of the people you discuss vital things about your life with every day. There are those who are dull and void; they cannot separate themselves from the conversation; they will make issues about them; they will personalize your traumas as if the entire world begins and ends solely with them. This type of thinking in psychology is known as "Egocentrism," which is the inability to differentiate between oneself and others. Pay attention, pray in privacy, pray in secrecy, pray diligently, trust yourself, trust the voices in your mind, know how to distinguish between your ego and intuition, and keep your joy under control. Do not allow what you want to blind your eyes to what is and is not.

When you are not in alignment with yourself, you will doubt danger. You will even see the evil being done to you and call it love. Love yourself so that you can recognize those who do not love you. Never get too close to those who struggle to love themselves and yet do not attempt to make any changes. There are those who need a helping hand, and then there are those who will break your hand so that you will never climb from the bottom. Keep your eyes and ears open; know where, when, who, what, why, and how you should use your words; understand that once they are out, you cannot correct them; your words can either give or take a life; they can either defile you or destroy you. I am in the spirit of understanding, and I am here to inform you that not everyone deserves the same version of you. Each person will experience you according to whatever unhealed trauma they have not healed from or whatever self-love they are operating from; the unconscious choice is theirs.

Learn to be still and meditate within your space of peace. You can tap into another of my virtues, the spirit of intuition. This virtue will merge with your sense of discernment to guide you throughout your life. Again, you must be willing to be aligned with your purpose, and you must also be willing to be present and emotionally available. Understand that once a snake shows its head, do not lie to yourself and tell yourself it is not a snake to appease that snake; a

VOLUME 2. Confronting the unseen self is a giant task, which can become quite painful. Can you think of a time where you were faced with your shadow?

snake is what it is, and there is nothing you or the snake can do to change its nature. Know people by their nature. Associate with them also by their nature; in other words, no matter if the rabbit becomes friends with a fox, no matter how friendly, kind, or humble the fox is, it is still a fox, and foxes eat rabbits; that is the nature of the fox and the misfortune of the rabbit. If you, a rabbit, find yourself becoming friends with a fox, do not be common; greet him on your way and keep going; do not pass by his gates every time at your leisure throughout your path; he will, one day, plot against you while smiling in your face. Again, understand that that is its nature.

Nonetheless, I am hoping you have understood what I am implying here. I use the idea of an animal to help you understand what I am saying here. I must speak to the child in you for you to understand here. They will seek understanding.

Selah.

THE FOUNDATIONS OF TRADITIONAL TRAUMA

Let us first examine the terms "tradition" and "trauma" before diving deep into traditional trauma. Tradition is an act passed down from one generation to the next. It is a cycle meant to align with the culture; it was created to maintain the culture or for some situations. It is what created the culture or its means of survival because some cultures are still stuck in the trauma that might have created the culture. Each moon cycle, they would celebrate one hundred years since colonization started. It was not simple to rule over the land; the trauma that this distraction caused gave birth to many things that are still deemed normal today, such as eating habits, the food they eat, and the way it is prepared.

Trauma is also an emotional response to a terrible event like an accident or incident such as rape, a near-death experience, or a natural disaster. Immediately after, denial and shock are normally typical. Longer-term reactions include unpredictable emotions, flashbacks, strained relationships, and even physical symptoms, like in the etymology definition, 1690's "Physical wound." In medical Latin, from Greek, trauma is "a wound, a hurt; defeat extended form of root tree to rub, true, with derivatives referring to twisting, piercing, etc." It is a sense of psychic wound, an unpleasant experience that causes abnormal stress.

Now that we know the etymology of trauma, let's consider the contrast between contagion and detonation. We must keep in mind that in each culture, trauma expresses itself in either a connotative or denotative form. The perception of one's experience is needed to know their culture, understanding, environment, and the minds of those with whom they associate themselves.

Nevertheless, whichever one's trauma is rooted from, I, the author, send mercy, send tears of empathy, I send my understanding heart, I send my patients, I send my listening ears, I send compassion over killing; I send all this with no strings attached, and I am able to do so from a place where I once was, a place from which I have healed.

VOLUME 2. Confronting the unseen self is a giant task, which can become quite painful. Can you think of a time where you were faced with your shadow?

In a place where I was once a victim of volunteer trauma. I said volunteer; however, one should not allow their traumas to define who they are.

Trauma can be defined as a deeply distressing or disturbing experience in one's past that can affect one's worldview. However, do not let your trauma define who you are or how you interpret hurt in a relationship. Trauma can keep you enslaved, depending on how you perceive it. Like taking an ox by its tail, you must take control of what you apprehend, whether short or a rape. Be in control of the pain. I know this might sound crazy to you as you read, but of course, it will; it would sound crazy to me as the author as well. A book like this would offend me if I were still operating from a victimizing mindset. I would even go as far as hating the person who wrote it, the publisher, the graphic artist, the thought, or any concept of books like this one. However, it would not go boom, and those who created it would be my problem; the book would only be a scapegoat, so I would not have to be accountable.

VOLUME 2. Confronting the unseen self is a giant task, which can become quite painful. Can you think of a time where you were faced with your shadow?

Studying the book of Genesis, where Adamah (MAN), and Khawah (Woman) were removed from the garden, was quite a traumatic experience. However, I will not say it is the beginning of all traumas but the beginning of traumas to come. We must acknowledge it is a part of life's development; it is the thin line between life and death that can be grasped and remolded into positivity, such as by many Jamaican reggae artists who, suffering from a traumatic act such as poverty, created such an extraordinary melody as reggae music. This music has touched the entire world, from artists like Robert Nesta Marley and Richie Spice to hip-moving musical rhythms like dancehall. But you should get my point by now, and if you are still offended, you are not ready to heal. Healing is a stage of acceptance and maturity; you cannot take your trauma personal.

Yes, I know that is hard to swallow. I know by now that you are probably offended by what I have written. If you are not, keep reading, for I want you to get angry. I want you to feel what I am writing here. I want snot to run down your nose. I want your eyes to be swollen from crying.

I want you to sit in your devastation, with no one there to rub your back, telling you it is okay, it is not okay, damn it, it is your breakthrough, it is part of your eyes being open, it is your subconscious thoughts aligning with your conscious thoughts, and you must go through a breakdown to get through the breakthrough. I do not mean meanness or wickedness here; I am being frank, with no apologies, so do not look for one. Not from me, as Don Ruiz Miguel stated in his book The Four Agreements: "Whatever happens around you, do not take it personal." Nothing other people do is because of you. It is because of themselves. All people live in their own dreams and minds; they are in a completely different world from the one we live in. When we take something personal, we assume they know what is in our world, and we try to impose our world on theirs.

Even when a situation seems so personal, even if others insult you directly, it has nothing to do with you. What they say, what they do, and the opinions they give are according to the agreements they have in their own minds. Taking things personally makes you easy prey for these predators, the black magicians. They can hook you easily with one little opinion and feed you whatever poison they want because you take it personal" -The Four Agreements. What they say, what they do, and the opinions they give are according to the agreements they have in their own minds. "Their point of view comes from all the programming they received during domestication." — Don Miguel Ruiz.

Now, with this statement from Miguel, he is not saying that. Your emotions or feelings here are not valid; we are just saying that you, the reader, must not get stuck in what transpired in your life. Please make up your mind to use what has happened to you as a lesson and push through the web; if not, you will be forever lost mentally, and in that realm, this would be the true meaning of "everlasting hell" or "doomed." It will take time, patience, and consistency. I am not trying to invalidate your experience; I am just telling you not to let your experience steal your identity because it will. Your trauma is fearless; it has no manners or boundaries; it does not have parental guidance; it lurks behind your shadow, ready to become you,

VOLUME 2. Confronting the unseen self is a giant task, which can become quite painful. Can you think of a time where you were faced with your shadow?

leaving you in an identity crisis. Free your soul from your experience; embracing it will become how you see the world around you. You will operate from how damaged you are.

Whatever the mind does not heal from will be adopted. For example, if a family member molests you at a tender age and you do not bring that demon to light, it will persist. However, if this is brought to light and your caregiver or parent does not get you to see a trauma therapist who specializes in child molestation, left untreated, it will become your personality. Either you will become promiscuous, withdrawn, shy and timid, with resentment towards the gender or race of your molester. With this, you will live your life as a constant victim, even victimizing others, causing them to emotionally pay for the trauma you have experienced, which had nothing to do with them. Lastly, please work on your trauma because that is the only way to be free. It is in your hands and mind; it is all about the perception of deception.

Peace.

VOLUME 2. Confronting the unseen self is a giant task, which can become quite painful. Can you think of a time where you were faced with your shadow?

BREAKING THE CHAINS OF GENERATIONAL CURSE

"The sins of the fathers are to be laid upon the children."

If we look into the book of Deuteronomy, it is stated, "We can either choose life, and blessings, or death and cursing." Before we can break the chains of a generational curse, we must first define and understand the concept of a generational curse.

A generational curse is believed to be passed down from one generation to the next through our learned behaviors, thinking, or way of doing things in rebellion towards "God." If your family generation is marked by divorce, incest, poverty, abortion, or anger, most likely, you will continue to carry on the legacy. But even these curses are much deeper than the unknown behaviors adopted that are sometimes measured to survive a traumatic experience.

There are behaviors within our culture that are learned because of the need to survive an ordeal; this, therefore, leaves these individuals with one of the five trauma responses: Flight, Fight, Flop, Freeze, and Fawn, or even all responses such as the Fawn response, involve immediately moving to try to please a person to avoid any conflict. This is often a response developed from childhood trauma, where a parent or significant authority figure is the abuser. Children go into a fawn-like response to attempt to avoid the abuse, which may be verbal, physical, or sexual, by being a pleaser. In other words, they preemptively attempt to appease the abuser by agreeing, answering what they know the parent wants to hear, or ignoring their personal feelings and desires. They do anything and everything to prevent the Freeze: threats, real or perceived, and this can be shocking.

Instead of fighting or running, the threat can create a deer-in-the-headlights sort of response. The possum is another animal that uses this response, often to its demise. When approached by a car or a human, a possum will fall over and play dead. The Freezing response is a sign that the brain cannot process what is happening, so it simply goes into shock until it can decide what to do next. Flight: Our flight response is one of our more animalistic responses.

Rabbits, for example, have evolved to be fast to escape quick predators like foxes, who have also evolved to be fast. We take flight and run when we cannot fight or connect with another response form. People can experience an unhealthy way of life when they become conflict-avoidant entirely and never stand up for themselves or fight in any way. Flop: like freezing, except your muscles become loose, and your body goes floppy. This automatic reaction reduces the physical pain of what is happening to you. Your mind can also shut down to protect itself.

At some point in our lives, more so during developmental cognitive growth stages, the subconscious mind is wide open to the events: the circumstances, the programming, the talks, and everything in your environment. Your subconscious mind controls ninety percent of your entire life, including your income, status, and health. Your subconscious mind is the land of habits. These habits become an inheritance, inheriting behaviors that were not broken or affecting the present and future generations.

When it comes to breaking the chains of generational curses, one must understand the root of where the curses began. Breaking the curses is not just to break a link; it is to uproot the stem and destroy the fruit it bears. There will be a great uprising of emotional aggression that will reawaken within your mind. Know that the curse is not outside of you; it is within you; it is within your mind; it is the War in the Heavens (mind, the consciousness), its generational war of unforgiveness, heartbreak, disappointment, emotional unavailability, toxic positivity, abandonment traumas, miscarriages, parental neglect, the narcissistic parent, and the emotional surrogate are all seeds of your generational curses. Most of those same curses began with a simple misunderstanding that went unresolved.

That unresolved issue then morphed into a seed of bitterness that was planted in the womb of a developing fetus to give birth to the next generation of misunderstanding and ineffective communicative languages (confusion) or through the scrotum of an unborn male child to plant the seeds of children with resentments in their hearts and heartaches that they do not own or understand. When breaking these curses, you must be willing to be the outcast. Your generation

VOLUME 2. Confronting the unseen self is a giant task, which can become quite painful. Can you think of a time where you were faced with your shadow?

before you will not support you; they will curse you, call themselves the victor, and see you as the velour. You must understand that they are conditioned, programmed into, and dedicated to the spirit of the curse. This spirit is roots are deep within their minds. You must be very careful in your attempt to awaken your family members, who do not want to be awakened, so be wise. When you blow your trumpet, the beast of your generational curse will be unpleased, for this beast (curse) has no thoughts of letting go of your mind. It is here to stay; it has planted its roots far beyond your imagination; it has made love with your mother's mind and impregnated her concept of how to raise you; she made love with this beast each time she stole you.

Each time she prepares meals that oppose your gut flora, breaking the chains of your gut-brain relationship and affecting your rational way of thinking, she makes love with them. Each time she teaches you unconsciously about how not to love yourself, resulting in the poor choices you make in your relationships and the poor choices of friends that cause you to be emotionally unavailable and therefore Codependent; the same curse that caused her to fight with her eleven-year-old daughter as though she were a stranger. The same curse would allow her to give up her fifteen-year-old virgin daughter to a forty-five-year-old man to be his woman so she could have enough money to care for her other children. These generational curses are not too far from the ones in the Bible, nor are they from the times of slavery. Let us reiterate it was the same way they made Yeshayahu modern-day "Jesus" a sacrificial lamb, the same way even in the time of the "Black Holocaust." The babies of the enslaved people were used as sacrifice; this traumatic legacy runs deep into our epigenetics, so even breaking away from the injuries is a massive blow.

To sum this all up, I cannot tell anyone specifically how to uproot their curse because it is a very bold yet dangerous task. A task that may cost you your life; it is a task where you might have to lose your mind or even think that you are going mad. When or if you begin to feel this way, you are clearly not losing your mind; you are gaining it. You are going through a transformation. Your eyes are beginning to open; all your senses are beginning to wake up, and your sense of discernment begins to speak to you. You might believe that you are hearing voices talking to you. You are hearing your voice - the voice of your shadow. You could not hear it before because you were distracted by your learned dysfunctionalities and the dysfunctionality in your environment. Does that make sense?

Let me explain a little more, but I must go after this because today is my birthday. You are losing what you thought was your mind (understanding, concept); those ways of thinking were not your thinking; it was a pre-programmed way of thinking; it is the way of the beast (curse); you must be dedicated to breaking free from it. You must be willing to disassociate yourself from your environment, family, and friends. You must be willing to separate without looking back; you must not be like the biblical Lot's wife, who became a pillar of salt because she looked back in her mind. The curse is deep; the beast is very crafty; the beast will affect your generation's emotional state; your parents' or caregiver's state of emotional avoidance will cause you to be emotionally unstable, resulting in you making irrational decisions about trying to fill the void because you are emotionally underdeveloped. You will go out into the world and produce a traumatized baby. Being brought up in a trauma-connected relationship and living a traumatic experience with the idea that you are doing the right thing will traumatize your baby the way you were once traumatized; the baby's soul will then cry out for redemption, for it knows that it was not brought on earth to be traumatized. The baby will go into survival mode, adapting to the trauma, for this is its natural animal instinct. You will feed your baby traumatic foods that would add to being traumatized; the food is seedless, inorganic, processed, and has dyes and preservatives that affect your emotional state and thoughts. Every decision you make is traumatic; your kidneys are out of balance, for they are traumatized, causing you to suffer from fear and frequent anxiety attacks.

Again, I cannot tell you how to break away from your generational curses. For each culture, curses are different according to how long the effect of slavery lasted. However, when I say slavery, I am not just talking about the Black Holocaust; I am also talking about the enslavement of every culture; no culture will go scotch free from the pit of hell(a deplorable way of thinking); the entire world has been and is still being affected; even the ones who have committed the trauma are affected. All I can tell you is to be patient with yourself, and when you have decided to break these curses, be prepared to stand alone. All this is also far-fetched for those who are not willing to do the same work within their family or cultural dynamic. Stay prayed up; this is spiritual warfare. Remember that most of those demons are not our own; they are terrible. Be willing to call upon your ancestors for help but be careful of which ancestors you are calling unto for help; some of them were the curse itself. They were the uncle that was the molester, the aunty that was not willing to divorce her husband after finding out that he was responsible for impregnating her twelve-year-old daughter, who is now the neighborhood mattress (whore), or the father who raped his son, affecting his sexual choices and taking away his sexual autonomy.

Understand the trauma of what these ancestors died from or the trauma they caused while on earth. Know these ancestors; not all are divine spirits. So be careful how you call them for assistance. If they were defiled spirits, they would end you; they would be those intrusive thoughts in your mind; they are no different from the adversarial spirit of Err. Also, understand that these spirits are in

VOLUME 2. Confronting the unseen self is a giant task, which can become quite painful. Can you think of a time where you were faced with your shadow?

your bloodline; it is a part of you; the spirit of Err is not outside of you, as I always make it clear that the spirit of Err operates in your mind; that is the only place; it can function from; it is "The war in the Heavens." Be willing to move away from your communities, which does not make you a bad person; if not, you will be a fool. Be careful about your learned behaviors; understand that your DNA can be reprogrammed, and do not let those lying scientists tell you any difference. I can only encourage you to free yourself in this life so that you will not be reborn as a captive in the next life. Free the mind of your next generation; redemption is in your mind. It is in your hands and your choice.

Do not share your move of breaking away from the curse with those who are not putting in the work to do the same; if you do, they will deceive you into staying; you will not even see the destruction coming upon you until you are knee deep in theirs' along with your own dysfunctionalities; you will even forget that you are even breaking away from the curse; and to those who are also on a quest of breaking their generational curses, watch them as well. Not all are willing to go all the way through; everyone loves you until you are ahead of them in the journey of your pathway; everyone's healing has its own depth; and you cannot judge the capacity of your healing by how far someone else has gone on their pathway.

Mind your business, stay focused, drink alkaline water, and eat your greens. Understand that there are those whose purpose is to distract you; they come as false pretenders and will even go as far as creating adversities in your life to pretend to be your savior. Do not trust them once you find out who they are. If a person cannot address and confront their own demons, they will not be able to help you confront your own. I must go now. As I stated before, it is my birthday, and I am about to go enjoy a bottle of raspberry kombucha (fermented tea).

Selah.

VOLUME 2. Confronting the unseen self is a giant task, which can become quite painful. Can you think of a time where you were faced with your shadow?

BREAKING UP WITH RELIGION
Unchaining the mind from what it was beating into thinking.

To break up with a religion, you must deal with the fact that you are breaking up with a concept. This would be a tough one to talk about, for I know I will step on the toes of many who will read this, but the truth is the truth, whether by free will or by force. It is a topic that must be mentioned, especially with the title of this book. The world crisis was built on the bedrock of religion. Before I continue, let's define the etymology of religion.

Middle English (originally in the sense 'life under monastic vows'): from Old French, or from Latin religion (n-) 'obligation, bond, reverence,' based on Latin relegate 'to bind.' What does "religion" mean in Hebrew?

The word is דָּת listen and repeat. In the Bible (most commonly in the Book of Esther), the word means "law" or "sentence" in the legal sense. And since religion can be described as a set of laws, over time, the word ת□came to refer to religion itself.

Now in Hebrew philosophy, religion means law. The law binds a construction of ideas to the mind that behaves, acts, congregates, speaks, and how we construct ourselves socially. Religion in this context has been the curse of many generations. I will not mention any belief system, but I am talking about the condition of the entire world.

Most religions are based on fear, specifically fear of death. Many who were colonized made up the idea of physical heaven to keep their captives from fearing death as a means of bondage and control. Therefore, if colonization can cause you to fear death, then there is nothing you, the captive, will not do for the captor. The effects of this all will forever help us in bonding at war with each other, all in the name of religion, while in most cultures, the religious beliefs that a lot of us have or believe do not belong to us but to a system that was created to keep us from ever being free. Religious beliefs can stem from anything; for example, some do not consume or partake in the eating of the flesh or a byproduct of an animal's carcass; they see this as inhumane. There are those who believe in this lifestyle too, yet many religions will say it is okay to take an animal's life for consumption yet tell you their gods say it is unlawful to kill a man. This ideology contradicts the balance of the scale; death is death. They are religions that will cause us to be biased against someone else's cultural beliefs.

In my philosophy, it is a man's own choice to choose his belief system. However, before exploring other ideologies or creating his own, he must first find himself, his purpose, and his self-worth and be willing to stand no matter the stones thrown at him.

Selah.

THE METAPHYSICAL HUMAN EYES
Wide Open Concept

The human eye was created for visual purposes. In some cultures, the eyes are said to be "the window to the soul," and the soul is considered to be the liver. The Hebrews define the two eyes as Ayin עַיִן (ayin) translates to "the windows to the soul." According to Eastern concepts, the eyes flow into the emotions, reflecting our psychological and physical health. However, in this said Hebrew philosophy, the eyes are also a determinant; it is stated that the most prominent emotion is jealousy based on what the eye has seen. Therefore, those with the letter Ayin in their names should be careful.

A Jewish text idiom states, "When wine goes in, secrets come out." We must grasp the understanding from this: the connection between wine, secrets, and the eye. More secrets come out because the eye desires wine more than the body needs it. In this case, the secrets also refer to our personal discipline, which is often let go after too much wine, and we should be careful to guard it. Now that we have an in-depth look at the Eastern etymology of the Eye. Let us now view the concept of the Western philosophy. It states, "The human eye is an organ that reacts to light in many circumstances."

As a conscious sense organ, the human eye allows vision. Rod and cone cells in the retina allow conscious light perception and vision, including color differentiation and depth perception. The human eye can distinguish about ten million colors. When light hits the retina (a light-sensitive layer of tissue at the back of the eye), special cells called photoreceptors turn the light into electrical signals. These electrical signals travel from the retina through the optic nerve to the brain. Then the brain turns the signals into the images you see. Let's examine The Culture of Traditionalist Chinese Medicine to wrap this up.

In this concept, the organ flow in the liver meridian is connected to the eyes, and the visual ability relies on the nourishment of liver blood. Therefore, the eyes can reflect the function of the liver.

Insufficient liver blood may cause dry eyes and blurred vision; hyperactivity of the liver fire will lead to pain and swelling of the eyes.

In light of the cultural etymology of the eye, it is imperative to recognize that the human experience goes beyond the physical senses and also involves the metaphysical senses. What I mean by this is that the eye is more spiritual than it is physical. There are times when the physical eyes can fail to see what is not there, but with the spiritual eye, one can see what is happening even if they are not in the presence of what took place at the time. Some might call this Clairvoyant, which is the ability to perceive events in the future. This is our third eye, which is connected to the pineal gland. This third eye is about enlightenment. It is a connection to the great unknown yet known; it is a connection within every human. Some say the third eye is historically a metaphor; an egg-shaped structure within the brain defines what it means to be human, which is the thymus gland. The egg-shaped gland is a relay station in the brain; all the information comes in through here. If the thymus is damaged, it will knock out consciousness. Some also state that the thymus is the open eye; it is the state of consciousness. This brain structure is a connection to yet another way of looking at things.

The third eye sees far beyond human conception; it might be said that it connects us to the things we normally do not see with our naked eye. Our naked eye cannot see everything, and not all that the naked eye perceives is always as it is. There is always a deeper understanding tied to what we see, and we must not only rely solely on this. Your insight, your sense of discernment, is also an eye that will see the things you are not able to see even when it is being displayed in front of your face, for there are deceitful spirits that are crafty; they are the imitation of life; they will pretend to be everything you want. Do not be fooled.

Once the spiritual eye has revealed its intentions, do not allow the physical eye to deceive you. Do not begin to doubt what your senses are picking up. The metaphysical does not ignore it. If you are unsure, stop and meditate. But do not allow your ego to influence what's happening, for something like that happened in the Garden of

---

VOLUME 2. Confronting the unseen self is a giant task, which can become quite painful. Can you think of a time where you were faced with your shadow?

Eden when the serpent-like spirit deceived Khawah and Adamah. That spirit is still alive and active, just with a different name, like Jezebel, Dalila, and Judas; those were some of the biblical names, but these spirits are in your mind; they are your parents and friends. They are to whom you reveal all your darkest nightmares and your brightest dreams. Watch out for them and be careful; they are your enemies.

Selah.

MENTAL ILLNESS AND THE PSYCHOLOGICAL EFFECT OF THE GENERATIONAL BEAST

When it comes to breaking generational curses, your mental health will play a major role because that is where the war stems from. In doing so, your perception of what is happening around you in your mind, environment, or family dynamic will dictate whether or not you make the necessary changes to free yourself. Within the spirit of perception, birth deception. What you believe you are seeing results in what is actually occurring.

Let us use those who are descendants of the Adamic race (the Hebrews) as an example. I, however, can only use these races of people, for they are who I am a product of; therefore, I can only speak from my reflection; anything else would be a lie. Let us proceed to the psychology case and "Black Mental Illness." This Spiritual Disease (Mental Illness) is most commonly associated with those from this race. Schizophrenia is a mental illness. It has been termed a DSM - a split in the brain. Schizophrenia has been associated with many of the "Black Revolutionists" in the United States during the civil rights era; it was an illness marked by violence among angry protesters.

Many in the nation of Islam had taken up the term "schizophrenia" to mean that it was not an illness of the black mind but an illness to fight against white oppression, who were fighting for the equality of the Africans who were being treated with injustice and inequality. Mental illness amongst Afrikaans can be dated as far back as the colonization era during the Black Trans-Atlantic Slave Trade. Such traumatic experiences of being stolen, separated, beaten, murdered, raped, cursed, and misguided have left a deformity within the bloodline of the Afrikaans (Hebrews). The impact has trickled down the lineage of cause and effect; the responses are indeed mental illnesses affecting self-value, self-esteem, self-worth, identity, languages, perception, philosophy, and thought processes, all of which are dismantled and oppressed. These traumatic psychological events breed separation, anxiety, bipolar personality disorder, and body dysmorphia. Identity crisis, depression, colorism, individualism, and autism result from the Afrikaans (Hebrews) being separated from their culture, their God, their ways of praying, their languages, and their diets to only be replaced with all these.

Identity Trauma is the biggest influencer of mental illness.

We are talking about both historical and present trauma, a trap that causes the same people to pledge allegiance to their oppressors, traumas like the Black Holocaust that do not belong to them. This will indeed keep them mentally deranged for generations. The cycle of Post-Traumatic Slave Identity is passed down through each generation, with no one to challenge the beast of the generational curse. The curse becomes a part of the family, and the family will never see themselves as a whole; they see each person in their family as an individual instead of an important factor. Therefore, when the individual's mental state has been affected, they will claim that the individual has a mental illness instead of the family having a mental illness. They would believe willpower, faith, or race controls black mental illness.

The effect of breaking the curse will destroy the mental health of those who attempt to carry out such a task. Onlookers will see this transformation and, in return, label it as an illness. Unknowingly that it is a journey they all will need to go on; no one will want to go on that journey of healing; they will all stand apart and watch from a distance. The generational beast is crafty and aims to conquer you through fear. This beast will use your organs to attack your thinking and use individualism to take revenge. Its mission is to leave no stone unturned. A famous quote by Marcus Mosiah Garvey once says, "The people perish because of lack of knowledge." When people are cut off from ways of knowing who they are, they will perish in nothingness. As long as they are divided, they will forever be lost. The mental illness system was created with the captivity of the people; mental illness was not designed by nature for it to be this way. Yes, I know and am very aware that the polarity of life must have good and bad, but I will never agree to this extent. The extent of the people's existence, no way. The recovery is even more damaging than the effect itself.

Mental illness will not look the same in each culture, for the devastation of the beast's strike or blow was not the same for each culture, for the Adamic people have the effect of mental illness in their culture, whereas the Afrikaans are on the continent. The mark on the mind from the generational beast is the impact of the beast on humans. As a result, it is the only thing the beast holds onto, and it will forever lead its victims through mental illness.

The miseducation about mental illness is also part of the curse; it is become an illusion that it does not affect a specific race. Well, I am here to tell you that as long as everyone has a mind, they are always subject to mental illness. There is one thing about this beast: it has no partiality to whom minds it takes over. No one is exempt from this beast; in fact, the entire world is affected. Mental illness does not just affect the captive; it benefits and destroys the captor. The captor might seem to be in control of those they hold captive, but they are mentally ill and mentally enslaved to an idea. The concept of "mental slavery" began to yield a more sophisticated form of mental illness. We have been hung up on the lie that the conqueror is the bringer of all civilizations.

Overall, the stigma of mental illness must be addressed; sweeping the trauma under the rug will eventually show up in our everyday behavior. The Adamic people's stigmas towards mental illness are not easy because they expose their vulnerability and remove the curtains covering toxic masculinity or feminine strengths. For many women in the Adamic culture, where poverty, another feminine mental illness, is prominent, the ability to be vulnerable is a luxury; the ability to be present, to be still, to be alive, is all a luxury. That will keep the mind in the rat race cycle, chasing what is designed to be mental freedom. The thing is that the oppressed cannot seek freedom from those who have kept and invented the slavery factory that they are living in; it would be a conflict of interest.

Selah.

Chapter One

VOLUME 2. Confronting the unseen self is a giant task, which can become quite painful. Can you think of a time where you were faced with your shadow?

THE GREAT RETURN

As the damsel returned to America, she found out eight weeks later that she was with the child of the man that raped her, her prince charming's baby. Confused and afraid, the damsel reached out to prince charming, telling him what was going on, but with fright, fear, and only plain old immaturity, the prince slammed the phone in the ears of the damsel. However, this may have been, the damsel was persistent. She called back several times, and the more she called back, the more he refused to pick up the call. Feeling the emotions of fear, despair, and confusion, the damsel thought to herself that she would try to drink herbs that would kill her baby. The damsel even tried using her fist to punch her stomach, hoping to kill the moving fetus inside her.

When she woke up the next morning and found that she could still feel a movement inside her, she realized it would not work before her mother found out. She then ran to get her friend - the same friend that violated her femininity. The same friend used to touch her in places she was not ready for, the same friend that molested her innocence, the same friend that took advantage of her low self-esteem and then justified it with his intentions for good. "It is amazing how others justify their intentions towards others, no matter how much their intention damages the other person. The main focus here is that their intentions were in the right place. This act is the act of the Grandiose Narcissists" — Author- Gem C. Collie.

She ran to him to ask him what she should do. With jealousy in his heart for leaving him and getting herself pregnant, giving away her body to another man, and with a deceptive mind, he told the naive damsel to get rid of it, for it would be too foolish for her to carry and give birth to a baby that was conceived out of pain. He told her he could only give her $30 towards the abortion. He told her to deceive her mother that she needed the money towards her college tuition; being that her mother was so hell-bent on her returning to school, she would jump at the idea of the damsel needing the money towards her education to fulfill her mother's dream of becoming a nurse like her, even though the damsel wanted to be an author.

With fear accompanying her, the damsel asked her mother for the money she needed to go to the abortion clinic. With joy, her mother gave her the money, thinking she was paying for the damsel to attend college. The damsel called her younger cousin to open up to her about her secrets, for she could not hold them in check anymore. She confided in her, thinking that her secret was safe. As the appointment for the Wednesday afternoon approached, the damsel took a bus to the clinic that was tucked away in the neighborhood, where the average person would not have known. As the damsel knocked on the door of the clinic, a young casual girl answered the door. When the damsel walked into the hallway, several young ladies were sitting on the floor awaiting their appointment. Even one young lady was accompanied by her boyfriend, who was not ready for fatherhood. As she moved closer into the hallway, she could see the faces of the other girls dropped with their mouths gaping open at the size of the damsel's stomach.

Not understanding their social cues, she thought nothing of it. One by one, the nurses called each patient for their appointment. When it was the damsel's turn to be brought back to the nurses, they took her vitals and a urine sample for a pregnancy test to ensure she was indeed pregnant, and she was. They then asked her to remove her clothing and replace it with a hospital gown. After that, the doctor explained that they would inject her with a dose of medicine so that she would feel no pain. But before they could do so, a counselor would come into the room to counsel her before her operation.

As the counselor walked into the room, she greeted the damsel.

"Good afternoon. I will be your counselor. I will be conducting your pre-abortion counseling. My job is to help with your decision-making and to maintain your emotional and physical state throughout and after your procedure. This consists of the effect of regarding the potential effects of the abortion, such as long-term mental health consequences after an abortion or a fetus' ability to feel pain. I will be asking you a few questions.

"Okay?" "Please just say yes or no to the following questions."

1. "Do you smoke or smoked before you got here? How old are you, and how far along are you?"

2. "Did you eat or drink anything, including water, in the last six hours?"

3. "Do you come with sanitary pads?" "If not, we will provide them."

4. "Do you have your blood group card, or do you know your blood type?"

5. "Is there anything about which you are concerned?"

6. "Is this your first abortion or your first pregnancy?"

7. "Are you afraid?"

"No, I did not eat anything or drink any water. I am twenty-one years old; I do not know how far along I am. I know I did not smoke, nor do I smoke. I am afraid. I did not bring any pads; no one told me to do this. Yes, this is my first baby; I have never been pregnant."

"Oh, will I be able to go to school tomorrow?"

"No, I am not scared; I am just curious about what would happen."

"Well, you will feel a relief once everything is over." "Did you come with anyone?"

"No, I am here alone."

The counselor then left the room, and the nurse came in and gave the damsel two tablets to take with a cup of water. They told her it would help open her cervix, and the damsel did as instruct. After some time, a male doctor returned with a female nurse.

"Did anyone accompany you here, young lady?"

"Well, do not worry; someone here, like the nurse, will hold your hands." "Are you comfortable with that?"

"Yes, I guess so!" As the doctor began the operation, installing the suction tube inside the damsel's cervix to extract the destroyed fetus' body, she could see the gasping fright on the nurse's face as she saw what was happening. The nurse's body language was not alarming to the naive damsel." It is amazing how trauma and a lack of social cues can affect the discernment of a person's mind, that even when their hands are in the mouth of a lion, they do not recognize the danger." - Gem Collie.

Within an hour, the doctor had completed the task the damsel had come for. She was given antibiotics and then sent home with instructions on how to take care of herself and what to expect. The damsel got dressed and quickly left the clinic. As she waited at the bus stop, she could feel the sense of relief the nurse had told her she would feel; she was not afraid or guilty.

The damsel hurried home and called prince charming back in Jamaica, telling him what she had done and that he did not have to worry anymore, for he had completely broken her heart, a heartache she had never known. The prince had snatched back everything that she thought he was to her; the promises he used to charm the damsel were beginning to wear off; the damsel was beginning to open her eyes; and the spell cast upon her was beginning to disappear.

Brokenhearted and confused, the damsel decided to follow her mother's rules and return to college as she promised she would while keeping her secret tucked inside her womb, where her baby once occupied. Her womb now became the place where she hid all her lies, all her unforgiveness, and all her disappointments. As the damsel readjusted to get on a new path, she began to lose herself. She was no longer the modest damsel that was so cultured-driven. Instead, she had begun to dress in revealing clothing, smoked cigars, and returned to the arms of the people who had inflicted pain on her. The damsel became another person lost in her trap.

VOLUME 2. Confronting the unseen self is a giant task, which can become quite painful. Can you think of a time where you were faced with your shadow?

THE NEW IDENTITY
Hiding The Shadow in The Mirror

The damsel began to reassociate herself with the same group of people who led her down the path of hell before the same people who had a hand in traumatizing her, the same people who denied her, the same people who saw her light and threw their words like a stone to break her light bulb from being too bright, the same people who stole from her. The poor, naive damsel tried convincing these same people to love her and that she was now acceptable and willing to hide her true identity for her to feel validated.

However, the damsel's behavior was a manifestation of her trauma-based associations with love and family dynamics. She was suffering from an attachment style known in psychology as "Preoccupied (Anxious) Attachment." This type of attachment identifies as insecure in an intimate relationship, constantly worried about rejection and abandonment, preoccupied with relations,

Gem C. Collie

hyperactive attachment needs and behaviors, and needs and requires ongoing reassurance. Yet no matter what she did, she would still be mistreated, but she was willing to accept this, for at least she was not alone. She could identify with someone, no matter how toxic it was, for she did not want to experience the trauma she experienced when she ran away to Jamaica; she did not want to be punished again like how her father punished her for deciding to find her autonomy. She was willing to sell out her freedom for acceptance by any means necessary, so she ran back to the arms of danger.

The damsel was no longer the person who ran away to Jamaica. She also allowed her identity to die in secrecy when she decided to abort her baby. She wore her new identity for survival and became a stranger to those who knew her. Whenever familiar people who knew the damsel saw her, they thought they were seeing a ghost. They could not believe the transformation they were seeing, but they did not understand that the damsel was in an Emotional state of Dis-Stress and that she did not understand her path.

VOLUME 2. Confronting the unseen self is a giant task, which can become quite painful. Can you think of a time where you were faced with your shadow?

The damsel's new identity attracted new pathways she had once vowed never to venture into. These pathways included attending nightclubs, smoking cigars, drinking liquor, and having reckless sexual relationships with a young man making the damsel feel like a princess. After all, the damsel had now escaped only to find her way into the mouth of the dragon, but there was one prince who loved the damsel for who she was and would sacrifice his identity to rescue her, but she was too frozen to be melted by his fire; his fire did not have the amount of heat she desired. The damsel found faults in him she did not like, yet she refused his love for her; her self-hatred blinded her judgment. She refused the young man, only to chase behind a fool who was also participating in the same self-hatred behaviors she had towards herself. She enjoyed the beating, the occasional slaps in her face, the dismissive arrogance, the cat chase, and the unbearable, unpleasant thrust of his manhood inside of her, dumping his frustrations, his insecurities, his anger, his domestic quarrels, and all his dysfunctional family dynamics on her. Her womb became his dumping ground, where he would meet with her every week to dump his unfiltered garbage. She would proudly accept this type of relationship with the dragon, for at least she did not have to sit with the traumatic experience of getting her heart broken by the prince charming or feeling such a violent act against her womb. The damsel made sure the young prince who wanted her was turned off from her; she did not understand that breaking the prince's heart would also cause a trickle effect in the future when she, too, would love someone like the way the young prince loved her. She, too, would feel the pain she had inflicted on him. "The act of self-hatred is so deep that, when love comes to appease its cause, a person would be so dedicated to their brokenness that they would destroy love's attempt to touch their heart while participating unknowingly in their demise. "I pity the heart of such a person; I send healing your way."

No matter how much the young prince tried to woo the damsel, she found more reasons to turn him off. Just so she could be with the dragon, whose aim was to destroy her essence, she was of no value; but to get her horny. With the damsel being so lost in her darkness, seeing the dragon's fire was like mistaking it for the light at the end of the tunnel. Lost and confused, the damsel decided to withdraw from school. She had gotten herself caught up in a group of men whose aim was also to turn the damsel into a masculine female or to have her as their fool, but she was supposedly saved from them by the ringleader, whom himself had an ulterior motive towards the damsel. He wanted her to be his woman; he wanted her to be what she did not understand. This man was the same man who told her to kill her baby, who touched her in places at seventeen years of age while he was thirty-three, and who deceived her into believing that if he broke her virginity, it would stop her from feeling pain while her monthly cycle visited her. He was the same man at a different time and age. He was determined to get from her what he wanted.

As for the damsel, all she was looking for was her mother's love and her father's security. She wanted to be thought of and guided, and she was not ready for a relationship with a man. After all, how was she supposed to be someone's wife when she did not understand her dynamics? She did not understand womanhood; she did not even understand how to trust, and her boundaries had no lines. All she

Gem C. Collie

knew were her tears: tears that she made friends with, tears that kept her face wet, and tears that were misunderstood.

The damsel was lost as though her soul did not board the plane back to America, and it did not; she was lost at sea as it traveled across the Atlantic Ocean. This ringleader and his friends tried to take advantage of the damsel, but because she had already tasted hell, she had to master her idea of outwitting the devil. She could not allow herself to be hurt anymore. The damsel was numb to pain; she was on a mission to trick them without letting them have their way with her. She intended to not go down with them, and she didn't.

She quickly differentiated between playing chess and checkers. She learned her role on the chessboard: each time they figured the damsel out, the damsel would find another way to maneuver her way around the chessboard in their environment without being manipulated. After all, she was stuck in survival mode, and there is nothing more interesting than seeing a broken person operate throughout life. For survival's sake, they are more clever, witty, crafty, and quick thinkers than most of their peers, who are not

---
VOLUME 2. Confronting the unseen self is a giant task, which can become quite painful. Can you think of a time where you were faced with your shadow?

exposed to everyday trauma. Their animal instincts are immediately activated, which prevents this individual from being their true self. They will not be able to be soft or trust easily or at all; no matter if the love is shown to this type of individual, they will not be able to receive kindness; they will steal from those who are kind to them. They would lie to those who are honest with them because they were never shown love, so love seems like a danger to them.

Their parents or caretakers abused their concept of love or kindness. Being cared for by someone else is something the brain cannot conceptualize outside of trauma. Therefore, whenever any form of assistance comes their way, they will sabotage the idea. The abused will always seek validation on what to do because their boundaries were violated; they will operate out of violation; their words will not be circumspect; their self-value will be faulted; red flags will become green; and they will forever chase the idea of their parents in the shadow of someone else. This is where the damsel was operating from. Even though her mother brought her back from Jamaica, she did not seek help for the damsel. She believed that the damsel's opportunity to return to her home and go back to school was what she needed.

However, this was just a little too much of the truth: she needed a therapist, she needed a hug, she needed direction, and she was only brought back to a familiar place with no parental structure. This, however, caused the damsel to be caught up in the spirit of misdirection. "Life does begin at forty. Up until then, you are just doing research. — Carl Jung.

Chapter Two

VOLUME 2. Confronting the unseen self is a giant task, which can become quite painful. Can you think of a time where you were faced with your shadow?

SEEKING BETTERMENT

Confused about what to do, the damsel was uncertain about her next move. Going to school for medical assistance did not pay off for the damsel; she simply could not afford the tuition the school was asking for, but the young prince was willing to assist the damsel. He was willing to put his name on her loan to help her pay for her tuition, but being who she was, the damsel vowed not to take the money from the young prince. She felt like she would be obligated to him. She felt she would be signing a contract of commitment to the prince, which would have been a great move for the damsel because the prince had a promising future ahead of him, and he wanted the damsel to be part of him.

However, when an individual was not created in love or raised on how to love themselves, they will surely curse the idea of love. They will play around with it like a young lion cub who plays with its

VOLUME 2. Confronting the unseen self is a giant task, which can become quite painful. Can you think of a time where you were faced with your shadow?

prey when he has just begun to discover it. The damsel did not want the commitment; she even refused the prince's idea of assistance, for she figured that it would not be good for him to help her on such a great level, knowing that she did not have the same desires for him the way he did about her, She thought that her actions were the right thing to do.

As I write this story of the damsel, I grieve for her, for the poor damsel was unaware of or even understood what she was doing. My soul hurts as I write these words, for I can relate to her self-inflicted trauma, which I experienced enough to understand better now. However, growing up in a world where your parents are physically alive, yet emotionally and psychologically uninvolved, putting little or no effort into parenting, and focusing more on other areas of life, in extreme cases uninvolved parents neglect their child's need for food, water, shelter, and love. Uninvolved parents may even abandon their children and leave them in the care of others. Uninvolved Parenting is also referred to in psychology as NEGLECTFUL PARENTING STYLE. This form of parenting style affects how the child views themselves because they never receive any feedback or attention. This will cause the child to have a lack of trust in themselves and others. They will become insecurely attached and will be unable to develop healthy relationships with others. These parents limit their affection for their children because they are too focused on themselves, set few or no expectations, or demand behaviors.

Now that we understand the type of parenting the damsel was raised by, we now understand her decision-making. As I was saying, "My heart reaches out to her, and I could not wish this type of experience on anyone, even though there are those whom I am sure have gone through an even more disgusting experience than what we're reading about the damsel in this book." This is not to take away from her experience, for we must understand that everyone thinks their burden is the heaviest. I will show empathy for the damsel, yet understand that to refine a Gem, the stone must go through some rough times."

VOLUME 2. Confronting the unseen self is a giant task, which can become quite painful. Can you think of a time where you were faced with your shadow?

However, the damsel did not accept love from the young prince; she denied him, thinking she was doing the right thing. Instead, she chose her pain, for this was what she was familiar with; it was what she knew, so she ran away from it only to run into the arms of the one who did not know himself. The madness with the dragon went on, but for a little while longer, before he suggested to her a vocational trade school, where she would more than likely receive a certification in the nursing field, being that she could not afford the school she had just attended, being that the damsel would do anything the dragon asked, to win his affection and his love, in order to gain his tender touch instead of his brutal slap or abusive truths, that he would aggressively give to break her down. The words he used to break her height down were familiar to the damsel; they had the same tone, structure, and vocabulary that her mother would use towards her whenever she was angry or hurt, so the damsel loved the words.

She kneeled at his command, which meant he would finally accept her. The damsel took her head to the dragon's demand and reached out to the necessary people to complete the application to attend this school. There was a high expectation that the school would accept the damsel. She then notified her mother and the dragon of the school's acceptance. Her mother was excited, for this meant the damsel would be away from her for a while. She could finally breed without the damsel interrupting her breath; she could finally open her front door and come home without having to see the damsel. She was more excited than the damsel, especially because this meant that her mother would not have to endure the smell when the damsel disobeyed her by lighting the candles she had asked not to be used in the house. Her mother even went out to buy the clothing and hygienic necessities that the damsel would need to attend this school. The dragon came to wish the damsel farewell, but nothing was well about what he wished for the damsel. On the appointed day of traveling, the damsel took the city's public transportation to Washington, DC, to begin her new journey. This journey would pave the way for her future going forward.

VOLUME 2. Confronting the unseen self is a giant task, which can become quite painful. Can you think of a time where you were faced with your shadow?

ALL ABOARD

The Next Stop a Different Destination

As the damsel boarded the bus to Washington, DC, to begin her new life. She met the next chapter of her life, which would mold her for the future. The damsel and twenty-two other youths from the Baltimore, Maryland, area arrived at their new destination, their new place of residency. The group was separated by gender into a dorm that houses over eighteen teenagers and young adults ranging in age from eighteen to twenty-four. The damsel was placed in a room with six different girls besides herself, all of different ethnicities and races.

The friendly damsel quickly acquainted herself with two other girls; they were all born around the same month (October), so they found their familiarity with each other there. The three girls bounded together to ensure each other's safety. The dorm leader of the room, a young Caucasian girl in her early twenties, warned them to be

VOLUME 2. Confronting the unseen self is a giant task, which can become quite painful. Can you think of a time where you were faced with your shadow?

mindful around her, for she was HIV positive. They were shocked and appalled, not just because the young woman was HIV positive but also because she was so bold to share such intimate information after only meeting the girls for five days. With their mouth gaped open and silence taken over, the damsel, whom she would decide to break the ice with, asked, "Hmm, how did you get Aids?"

The room leader: "I do not have AIDS; I have HIV. Were you not listening? Anyway, I got it from my boyfriend."

The damsel: "Your boyfriend, do you mean your ex?"

The room leader: "No, I said what I said the first time. I mean, my boyfriend, we are still together."

The damsel: "What the hell, no?" – proclaimed the damsel and the two other girls.

The room leader: "Yes, we are still together. I mean, he did warn me to use a condom, but he never said why. I knew he was cheating on me, but for some reason, I still trusted him because he would come home to me every night; it was what I was used to seeing. My stepfather would cheat on my mother, but she never complained; she was silent; they never argued; she would get up every morning and make him breakfast, wash his clothes, and make sure that the house, children, and dinner were ready by the time or whenever he chose to come home. I saw my momma do this, so I figured I should do the same."

The damsel: No, just because your mother did that does not mean you should; plus, he was cheating. "Girl, why do you hate yourself? Is it because you are so big and fat?" The damsel asked in a very frank manner.

After being very upset by her harsh, immature, bold, and daring questions, the young girl responded to the damsel.

The room leader: "What? How do you get that? I hated myself because I wanted to serve my man, not because a man cheated. That does not mean you cannot trust or cook a homemade meal for him. Where the hell do you get that "I hate myself" thing from? So

Jamaican men do not cheat? I know they do because one of my friends dated a Jamaican man who always cheats."

The damsel thought long and hard before responding to this young lady. After all, this was an opportunity for a new beginning. She did not want to leave a nasty taste in their mind about her; this reputation always followed the damsel everywhere she went. She sometimes did not know how just to be quiet; it was of a Jamaican nature. Jamaicans are known for being very frank in their speech with no regard for perhaps "what I am saying should not be said." Nonetheless, the damsel, being who she was, of course, said something.

The damsel: "Well, yes, Jamaican men do cheat. They do it so much that it is part of the culture. It is what's to be expected, but that was not my point. This man was cheating on you, warned you, then came back around and knowingly inflicted you with a deadly virus that will forever mold your life from here on, and whatever. You also were dedicated to your death by staying with him because you saw your mother do something. That is so stupid. Young woman, he did

---
VOLUME 2. Confronting the unseen self is a giant task, which can become quite painful. Can you think of a time where you were faced with your shadow?

not give you that virus. You asked for it, and he delivered. You wanted it so that he could accept you, no matter the cause; even if it meant you lost your mind or your life, you were willing to do so to be loved and accepted. You wanted to be like your mummy girl, but your mommy is a broken woman. Oh no, I should not have said that."

The room leader: "What the... No, you shouldn't have said that to me; you had no right; you went too far, for real. Please shut up."

The damsel: "You permitted me to say something; once you started to open up and tell me about your business, that was an invitation for me to say something. You need to love yourself instead of telling me to mind my business. You should be trying to lose some weight. I can help you, girl."

Coming from a broken home herself, the damsel had no room to inform anyone about love. She needed healing, maybe not as much as the young lady, but it still was broken. This is where a lot of confusion in the world lands. Many think that because their burdens, or theories of traumas, are not as damaging as the next person's, they feel entitled to have the idea of someone else being less than they are because their traumas are not as equal. However, this is not the case; it is how someone perceives their experience. For anyone to achieve greatness, some sort of rough experience must be tied to it.

We will not find an excuse for the damsel in this story, but we must also keep in mind that the damsel was naive and young. The damsel was not raised with boundaries. So, she did not know when or with whom to use her truth.

The damsel and the two other girls she had befriended together left the room to avoid the emotionally provoked young lady; even though the damsel's words were harsh and forthcoming, it was an awakening of truth. A truth that was not said in the manner that wasn't supposed to be said to this young lady. Many times, in life, we grow up being conditioned to what we were taught in life: what is and what is not.

As the damsel and the two other girls she had become acquainted with left the room for lunch, they warned the damsel of her mouth not to utter anything about the girl's condition. Even if she was the one that brought it on herself, they reminded the damsel that it was their second week there and that she should be careful before they kicked them out of the program. The damsel thought deeply within herself about what her newly found friends had told her; she knew that going back to Maryland to her mother's house would not be a good idea; after all, she wanted to impress the dragon, for he would not be too pleased with the damsel for being kicked out of the program. Even though he did not have the damsel's best interest at heart, the damsel did not recognize this: she was doing it to be accepted by the dragon; she needed his validation; she needed his approval; he was filling in the broken pieces in that, for at least that was what she thought; she did not want him to punish her with absence like the way her mother did to her, she did not want to be crushed by his words like the way her mother would crush her; even though the dragon would do even worse to the damsel, he would beat her with both his fist and his words, or simply humiliating the damsel in public. Trauma was all she knew—unhealed connections, disloyalty, betrayal, and deceit. Generational curses were all the ingredients that created the mind and personality of the distressed damsel.

This type of treatment the damsel was experiencing with the dragon in the world of social science is known as Psychological or *Emotional Abuse,* in which the individual exemplifies humiliation or constantly criticizing, threatening, shouting, or name-calling, making the individual the subject of jokes, or even using sarcasm to hurt the individual.

Every adversity, every failure, every heartache carries with it the seed of an equal or greater benefit." "You may be hurt if you love too much, but you will live in misery if you love too little." "A quitter never wins, and a winner never quits." — Author: Napoleon Hill.

OUT GOES THE OLD IN WITH THE NEW

The damsel and her new friends did everything together; everyone called them triplets because their birthdays were all in the same month and on the same day, yet years apart. The damsel was close with the girls; they were her new trauma mates who were far from understanding themselves. One day, one of the other girls from another dorm wanted to fight one of the damsel's mates. The most aggressive one in the group walked over to the damsel's friend and began to talk disrespectfully to her, saying that the damsel's friend was from Philadelphia, and she wanted to represent her home. Ever since they got there, all they heard was each student representing where they were from and how much their state did not like the other states. They named Baltimore "the state with the most drug addicts, Abandon houses, and dirty people." And, of course, the students who were from Baltimore saw this to be disrespectful.

VOLUME 2. Confronting the unseen self is a giant task, which can become quite painful. Can you think of a time where you were faced with your shadow?

Nonetheless, the damsel's friend was not compelled to back down from the disrespect. She needed to stand up to the "Dirty Girls" from Baltimore. She wanted to destroy them and felt ever so confident having the damsel around to support her in her fight. Unfortunately for her, the damsel was thinking otherwise; she was representing neither Baltimore nor Philadelphia; she was representing her green card and her status in America. She was making sure not to get herself into any trouble that she knew she could not vet herself out of. She understood what would come along with her fighting was not wanted; she knew her mother did not love her enough to rescue her from any more trouble.

The damsel knew how to run her mouth, but she also knew enough to run from trouble; she knew how to choose her battles. Moreover, she did not want to get beaten.

But the damsel's friend wanted the fight; she wanted to war, and she was willing to go for it as long as she had the imaginative idea that the damsel would be her co-supporter. But what the poor damsel did was beg her friend not to fight. However, the more she begged, the

---
VOLUME 2. Confronting the unseen self is a giant task, which can become quite painful. Can you think of a time where you were faced with your shadow?

more intense her friend's ego became and the more outraged the other parties got. It became a war against the egos; each ego war would cast words of the dagger against the other. The egos eventually got out of control, so the war became physical as they began to throw their fists at each other. Each ego through words of disrespect, while each co-supporter ripped away their self-esteem, weakening the opponent's strength to fight. The aggressive battle between the girls got out of control, with the poor defenseless damsel literally standing in the middle without any hits at her. She was like a deer in headlights, caught in the Freeze Response. She did not know what to do; her body would be paralyzed, and she could not move until the counselors rescued the damsel from the ordeal. They, however, had to fight frankly to stop them. When they finally got them away, they brought the damsel and her friend into one room to calm down. The damsel's friend asked her, "Where were you?" "Those ugly girls got the best of me, man; they pulled my braids from my skull; my shit is burning me; why did you not help me; are you, my friend?"

VOLUME 2. Confronting the unseen self is a giant task, which can become quite painful. Can you think of a time where you were faced with your shadow?

The poor damsel was still stuck; she could not find her words. She was humiliated for letting her friend down, yet at the same time grateful that the first of none of those girls had caught her. "Well, you wanted to fight and represent Philadelphia, so that's why you got your ass beaten." What did you want me to do? Jump in and fight those big girls who looked like someone who weighed three hundred plus pounds and was six feet tall. "I know what I can do."

The damsel thought silently to herself, but all she said was nothing, nothing at all, but staring into space. The uneventful experience was a trigger for the damsel; it reminded her of when her mother would team up against her, with her grandmother and brother acting on her to kill her. The damsel's mind was all trauma-based; she felt as though she was always under attack, her experience resulting in her never knowing how to identify peace. If she did not bring the attacks up directly, her thought process, the idea of how she saw, did. Luckily for the damsel, her friend was understanding;(or so she thought). Nonetheless, she was also traumatized. Her trauma response, however, was different; it was the Fight Response. The

---

VOLUME 2. Confronting the unseen self is a giant task, which can become quite painful. Can you think of a time where you were faced with your shadow?

young lady's mother was notified of her fight with the other girls, and her mother immediately responded for her to retreat. She wanted her daughter to come, and she wanted her to be safe. Unfortunately for the damsel, she did not have that option. She knew she was not going to be rescued by anyone; she knew no one was coming to get her; she knew her tears were the only thing that would show up to rescue her; she knew that empathy for herself was all she had; she knew that if she fell, she would have to find her own way back up. But that was her secret. She knew how to pretend, lie, create a false image of having a support system, and have others believe her mother was too busy being a nurse, so she could not rescue her, as oxymoronic as that sounded. It was the damsel's reality, unlike her friend's parents.

There are times when the human mind goes into adaptation mode, believing the lies it tells itself. These lies now become a shield of armor, protecting the individual from uncomfortable experiences. There are those in many cultures who believe that the human experience is what they choose before manifesting themselves in the human form; they have chosen the families they were born into to learn a karma lesson. The damsel's friend's parents came to rescue her, luckily for the damsel. They decided to take them out to dinner to soothe the embarrassing experience. Unfortunately, the damsel's friend was shipped away from her after dinner. She left with her parents, leaving the damsel behind without anyone to relate to. This, however, was all short-lived.

The damsel later found a group of people to whom she could relate. However, there was one new girl among them; she was different, very intuitive, and culturally aware. She wore her hair matted (dreadlocks) and would wrap it with native Afrikan fabric. She was a poet; like the damsel, loyalty, and honesty were also part of her personality. She also grew up in a home where her mother was emotionally abusive. Another trauma mate for the damsel to relate. The newfound friend's name was Empress. The damsel was grateful to have finally met a friend she could relate to, one who embraced areas of her life from which she had been running. If running away from one's trauma was a career, the damsel was indeed a master at it.

VOLUME 2. Confronting the unseen self is a giant task, which can become quite painful. Can you think of a time where you were faced with your shadow?

"There are times in one's life when they have to master the art of distraction to escape the reality of their pain, so they create a fictitious reality in their mind. Their belief even goes as far as attracting broken people who can relate to the same wounds; together, they become "WOUND MATES," with no intention of healing, only to go around being victims. Victims of their perception find people, places, and situations that can assist in the depths of victimization. Until these individuals are challenged by their reflections, they will not change. They will give birth to children who will eventually be carriers of the trauma that does not belong to them, but they are forced to carry on the generational curse."

The damsel and her new-found wound mate got along very well; they became close, but the damsel kept a bridge between her and her friend. She did not want to get too close to her, for she challenged the damsel's mind. She would constantly tell the damsel to go back to her roots — to return to the person she was before she was ripped apart in Jamaica. She would tell her to go back to eating naturally. Because eating fish was causing an infection in her body, and the sexual relationship that she had with the dragon was making her sick. But the stubborn-headed damsel did not want to hear this. She instead found others who were running away from their pain. Together, they formed a track team of runners from the four corners of the earth: Jamaica, Puerto Rico, the US Virgin Islands, Panama, Richmond, Virginia, China, Ethiopia, etc. Together, they would sit and imaginatively smoke their traumas away. At times, they would embark on adventures to explore nearby abandoned asylums, seeking to uncover fictional hypotheses about why the buildings were deserted. Sometimes they even expressed how they saw ghosts in the buildings, but the only ghost they were was thein or deflection. This went on for a while until the damsel began to yearn for the feeling of the dragon inside of her. She decided to go home to visit him. But unfortunately for the damsel, her mother did not want her around; she was indeed pissed at the sight of the damsel's return.

The damsel's mother: Hey, what are you doing here?" "Why did you come back?" Her mother asked her. The damsel did not reply;

she just retired to her room. She began to call the dragon and her old schoolmate from middle school; they had not connected ever since the damsel returned from Jamaica, even though the damsel had no reason to reconnect with this young lady, for she was the same person who would stab the damsel in the back at every chance she got. She was always looking to see how the damsel did; even though the damsel was not in a competitive agreement with her, they were mutually relatable because she had chosen another different path. They had nothing in common, but memories of their jovial childhood played out, and the damsel, being who she was, had a deep-seated tendency to time travel. She would frequently go back to places where she was wounded, back to the same people with whom she once trauma bonded, even though she had matured away from the type of thinking they once shared. She was expecting them to embrace her, but they could only bring Miss Damsel back to destruction, and they did. They would either steal from her or hurt her feelings, disappointing her expectations of them. The damsel craved to be desired and accepted; she yearned for the reassurance that they were proud of her. She longed to be cherished as deeply as she wished to be by her mother. However, they couldn't fulfill these desires.

There is a quote by the late Marcus Mosiah Garvey: "Afrikaans in the diaspora is like crabs in a barrel; whenever one tries to rise to the top, the other would pull it back to the bottom." This quote represents the damsel's environment.

As I, the author, write about the damsel's experience today, not because the damsel is the worst perceived daughter in the world or because you, the reader, should feel sorrowful for the damsel. I want you, the reader, to understand why I am so brutally honest about the damsel's experiences. I will share her story with you as it unfolds. The human mind can only relate to reality, whether or not we want to admit it as the truth. I am not writing this book to seek validation of my truth. Yet I know that my truth, this story, and this book are tools that will help others recognize the devil (dysfunctionalities) within their minds. It is to bring awareness; it is to bring light to the dark places.

The damsel got up the next morning as early as possible to visit the dragon. She was excited to see him, and she would show him this emotion by giving him her body, lusting for his touch, as he would grab her fist-full cup breast with his hands while kissing her on her neck, as she would gracefully open her legs to request, as he stroked her with his manhood. He left his frustration, heartbreak, mental abuse, confusion, and the flakes of scabs from his wounded ego in her womb, as together they made love in the name of dysfunctionality. After the dragon released on her back, he would clean her up with his wet towel. After this, they would lay together as he picked a fight with the damsel, questioning her integrity.

The dragon: "So, how many of those guys have you slept with? And do not lie to me because I was once a student there. I know that place; those guys there always try to sleep with the new girls coming in, and many of them always end up becoming pregnant. So, tell me the truth: how many of them did you sleep with?"

The damsel: "I did not sleep with any of them; that is not a question you needed to ask me. Did you not feel how hard it was for you to enter me? Did you not feel the resistance between my legs as you forced your way in? Moreover, I only have a desire for you. Even when the gynecologist was taking my exam, I was thinking of you as the sexual desire came over me while he gave me my Passmore, so there is nothing for you to worry about. Moreover, Yuh brings uh bookplate (you are too presumptuous).

The dragon "HEY GAL AH WHO YUH CHAT GUH SUH DEH?" (Hey girl, who are you speaking to, ah?")

The damsel: "YO, I am talking to you and am not afraid of you either. I am tired of you disrespecting me; after all, I just gave you the best thing you ever had."

The dragon: And what was that best thing because I do not remember what you gave me? If you are talking about what's between your legs, then you need to think again because it is not all that; I have had better."

The damsel: "Better? Then if you had better, why are you wasting my time? Then stop me."

VOLUME 2. Confronting the unseen self is a giant task, which can become quite painful. Can you think of a time where you were faced with your shadow?

The dragon: "You went to Jamaica with your virginity; now you came back with it all taken away as though you thought me, as a Jamaican, was supposed to rave about that? If what you had was as good as you proclaim, that bwoy (boy) you were with would have a wife you."

"Listen, I sincerely do not like the manner in which you are speaking to me. Moreover, if a man wanted to marry me, he would have done so. Yes, he did not marry me. Yes, he is a fool just like you, or even worse, watch your words with me. I am not going to take too much more of your respect tone."

The damsel finally got bold enough and stood up to the dragon. She was coming to her wits end with him, but the dragon, being a native of Jamaica, would not allow his ego to be bashed by the damsel; he had to keep her head down on the ground. How else was he going to remain the dragon? How else was he going to use her? How else would he manipulate her self-esteem, beat her down, and then bring her back up to glorify him?

VOLUME 2. Confronting the unseen self is a giant task, which can become quite painful. Can you think of a time where you were faced with your shadow?

The damsel coming from a broken home with an emotionally unavailable mother who, too, was participating in her own demise was the best example of being broken, chasing behind a man who did not want her. This was a pattern for the damsel's mother; no wonder she was not emotionally present in the damsel's life because she was not present in the reflection of the mirror, but she knew very well how to hide her pain. She knew how to buy the latest dresses from Macy's, JCPenney's, etc. She knew how to chase the American dream, which was a nightmare for her own children. The quest of foreigners journeying to America, Canada, and England as single parents without support, they struggle to the point where their children will eventually become the sacrificial lamb. The child's emotional and mental state is sacrificed for survival; they are emotionally disconnected from their wombs. If any harm were to arise with being separated from the child, her motherly intuition would not detect it. The child would have been left to the mercy of the Creator.

This was the unfortunate story of the damsel and her mother. Her mother's resentment towards her was not personal; her mother was damaged; she was only acting out her trauma; and she had gotten pregnant at the tender age of eighteen, which was considered taboo for someone her age to get pregnant; abortion was out of the question for her. So, she had no other option but to carry the baby. Her best friend later betrayed her by having a baby with the same man, which destroyed their friendship. Then again, at twenty-one, she found herself pregnant with the damsel, impregnated by a young soldier from the eastern coast of the Island of Jamaica.

This soldier at the time was already married, with two children by his wife and two other children outside of his marriage. This behavior was very common and acceptable among men in Jamaican culture. It was acceptable for many of the young girls in the ghettos to become pregnant by a married man from the upper class so that he would be a means of stable income. It would mean that they could contribute to a way of getting them out of poverty. It wasn't necessarily because they were in love with these men, but rather a means to survival, pursued in any way possible.

The damsel's mother was now caught in the web of being a single mother at twenty-one by two different men who were not present to help her, so she took the best opportunity to leave the Island for betterment, leaving the damsel and her older brother in the care of their grandparents, uncles, and aunties. This decision sparked the separation trauma between the damsel and her mother.

Separation Trauma, according to psychology, "Studies have shown that if a child suddenly loses a parent, either through death, abandonment, or a prolonged separation, the child experiences intense fear, panic, grief (a combination of sadness and loss), depression, helplessness, and hopelessness. The child has lost his lifeline and often his sense of self. The three phases are protest, despair, and detachment. The protest phase begins immediately upon separation and lasts up to weeks on end or prolongs into adulthood." This separation from her mother has carried on into the damsel's adult stages. Even though she and her mother were reunited when she migrated to the United States, the connection between them was broken; it was like strangers living with each other. The damsel's ability to cope with her distress was adopted in her mind; she did not know how to be vulnerable enough to allow her mother to love her, and her mother was so damaged by the separation that she did not know how to present herself enough to love her child.

"We love because we can lose. If there was no threat of separation, no death to shake us to our core, we would not love much at all."
— Donna Lynn Hope.

Chapter Three

VOLUME 2. Confronting the unseen self is a giant task, which can become quite painful. Can you think of a time where you were faced with your shadow?

GO BACK TO WHO YOU WERE

The damsel and the dragon's argument continued until it was interrupted by the ringing of her phone. It was her old friend from her middle school. She wanted to see the damsel and felt like the damsel was the right person to talk to about what she was experiencing. She had gotten pregnant with her boyfriend, who was married with four children at the time. The damsel had already warned her that getting into a relationship with this man was not a great idea. But just like the damsel, she was in dis-stress and denial; somehow, she figured the damsel was the best person to talk to about her problem. This idea, however, was terrible for the damsel's tongue and guard. It was brutal and straight-coming; the damsel had no structure, and neither did her words.

Nonetheless, the damsel decided to end her visit with the dragon to rescue her friend, who did not want to be rescued. She wanted a co-

Gem C. Collie

supporter in her dysfunctionality, and as always, the damsel would put herself last to give from a place she could not afford to give from. The dragon was dismayed by the damsel's choice to leave him to see her friend, even though he hurt her feelings with his disrespectful words. He still expected the damsel to stick around until it was time for her to go back to Washington, DC, but she did not; she left him. This was the beginning of the damsel taking her power back from the dragon. The damsel met up with her so-called old friend; she complimented the damsel on her appearance, and the damsel did the same.

The friend: "So, girl, what happened? How come you are back in Baltimore? I thought you would have been married in Jamaica and at least have a baby by now. What happened? "How come you are now living in Washington?"

The damsel: "Yes, I did go to Jamaica, but it was not a good idea. Girl, I ended up in nothing but drama; it was not what I expected it to be. I did get pregnant, though, but I was raped. I did not know I was pregnant until I came back. My sister put me out of the house;

VOLUME 2. Confronting the unseen self is a giant task, which can become quite painful. Can you think of a time where you were faced with your shadow?

when I was there, I was waiting for my father to come and get me, and he never did. I made the stupid choice of going with the Gardner to stay the night at his place; he raped me, and the crazy thing was that he was also planning on gang-raping me. I will never forget that dark evening."

The friend: "What are you saying? What do you mean he raped you? How did you know he was going to gang rape you? Oh my gosh, you were pregnant. Where is your baby?"

The damsel: "My baby is dead, the damsel cried bitterly. Yes, I was raped; my sister put me out on the street. She hated me and treated me like I was nothing. She embarrassed me at every chance she got. I even broke my foot while I was there, girl; I wish I had listened; I should have never gone."

The friend: "What, did the baby die? How did it all happen? Was it a late birth? What happened? So many questions, and you are not being honest. Tell me what happened. Did you have an abortion? "Oh my gosh."

The damsel: "An abortion? Like, really, that's what you think of me? (The damsel lied, hiding her embarrassment from her friend; she did not want to be judged bitterly; she wanted to avoid reliving her guilt.) "No, I had a miscarriage."

The friend said, "You are lying. I do not believe you had a miscarriage. I think you had an abortion because you were too scared of your mother, given how irrational and wicked she can be towards you. Moreover, you are probably still scared of her, aren't you? Honestly, she needs to show some level of respect for you; you are twenty-two years old now, so it is high time she allowed you your freedom. She should be able to understand that."

The damsel's naïve friend did not understand that the damsel's mother was suffering from a severe anxiety attack. She could foresee the danger that was about to repeat itself, the same danger that she went through at the damsel's age, but because her mother did not know how to communicate this with the damsel effectively, she instead responded the best way she knew, which was with resentment, anger, and aggression. It was as if she wanted to cry out to the damsel to stop her, but her words did not know how to release themselves.

She could foresee the damsel going down the same pipeline she herself went through. However, she did not know how to correct the damsel. She didn't know how to guide her; it was like watching two trains collide while the drivers lost control, leaving her only able to yell at the damsel. She no longer knew her; her daughter was lost in her own reflection, all that was left of her flesh.

The damsel: "I did not have an abortion. Why would you say such a horrible thing? (The damsel responded in a soft and shallow tone while holding her head down in shame.) I am not afraid of my mother. I am grown; in fact, enough about me. How did you get pregnant by a married man? Did his wife kick your ass when she found out? Ha-ha, what did your mother say about that? I hope you do not think that this man will leave his wife for you because it will not make him love you, girl. I am telling you the truth; giving him children will not keep him; he is already a father and is using you."

VOLUME 2. Confronting the unseen self is a giant task, which can become quite painful. Can you think of a time where you were faced with your shadow?

Gem C. Collie

The friend: "So, what do you want me to do? Have an abortion or lied to people that I had a miscarriage? Yes, I know he was married, but he is not anymore; she left him, and now we live together. All I asked was for you to help me pick out baby items, not to judge me

I am sorry that you went to Jamaica and experienced that, but you also did not listen. We were all trying to tell you not to go to Jamaica, not on that term anyway. You should have just kept your job first, moved out of your crazy mother's house, and gotten your own apartment. Then go to Jamaica and visit him to see if he really is what he was about, as he said on the phone. He could have killed you or set you up to be killed. He'd basically tricked you into thinking he was a certain way, but you couldn't see that because your pain blinded you. Listen, I am sorry if I said the wrong things to hurt your feelings, but it is the truth."

What both the damsel and her friend did not understand was that they were seeing their reflections in each other's lives. They thought they were advising each other, but they were advising their shadows. There are moments in our lives when we tend to see our hurt in others, not knowing it is our reflection. It is easier to judge the external selves we perceive in others. I am not saying either the damsel's or her friend's words were incorrect. I am merely saying that neither one of them was any different than the other; it just showed up differently or seemed to be different based on the choices and extreme experiences that were made. This is why it is so imperative that before judging someone, we ask ourselves, "Is that me?"

The damsel: "I know (the damsel broke down in tears because it was the first time, she allowed herself to be present to her pain of what transpired after she aborted the baby, and she, in return, filled its space with her hurt). But I was hurting; I did not know what to do. My grandmother and mother teamed up against me. I remember when they called my brother to beat me up. He used a metal rod to hit me in the eye, and my eyes still hurt three years later. They destroyed everything I owned. I could not sleep at night; my nervous system was shot. This is why I had to leave. I was scared for my life, so I ran away. My ex made me feel safe over the phone, so I thought he would also make me feel safe in Jamaica. But he was lying to me. He did not have a place of his own, and he was not who I thought he was. Girl, his baby's mother gave me hell. His mother was so fake. She would lie because she did not want us to be together. She was pretending. The only person that cared about me was his father. There was even a time when he was about to kill me; if not for his father, I would have died."

The friend: "Wait! What are you saying, ha-ha, ha-ha? Are you serious, ha-ha?"

The damsel: "Yo! What is funny?"

The friend: "No, girl, I am not laughing at you seriously; I am not laughing at you. I am laughing because he convinced you to come to Jamaica and then attempted to kill you. That is wild to me, and that is why I started laughing. He knew what you had to go through just to escape your mother and her wickedness; then, did he love you? Look at what you were running from, and then look now at what you ran into: "Okay, so what did your father say? Did you even tell him?"

The damsel: "No, I did not tell him. I did not know how to, but my sister knew about it before I even told her about it."

The friend: "Wait a minute, how did your sister know? How did she find out? This is getting edgier by the moment; I am starting to feel like you were set up. How did she know?" (She screamed)

"The damsel: "She said she heard them talking about it next door when she got up in the morning. She said that this was why she knew I would have been gang raped."

The friend: "Wait! You are not being completely honest. How did she know that they were talking about it for her to say she knew it was you, and why did she not tell your father? That was the moment she could have rallied people in the community to kill this man! I know Jamaicans do not play, so why did she not call the police? All these options, yet nothing was done. She set you up."

The realization of all this new awakening information made the damsel rethink what happened that dark Friday evening when she was raped. She had never thought of what her friend had proposed to her in that context before. The damsel was stuck in the conscious part of her brain. The conscious part of the brain\mind, the logical part of the brain, believes that we are conscious of what we are experiencing or have experienced. The subliminal part of the brain, also called the subconscious, is the emotional part. This is not the part we are conscious of, which has more influence on us.

"In cognitive psychology, unconscious information processing has been equated with subliminal information processing, which raises the question, "How good is the mind at extracting meaning from stimuli of which one is not consciously aware?" (e.g., Greenwald, Klinger, & Schuh, 1995).

The subconscious mind is a database for everything not in your conscious mind. It stores your beliefs, previous experiences, memories, and skills. Everything you have seen, done, or thought is also there. It is also your guidance.

VOLUME 2. Confronting the unseen self is a giant task, which can become quite painful. Can you think of a time where you were faced with your shadow?

The damsel's experience was stuck in her subliminal thinking. She did not realize that she was also operating from that place, and the damsel did not understand or was even self-aware to see what had recently transpired. She was not in an environment that provided self-awareness. When an individual is in an environment where love is not the foundation, they will operate from a survival perspective.

The damsel: "No, my sister did not call for help; I just told her it was me. I do not know how she knew it was me. She said she just knew. I, however, saw the guilt on her face, like she knew it was her fault, and to be honest, in a way, it was, and my heart is cold towards her even now. She almost cost me my life because of jealousy. You know, in Jamaica, the older people would say that "jealousy is as deep as the grave," and they are not lying. My heart is broken by what my sister did to me. Her mother treated me like I was nobody, all because I resembled the physical feathers of my father. Death has also been chasing me around for a very long time now. Death is a bully; it is like death is jealous of me, like I am the one who took its life."

The friend: "What are you talking about, now, girl? You are always on another level with your thoughts, always talking like a philosopher. Who do you think you are, Marcus Garvey?

How can the dead be jealous of you? You are crazy, ha-ha-ha."

The damsel: "I forgot you were a dummy; why did I ever say that to you? All you know is nastiness and stealing (the damsel mumbled to herself)." "Nothing just do not worry about what I just said. I am just saying that all I know is that I have had so many near-death experiences, which is all. Anyway, can we not talk about me right now? Let us hear what is going on and what you needed me here for before I begin to think that you called me here only to find out about my business."

The friend: "Okay, no problem. I need you to help me pick out baby clothes. Please, then, I will let you go home or to your new boyfriend."

The damsel: "Boyfriend? No, I do not keep boyfriends. He is my man."

The friend: Oooh, okay. Do you not think that it is too quick for you to have a man already? Did you not just come back from Jamaica?"

The damsel: "It is been almost two years, so what should I do? Be lonely?"

The friend: "No one is saying that you should be lonely. I am just saying that with what happened, you might not be ready for another relationship, especially because you still live with your mother. How do you think that looks?"

The damsel: "No, I do not care to be honest with you. I have been back now for two years, and I have moved on from what happened to me. I am not living with her; I am now in Washington, DC. I am only here to visit."

The friend: "But will you live there forever? No, you will be returning to her home. It is time now that you think of getting into your place. If you do not do so, you will always be disrespected by her. You also cannot say that you have a man if he is not assisting you in being better. If that is the case, you need to rethink your

---
VOLUME 2. Confronting the unseen self is a giant task, which can become quite painful. Can you think of a time where you were faced with your shadow?

choices and not just have someone get between your legs when their nature is riding them. Man, listen, I hope you have learned from what happened to you in Jamaica for real."

The damsel: "Are you lecturing me? I do not believe you are in the position to tell me that. After all, you destroyed someone's entire marriage because you are selfish. You do not have any boundaries. You just did whatever you wanted, yet you are bold enough to advise me."

The friend: "No. I am bold enough to tell you not to be stupid. Do you know what? You can leave. I am good; thanks for coming."

The damsel: "Okay, thank you."

The damsel took her belongings and headed toward her mother's home, not knowing that was one of the last times she would see that friend for now.

There are many times in our lives the truth visits us in ways when we are simply not mature enough to understand its plight, so we,

---

VOLUME 2. Confronting the unseen self is a giant task, which can become quite painful. Can you think of a time where you were faced with your shadow?

therefore, disengage ourselves from this truth because it is very frightening. The damsel was not ready for what she consciously knew was true.

The damsel's visit to her home was short-lived before she had to return to campus in Washington. If not, she would be marked as an unlawful absence, which would cost her the freedom to leave whenever she wanted to. Shortly after returning to the campus, her mates she associated herself with for the means of survival while staying there welcomed her. The thoughtful damsel brought back gifts of beedies (Tobacco rolled in Eucalyptus leaf), which was quite a treat for her mates.

It would replace their urge for marijuana, which they would sneak around on campus to smoke. The damsel's attention was split between her new-found friend and the mates she trauma bonded with. They did not challenge the damsel's dysfunctionalities. Being in their present allowed her to relax and not feel challenged. She could be her best dysfunctional self without judgment. After all, no one there was challenging their family's dynamics. They thought nothing of such. On the contrary, the damsel's new-found friend, however, related to the damsel in areas where there was culture, bug on the hand. When she challenges the damsel, she protests to the damsel about returning to who she was before she met the dragon.

The wound mate: "Go back to who you were before you started being this way and stop eating fish. It is changing your body odor. I am not being mean but check your health; you might have a kidney issue. Sis, you must go back to who you were; this is the only way to detach from your trauma. I know you are angry with your mother, but you must look for the message she is trying to convey. You cannot see it now because your mother just does not know how to express herself in a way that can get through to you."

What the damsel was not understanding or taking away from what her friend was saying was that her mother was operating from an unspoken secret that had been passed down from the "Black Holocaust." The secret of how the women would degrade their children whenever the slave driver would rally around her children, giving compliments of how "strong, hardworking, your boy is

---
VOLUME 2. Confronting the unseen self is a giant task, which can become quite painful. Can you think of a time where you were faced with your shadow?

coming along." The mother would disagree by verbally putting their children down to leave a distaste in the slave owner's mouth so that he would not sell her child. This is known as Appropriate Adaptation, or" GAS" Generalization Adaptation Syndrome, in a hostile environment. Renowned psychologist and author Dr. Joy DeGruy best define this conditioning as Post-traumatic Slave Disorder, which is a rare long-enduring adaptive survival behavior that is all normalized for the sake of survival. This can also be called Stockholm Syndrome; this phenomenon is classified as when a person is held captive for a while and, in return, has empathy and emotional attachment towards their captor.

The damsel did not want to hear what her newfound friend was saying to her. She felt resentment towards her friend; all the damsels knew was her pain. She cuddled and embraced her pain like a child emotionally attached to a teddy bear or blanket that was used to relieve his discomfort. The damsel did not understand that her pain was not pain but a lack of knowledge— knowledge of not knowing that she was being molded into the greatest.

Gem C. Collie

The damsel: "Are you defending my mother? (She cried with fire in her eyes.) You do not know the pain she caused me. You are telling me to go back to who I was, whom I used to be have caused me nothing but hurt. I hate that person. I wish I could even cut off my hair. The only reason I am still growing my long locks of hair naturally is because it is a covenant between God and me. I hate the person that I was. I was beaten, cursed, and torn apart. If you want us to remain friends, watch what you are saying to me about who I used to be; you do not know me."

The wound mate: "No, I do not know. You are right. However, once you go back and embrace your true self, you will stop suffering so much. You will no longer fight with your mother. I promise you will no longer cry if you just learn to stay detached."

The damsel's friend did not understand that what she was telling the damsel was way over her head, for you cannot heal what you do not know. You cannot go back to where you were, but you can go forward with acknowledgment of the past. Love is what the damsel needed to heal. Some will read this and disagree by saying no.

VOLUME 2. Confronting the unseen self is a giant task, which can become quite painful. Can you think of a time where you were faced with your shadow?

"Love is blind," therefore, it cannot heal. Time will do the healing, but love is not blind; trauma is blind. Trauma will make you feel broken, pretending that no problems exist. It will hope there are no consequences for ignoring all of it. Time does not heal. It is the step-by-step healing process.

The damsel could not cope with the information she was receiving from her friend. It was all too much for her, and it was beginning to trigger the unhealed wounds in her that she did not understand; the hurt that she had buried in her womb was starting to wake up from their sleep, but their awakening frightened the damsel; she could no longer recognize her trauma. They had become strangers to her and looked like an attack on her ego. So, the damsel became defensive, to the point that she was frozen in self-defense and always ready for war. The littlest triggers would spark the fire in the damsel's belly. The fire in her belly was sparked so many times that her gut became a volcano with a raging fire ready at any time to erupt on anyone. The damsel's fire had no mercy once it had started to bubble up; none was exempt from her flames.

Gem C. Collie

The damsel packed herself and walked away from her friend, not knowing that would be the last night they would be in each other's presence. Her friend was also struggling mentally, and her relationship with her mother was rough, but she used sex to cope. She used emotional attachment with men who were not emotionally available to cope. She was not much different from the damsel; she was just aware of her demons, while she had a secret hiding place of her own. The damsel's friend knew how to use her struggles to her advantage.

She would pretend to have a mental breakdown or hear voices talking to her so that no one on campus would provoke her. Instead, they labeled her "the crazy girl." She was willing to cope with that label rather than be ganged up on and toasted by the other girls, for she knew what they were capable of doing. She knew not to get along with them, unlike the damsel, who was diplomatically friendly with everyone.

The damsel, on the other hand, wanted acceptance. She wanted to fit in so she would not be a target, unlike her friends, who were ganged

VOLUME 2. Confronting the unseen self is a giant task, which can become quite painful. Can you think of a time where you were faced with your shadow?

upon and beaten. But this idea only highlighted the damsel and made her the target she tried so hard not to be. The other girls would pour water on the damsel's bed or do some other cruel act that would affect the damsel's mental health; it would be a glimpse of what she would be faced with in the future.

The damsel decided not to hang out with her friend too often, for she did not want to be labeled as crazy as her friend, so she would either leave to visit the dragon on the weekends or hang around with her other friends. But on one faithful night, the damsel's friend frequently tried to reach out to her, but the damsel did not respond fast enough, and her friend attempted suicide. By the time the damsel got to the building where she last saw her friend, all she saw was an ambulance passing by her. The damsel fell to her knees with streaming tears falling from her eyes, her chest tightening as guilt passed over her entire body. "Oh, Lord, it is my fault I did not come fast enough." She was calling me and even begged me to give her a moment. "Now that my friend is dead, I could have helped her, but I was selfish."

Hearing about her friend's condition traumatized the damsel; it was another add-on unresolved hurt for the damsel to store away in her womb. The damsel did not want to get close to the young lady because it would mean she would have to sit with her demons. Instead, she wore a mask, not just a mask, in fact, an entire body suit. This body kept her lost in a deeper identity that did not belong to her. After hearing the news of her friend's suicide, she escaped from the crowd to sit in the darkness of her room. Tears and guilt accompanied her as she fell asleep.

She was later awakened by the RA of the dorm, who asked her if she was aware of what transpired with her friend. However, the damsel was too weak to explain what might have caused her friend to make such a dark choice.

The next morning as the damsel rose from her bed, she felt herself awakening to a wet feeling. As she rose and sat on her bed to investigate what was happening, she saw that she was sitting in a puddle of wet redness. She gasped with confusion, for she knew it was not her monthly cycle time. This was not new; however, the damsel had this transpired before; each time she was traumatized, her womb would cry tears of red wetness. She quickly cleaned up the red-stained sheet before her roommates could see it and embarrass her.

After cleaning herself up, she got dressed and walked to the cafeteria to meet her other friends. They would sit outside in the chilled fall breeze, and as they held their jackets ever so tightly, they could see the changes in the damsel's body language. They knew that the damsel was usually the cheerful giver and would not think twice about sharing her joy, but it was far from a joyous moment for the damsel. However, they understood the damsel's emotional plight and did their best to support her heartbreak.

After her friend's misfortune, the damsel did not last much longer on campus. She eventually graduated with her certificate in landscaping. She then returned to her mother's home nine months after leaving.

Chapter Four

VOLUME 2. Confronting the unseen self is a giant task, which can become quite painful. Can you think of a time where you were faced with your shadow?

MOMMY, I AM HOME

The damsel returned home from Washington, DC, more ashamed and traumatized than when she left. She had experienced yet another traumatic experience of death. This experience, however, molded the damsel's heart to be hard enough not to be broken. She had learned to put her walls against the world.

As she entered the doors of her mother's home in the early hours of Tuesday morning, no one was home to greet her or welcome her back with open arms. Even if her mother were home, she would not be gracious toward the damsel's return. She went upstairs to her room to put her things away and fill her stomach with food, for she was so famished. She quickly called the dragon to inform him of her arrival, but the dragon was not excited about her homecoming. He was angry that she returned, asking the damsel to stay a little longer. You see, even though the dragon was abusive towards the damsel, he felt as if she needed to get away from her mother. His thought of the damsel's mother was that she was toxic and a setback to the damsel's growth.

There is something that always surprises me about the malignant narcissist and the psychopath: their agenda towards their victim is always the same: to manipulate, control, exploit, damage, or even murder, yet like a lion and a tiger after their prey, they will both fight to the death to capture their victim, all while wearing the sheep's skin (pretending to have their victim's best interest at heart), yet neither the damsel mother nor the dragon had her best interest at heart; they were all plotting secretly to destroy her.

Unlike the dragon, the damsel's mother did not care how the damsel was destroyed as long as she was not around to remind her of how she was guilty of mistreating her. It did not matter to her as long as she was not around to challenge her ego. As for the dragon, he wanted to rescue the damsel only to beat her down and control her. Whenever she would anger him, he would slap her or beat her in the streets, humiliating her to the point of breaking her self-esteem. This is the tactic of the narcissist: to break and mold his victim into the form they see fit for their good until they no longer see the need for their victim. They then dispose of them for another supply, defined in psychology as the "Narcissistic supply."

The damsel saw his behavior as love. It was what she had been subconsciously conditioned to believe was right. After all, she did not have anyone to interrupt her poor choices. She pledged allegiance to her dysfunctionality.

The damsel later decided that it would be in her best interest to find employment as a special needs teaching assistant in public schools, working with children with mental illness. This, however, did not work in the best interest of the damsel; she did not know how to understand the behaviors of children struggling with mental health disabilities.

There was one client that the damsel had — a bright and intelligent young boy around the tender age of eleven. This young boy's condition was classified as ODD (oppositional Defiant Disorder).

This disorder in a child is marked by defiant, disobedient behavior toward authority figures. This could also be seen as someone who is struggling with behavioral issues and hyperactivity.

The damsel's job was to ensure he was under control and follow the orders of his teachers and complete all his assignments in a timely fashion., However, the damsel's ignorance and lack of practical knowledge of the required tasks needed for the job made her unfit to work in such an environment.

She had first experienced how corrupt the educational system was; the teachers were just as dysfunctional as the students who claimed to have been diagnosed with a mental disability, not to mention that most of the parents were not knowledgeable about their own children's health.

This places responsibility on the educational system, cursing them for failing their children. But what concerned the damsel was how the child became the way he was. Luckily one day, while in a private setting, the young man allowed himself to be vulnerable with the damsel, for he could see she was of no threat to him; he opened up to her to properly educate her about where his dysfunctionality stems from. He reveals to the damsel that his mental health issues were an issue that ran deep in the family bloodline, stating that his mother, father, and sister were all suffering from the generational curse of mental health disorders.

The damsel inquired deeper. She asked the young man about the whereabouts of his father. He told the damsel that his father had been incarcerated for several years, which triggered his mother's behaviors; hearing of the lady's plight drove the damsel's level of empathy for him. But if the damsel were, to be honest with herself, she was truly overwhelmed by the young man; she could not handle his outburst and frequent classroom interruptions. Deep in her mind, she wanted to support the medication the school gave the young man to control his behavior.

Although she knew the medication was unhealthy and believed in a holistic approach to treating his situation, she wasn't opposed to it; she wanted to be free from him. However, the damsel's unconscious thoughts were seen by the young man. He told the damsel that he knew she was tired of him. Henceforth, the reason he missed class was to be suspended. He knew that the damsel would not have to come to work once he was suspended from school. Hearing this, she thanked her heavens that she secretly did not have to see this child for a week.

The young boy's angry mother swiftly came to his aid after being called to do so by the principal.

This was an everyday transaction for her; she would have to leave work to attend to the school complaint about her son's behavior. She infatuatedly trusted a broken system that only prepares children's minds to go from classroom to jailhouse. They were in no frame to support her, even if they were. They would not; they were not set up that way to assist little colored children of the melanated race in being successful in society. The educational system, the penitentiary, and the food and drug industries are collective measures to keep the lower class in mental poverty and to weaken and disable anyone who is not strong enough to stay afloat on the sinking ship of psychological slavery.

The broken family dynamic with no father in the household, or a mother who is present yet emotionally unavailable, struggling to raise a young man with no divine collective community support to back her, or a household where both parents are present but psychologically abusive to the children they are raising, or even where one parent is sexually molesting their child, all these spells "Generational curse": the beast that has designed this curse is the master of the culture of dysfunctionality.

This beast has no intention of freeing its captives, yet it creates the illusion of freedom, all while maintaining systematic bondage through self-destructive behaviors. Participants play the role of the victim, reproducing the same patterns in their children and hoping to be saved by a mysterious god, a creation of the very beast that perpetuates this generational curse. Many have tried, and many more will try, to break free from the grip of this beast. However, many have failed in their attempts. The truth is, you cannot demand justice from the beast while you remain in its belly.

Freedom is the beast. It is in the mind, and that's where the beast is attacking you from. It is attacking your bloodline. The world war is in the people's minds, and it is not necessarily outside of you; it is in how you raise your children. The way you talk to them will create or destroy their behavioral pattern. Whenever they act up, you will punish them for reflecting on you the war that is in your heaven's mind.

Dysfunctional behavioral patterns manifest as mental illness. Autoregulation activities are largely unconscious; henceforth incorporate many distractions and avoidance; they are not to be looked at as good or bad; avoidance and distractions are all a part of our human functioning. Self-regulation activities are different from autoregulation activities, and they are more conscious behavior patterns. They bring us a sense of presence and well-being. This is a part of the human behavioral pattern the young man fights throughout. He had inherited trapped emotions from his parents.

Trapped emotions are received during conception, and some inherited energy goes back many generations. These emotions are more likely to be passed from a parent to him, for the original emotional experience was packed full enough to recreate the demons he frowns at struggling with. We must understand that we, as humans, are neither good nor bad. We are simply humans. We create these mental categories as what we deem to be expectable and not execrable behaviors, and we form patterns of behaviors to survive in our environment. We are not separate from our surroundings and our parents but are deeply shaped by the beings we encounter. Although patterns can be negative, positive affirmations can move us away from Bipolar schizophrenia, Narcissism, and ADHD.

SEEKING A NEW START
The Rude awakening

The damsel's quest to seek betterment was all over the place, yet she could remember the voice of her friend, who would tell her to go back to who she once was, for she had gotten so caught up in the shadow of the dragon. She would constantly chase him each weekend in the Caribbean to feel the toxic flames of fire. She would not stop until the dragon's fire burned her to a place where it awakened her consciousness to what was causing her to self-destruct. Everyone around the damsel could see what was going on but her, but luckily, she was on for a rude awakening.

There was one cold December night, and the damsel planned to go to the Caribbean club to see the dragon. She was determined to spend New Year's Eve with him. So, the dragon decided to venture deeper outside of herself. She went to the nail salon to have fake nails put on her fingers, not to mention a new outfit to decorate her

VOLUME 2. Confronting the unseen self is a giant task, which can become quite painful. Can you think of a time where you were faced with your shadow?

body. She was willing to go all the way to impress the dragon and whoever would be in the club that night. It was a traditional Caribbean habit to be the best-dressed person at any event, no matter the cost. It was imperative to look your best, even if it meant not paying an important bill. The individual was willing to lose all or nothing to shine; there is toxic unconscious competition among each other.

Even though the fake nails the damsel was now wearing weakened her immune system, her body was not used to synthetic nails and polish chemicals. Her immune system was doing everything to fight it off. Suddenly, the damsel was starting to become weak; her throat was hoarse, and her body's temperature was rising. But the damsel did not care for this; she wanted the dragon's attention, which she did receive, and they partied the night away. Then, at 2 a.m., the club lights came on for the clubbers to now exist, and they did. The dragon waited for the damsel to exit the building, and as she did, he began to show her off to his friends. For the first time, the damsel felt some importance to the dragon. As the dragon turned his back, a

Gem C. Collie

soft touch was felt on the damsel's neck. As she turned around to see who was so presumptuous as to have touched her in such a private spot, to her surprise, it was the dragon's brother. With her mouth gaping in surprise, the damsel gasped, "Hey you, why are you so bold as to touch me there? Do you not have respect for me? You and I are not sitting together, and your brother is around. Do you not see him?"

"Of course, I know my brother is around. You look sexy in that skirt. What happened to you, and how did you just move on to my brother? We had something going on. You allowed me to taste your honey without allowing me to eat the entire honeycomb. I knew you had been in a relationship with my brother."

"My honeycomb?" Maybe because you were not the right type of beast to maintain the beehive. For years, I have wanted you, and at my most vulnerable moment, when I was homeless, I ran to you for help, and you neglected me. Maybe it was all for the best because you were or are drunk. Ha-ha, you are funny. How did you know your brother and I had something going on? Did you see my shoes at his door, or did he tell you?"

"Your shoes? Naahh, it was your scream. I heard you and him when you were having sex. I heard when you screamed out, and I said to myself, 'Bloodclatt, that voice sounds familiar,' so I put all the pieces together and realized it was you."

"My scream!! You are funny. I do not know how you recognize my voice when you have never had the chance to make me scream."

"Oh really? You forgot when you first came back from Jamaica. You let me put it at the tip. You screamed then."

"Listen, please do not let your brother hear us talking. The tip does not count."

The damsel quickly walked away to find her girlfriend, so she would come off suspicious to the dragon. However, it was too late, as the dragon had already seen them talking.

Gem C. Collie

He walked over to the damsel and grabbed her by her left arm while squeezing her tightly with his grip on her arm. The damsel knew he saw her, and she knew he was angry with her. He dragged her to the car, and they drove off together, heading to his apartment. As the two departed for his bedroom, the dragon pushed the damsel onto the bed and slapped her.

She screamed and jumped up. The damsel had had enough. At this time, she slapped him back as she held her sore, rosy cheek.

"What was that for?"

"So, you are bold enough to slap me?" The dragon responded with an angry Jamaican accent. "I knew you and my brother slept together before I met you. He told me everything. How tight you were, he confirmed things I knew were true about you."

"Your brother and I had nothing going on; he is lying to you. He is telling you that out of jealousy. By the way, he introduced you and me, so that's how you know me. Why are you acting like you already knew me before he hooked us up? Otherwise, since you

VOLUME 2. Confronting the unseen self is a giant task, which can become quite painful. Can you think of a time where you were faced with your shadow?

knew you had no right to slap me or even take me home, I am not taking any more abuse from you. It is bad enough that my mother and I can not get along, so why should I allow you to abuse me?"

The dragon pushed the damsel down on the bed as she rose to walk towards the door.

"Hey, bloodclatt gyal, you are not going anywhere. Who the hell do you think you are?"

The damsel sat on the bed and removed her clothing as he instructed her. She was very scared of his behavior towards her, and the saucy damsel did not understand why the beast was always disrespectful toward her. It was because she was a topic of conversation between him and his brother that she did not know that the two brothers were always at each other's throats. She did not know that the dragon approached her to get back at his brother. She was being used as a pawn in a family dispute. The damsel could not see this not only because the brothers pretended to get along with each other

Gem C. Collie

whenever they were in the public eye but also because the damsel was self-destructing, each layer at a time.

But this was the last night the damsel would ever allow the dragon to lay with her and climb between her legs. On this night, it was the eve of the damsel's unconscious action to break free from her generational curses. After they arose from the night of quarrels and toxic sex, they had their usual talks. The beast insulted the damsel with words of reinterment, taking away her self-worth. The defenseless damsel could take no more insults and fired back at him. Words of defense, to his amazement, the dragon's mouth gaped open with shock. He never thought the damsel would stand up to him, let alone speak up for herself.

There is nothing like the day of reckoning for abusers. Never in a lifetime would they ever think that the abused would be free, and never would they ever comprehend the ramifications of their actions. The damsel's literal awakening was much of a fright to the dragon. Her aim now was to blow out the dragon's fire. Unlike before, the damsel's stance was mightier than any sword that had

VOLUME 2. Confronting the unseen self is a giant task, which can become quite painful. Can you think of a time where you were faced with your shadow?

slewed any beast. She stood up and gave the dragon a slap across his face. With fire in her eyes, she stared at him. The dragon's ego stood taller than the damsel's, but she wasn't scared of him. He reached over to slap her down, but she swiftly moved out of the way. The two went at it for an hour, with their words attacking each other.

She stood up to the beast and demanded he take her back to her home. The dragon quickly did as she requested, but as they got closer to her home, he demanded she removes herself from the vehicle. With no fight left, the damsel did so. She decided not to fight any further, for she at least knew where she was. At least she could walk home from there. The damsel decided to stop at the nearby Caribbean Market, owned by a native Jamaican couple, on her way home. Everyone focused on the damsel as she entered through the doors. The shop owners greeted her by her name, for they had been familiar with the damsel since her preteen years. They had the opportunity to see her go through many transformations, but not like this one, where the damsel had lost herself in the ways of the dragon. She was so deep that she could not even see it, yet it was noticeable to everyone else.

She had gathered all she could, and as she was leaving the store, the store owner noticed the damsel looked drained and sickly. He turned to her.

"You know, young girl, the reason why you are feeling unwell is because you are not being true to yourself. When did you start wearing fake nails? "Apparently, it is weakening your immune system, and you need to go back to who you were before because this is not you. I also know that the relationship that you are in with the fool is not good for you. Everyone knows what's going on, but are you not ashamed?"

Hearing these words made the damsel so ashamed. She thought her relationship with the dragon was a secret, but it was the embarrassment she needed to set herself straight. She has often been told to reflect and return to who she was. The thing with telling a person to go back to who they once were for they were going in the wrong direction. You must be able to be provided directions for some because not everyone knows their way back to the road they had once traveled.

The impact of trauma can cause one to lose themselves; it will impact how they once viewed the world around them; therefore, they cannot go back to who they were; they must now go forward into a place within them that they had never traveled. They must now unlock their souls and walk on the healing path. It can no longer just be being aware of who you are but being aware you are not who you were thought to be. In the damsel's case, she was operating from a place of survival with a survival personality, which is why it was so easy for her to lose herself.

When you are operating in a survival state of thinking, you are not who you are. Instead, you just exist in a trauma mode of Fight, Fright, Freeze, Flop, or Fawn. The damsel was operating on the Fawn response to trauma, which is the emotional response to trauma. The fawn response (sometimes called "feign") is common among survivors of violent and narcissistic-type caregivers. It is "fawning" over the abuser, giving in to their demands, and trying to appease them to stop or minimize the abuse.

Therefore, the damsel moved forward. As she was leaving the market, a slice of her head told her she could purchase a reggae roots and culture CD (Compact Disc) from one of the Rastafarian brothers, who was a vendor at the store. He recommended she get the newest artist, which was now on the top charts. She took the recommended album and went on her way home. Halfway through her journey home, she ran into a young Rastafarian man she once liked. The bold young man majestically approached the damsel. He firmly addressed her behavior.

"Greetings, Sister Howard, thou? I have been noticing your behavior.

"Lately, you have been attending the clubs. Every weekend, I see you. When you enter, I also know about that brother you have been engaging yourself with. Listen, either you are choosing righteousness or death; those kinds of men are advocates of the devil himself. I am not disrespecting your man; I just want you to wake up so that you can see how you are self-destructing. Look at the way you dressed. This is not even the person I recognize; I am also aware of how he was beating you in the streets. Looking at my advice to you as Empress, you need to find yourself wherever you were lost and relocate that side of you."

With embarrassment, the damsel replied, "You are right. How did you know all this? I never see you in the club?"

"Listen, Sister, do not worry about me knowing all that; that's not your problem. Your focus is to get back to operating on the godly path you were once operating from. Know yourself, queen. Here are some herbs you can use while rethinking what I say. Here, take this frankincense and myrrh. Blessed love."

"Give thanks. I will do as you've said. I am done with those tools. Blessed love."

The damsel took her friend's advice; this time, she knew she must heed what the man told her. Even though the damsel was caught up in the dragon, a part of her still held her to who she once was. She was not too far gone. The words "Go back, you are heading down the pit of hell" had come to her one too many times for her not to heed the wisdom.

When she got home, she took a shower that lasted an hour and a half while crying away her pain and changed into something comfortable. She got the biggest trash bag in the house. She began to clear her dresser of all the chemical-laced lotions and skin care products into the closet and threw away all the short dresses and the clothing that did not align with her new way of operating. She then sat down to remove the bails from her fingers. She had decided to think differently and make the necessary changes to help her move forward.

She gathered herself and went to the local health food store to get the necessary herbs to cleanse her body from the dragon's infectious, spiritually transmitted disease. The herbs would cleanse her blood from his semen or any ties she had with him. It would also cleanse her blood from any generational patterns of his that she had unconsciously adapted. She wanted to cleanse her energy.

See, when you are going through the transitional stages of leaving a toxic relationship, you must also be willing to detach from the idea of who that person is and be ready to let go of the part of you who was once with that individual. You must cut all psychological and emotional ties!

Chapter Five

THE CROSS OVER

The damsel's mission now was to reclaim herself. She began to drink her concoction of bitter herbs that would cleanse and detoxify her from her ties with the dragon. She cut off all communication between her and him and went on a serious mission to turn her life around. The damsel had nothing but time to sit with herself this time. She had time to sit with all the funerals she held in her womb of all the disappointing news. She had time to be alone with her pain. The herbs the damsel took brought all her hidden pain to the surface. She sat in her room alone and cried for those who loved her but had passed away. The mourning she never allowed herself to have. She had decided to take the necessary steps to renew herself, and it was as though the universe was waiting for her to make her choice.

The damsel had begun to seek a higher perspective beyond what she knew regarding her spiritual belief system. She started to inquire about what she called the Black Jews; unaware they were Hebrew Israelites. The damsel could hear her inner voice guiding her toward the Israelites.

There was a certain bookstore that she started to visit quite occasionally. In the bookstore, there was an attractive young man that intrigued her interest. The color of his golden coffee-brown eyes would light up at the sight of seeing the damsel. His white teeth that glistened were even more charming than his personality. She would visit the store pretending to purchase items she already had at home, and there was even a time when all she had was her last dollars in her pocket, but her desire to see this young man was more exciting than anything. The sight of him would make any woman set ablaze. It was all nothing for her. She was determined to get him.

There was one thing about the damsel: whenever she wanted something, she would bet it all to achieve it. The tall sugar brown skin brother lit up when the rays of the sunlight touched him. His

VOLUME 2. Confronting the unseen self is a giant task, which can become quite painful. Can you think of a time where you were faced with your shadow?

height made him tower over the damsel as they stood close together. The damsel would use her beautiful smile to charm him, along with her lengthy storytelling. The charm of the damsel would weaken the young man, but not enough for him to fall to his knees, but his resistance made even more of a desire for the damsel. There was something about her. If a man showed her too much interest, she would lose the desire for the one she wanted. It had to be the right ingredients of a little resistance, a teaspoon of the cat-and-mouse chase, one cup and a half of interest, one cup of physical attraction, and a pound of intelligence with culture. This would ignite the damsel's light up; anything less was not what she wanted.

The chase between the damsel and the young man lasted two months until he informed her that in the spring, things would change. Oh goodness, this was the vaguest statement he could have told the damsel. He left her believing there would be an opportunity to come in the spring when they could be together. She did not understand he was seeing changes, for her, things that he could not explain. However, what she thought was not the case. A few months later, the young man called the damsel to ask her to meet him at the store, for there were some things he needed to discuss with her. With excitement, she called her girlfriend to let her know what was happening. Together, the girls stayed on the phone for an hour, trying to figure out what he could want to tell the damsel that could not be explained over the phone. They laughed to themselves after being unable to figure out what it could be. So, they came up with their logic of what they thought and wanted.

The next day the damsel eagerly went to meet the young man at the store. As she entered the store, she made sure she wore her best smile to entice the young man to desire her. Unfortunately, intimacy was not the reason he called her to meet him. He wanted to inform the damsel about an open position at a newly vegan restaurant where they were looking for a chef, so she was the first person to come to mind. A glance at the damsel's face would have been the perfect depiction of disappointment; her face fell to the ground as though it had reached its breaking point. In fact, the toxic damsel did not hear the blessings. All she was thinking about was what she wanted to hear. She wanted him to say he wanted to be with her, but he didn't.

The young man informed the damsel on where to go for the interview and whom to meet with to get the job. He wrote down the information for her and left. She traded between the lines and headed home. She rushed home to tell her friend how their logic was wrong. However, he told her a joke. They both laughed at the whole thing, but deep down in her heart, she was hurt.

When the damsel called the number, the vibration from the other end calmed her disappointment. It was a gentleman in his mid-thirties. She introduced herself and told him the reason for calling. He was pleased to hear that the damsel was interested in the position. The next day, she met him in person, and he informed her about the interview. He liked what the damsel was telling him, but he wasn't the only one who would decide to hire her. He told her to meet with his business partner the following day, and he would make the final decision. She nodded her head in agreement.

VOLUME 2. Confronting the unseen self is a giant task, which can become quite painful. Can you think of a time where you were faced with your shadow?

As the gentleman offered the damsel a ride home, there was something different about this man's attire that she didn't understand. The damsel inquired about his clothes and the red tightly knitted hat on his head; he informed her he was part of the Afrikaans, Hebrew Israelite of Jerusalem community.

He said that the Hebrews were direct Descendants of Avraham (Abraham). The Hebrews also believe they were also from the twelve tribes of Israel. They are a spiritual collectivistic base community that migrated to Dimona, Israel. They are also a vegan-based community that believes health makes us holistic. This information excited the damsel. She inquired where the Black Hebrew Jews were, but the gentleman informed her that although Judaism and Israelites were similar in many beliefs, they were not the same people. Nonetheless, it was the information the damsel needed to hear, and it was exactly what she was looking for to break her generational curse.

After the meeting with the gentleman, he brought the damsel home and instructed her to go to the restaurant to meet his business partner, who was also a part of the Hebrew community. She thanked him and went inside her home, happily claiming the job without knowing she had received it.

The next day, bright and early, the damsel gathered herself to do as she was told to meet the other business partner to be hired. As she arrived at her destination she was confused about where to turn, after asking several strangers she had arrived yet still confused for she was not sure if she had reached the exact place, unknowing to her she walked over to the owner, with such politeness to ask him if he knew the new vegan restaurant, the gentleman replied to her she was indeed in luck she had arrived at her destination. The person she was looking for was, indeed, him.

He asked her the reason for searching for him, and she told him that his business partner sent her for an interview. He looked at the damsel deeply in her big copper-tone eyes as though he was searching her soul. Without any further questions, he hired her on the spot and instructed her to start work the next day. After two weeks of godly working her new job, the damsel's life was in for a change as she had never seen before. Her new boss had invited her to their Afrikan Hebrew "Breath of Life" classes, again like before the gentlemen interviewed the damsel. This time, on her level of conscious reasoning and understanding, she recited one of her poetries for them to show that she was indeed capable of conscious understanding, heating the word choices. The damsel used in her poetry had truly impressed them. They asked the damsel if she would return to their classes, for she was indeed on the right path and the place of breaking her generational curses, but all this would soon be interrupted by a charming new prince, the owner's son.

There was one thing about the damsel; she had a pattern: each time she was close to breaking the curse cast upon her, she would always allow herself to be interrupted by a deceptive prince charming who would come under the guise of needing help. But the damsel did not understand that there are times in life when a wolf would cry. However, this would cause her to lose focus from breaking the chains of generational curses, leaving herself to be at a battle and always playing the victim she created. She would be so deep in the red flags that she ignored them only because the damsel wanted to be accepted. She would be willing to sacrifice her healing, her being only "Three feet away from gold' from her healing. The damsel later realized that it would only be so many times when the scale of life would give her so many beginnings before she would stop suffering from the savior's syndrome.

This book not only illuminates the journey and trials of a young lady's life but also highlights her unconsciously-chosen path and the constant war in the heavens that she is forced to endure.

"We are going to emancipate ourselves from mental slavery because whilst others might free the body, none but ourselves can free the mind. Mind is your only ruler, sovereign. The man who is not able to develop and use his mind is bound to be the slave of the other man who uses his mind." — Marcus Garvey.

To Be Continued...

The Author's Note to The Author

At last! You have completed the second book. This time I see that you have taken my advice on addressing yourself. I also see where you have matured emotionally. Excellent job! I must congratulate you on such a giant task as defeating your Goliath (the internal beast).

Addressing one's misfortunes and demons is not heard about every day, and being accountable for what has taken place in your life shows growth. Whereas before, you struggled so hard with being a victim of your trauma, misfortunes, and maladaptive thinking. I completely understand your pain, cries, and heartache.

I empathize with you, my beloved author. I am proud to know you are no longer a damsel in distress or even coping with Emotional Codependency behaviors. Life seems to have taught you a great deal. I am so sorry you had to fall on your knees with no one to guide you through your rights of passage. I am so sorry you had to

VOLUME 2. Confronting the unseen self is a giant task, which can become quite painful. Can you think of a time where you were faced with your shadow?

cry alone. I am sorry your lessons were so brutal. That's the way it is. It is life and rough, but it is your compass. It is your instruction. I know there are times, even now, you feel like giving up, you might even go as far as feeling like death is your answer, but the death of the flesh is not the answer. Even if you were to take your own life, you would still have to learn the lessons in the next life. Your lessons are your parental guidance, your teachers, and the lessons you learned on becoming a teacher. I empathize with a dilemma like yours.

You have done the work of addressing your broken shadow. This is something that many psychologists, therapists, and even scholars themselves have not even come close enough to have done so. Keep in mind that you did not only have to heal from your learning, behaviors, the environmental influences but also your cultural trauma. The work you have done is not a walk in the park.

I, the author, understand. I mean, I am not saying that I have done the same kind of work as far as breaking all sorts of generational curses. But I mean, I was among the first to graduate from college in

VOLUME 2. Confronting the unseen self is a giant task, which can become quite painful. Can you think of a time where you were faced with your shadow?

my family, and that's about it. I have not done such in-depth work as you have, and I am not the one chosen to do so. I have never heard my ancestors calling on me. I am still trying to distinguish the differences between my thoughts and intuition.

Yet I again command you to keep working on healing and forgiving your parents. I know it will be hard but do not allow their curse of not knowing how to be emotionally available to you to be your own. You have come too far and gone too deep. Your healing will be the healing for the next generation to come. It will not end with you but will begin at least with you. Forgive your culture. It is a broken one that carries the weight of the world on its back. Forgive your wounds, forgive your womb, even forgive your thoughts, make an atonement with your heart attacks, embrace your faults, and do not take anything personally. Everything is a lesson, beloved. Everything and everyone is a teacher. Everyone who has come into your life was a teacher in the school of life. When it is time for you or them to leave your life, do so with gratitude, be grateful for what you came to learn. Do not attach to anything or anyone. Understand the laws of detachment, but do not forget the laws of attraction.

VOLUME 2. Confronting the unseen self is a giant task, which can become quite painful. Can you think of a time where you were faced with your shadow?

Know your role in people's lives as you go forward. Do not play a role they did not cast an audition for because you were selected.

Learn to communicate effectively. Do not assume that the other person understands what you mean because you say, love. Love means something completely different for each being. Listen more than you speak. Be mindful of whom you share your life with; some are not mature enough for your conversation. They, too, are battling with their own demons and understand the laws of human nature. If you are not willing to lose it, do not share it. Keep in mind, beloved. You have taken the tone of breaking the generational curse. Those demons will not let you go Scott-free. They will come after you. Trust that. No monster who hosts your family's dynamic will allow you to easily move out of its grips. You must push on but do not run. You cannot outrun that demon. It is in your mind, and you have to be the dictator.

Selah,

Author, Gem.

We want to hear from you. Please send your comments about this book to us in care of gembouks21@yahoo.com. Or visit our website for more information www.gembouks.org. Thank you.

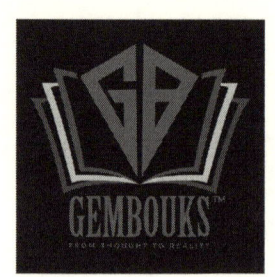